T0283555

PRAISE FOR

Dear Miss Perkins

"Rebecca Brenner Graham's *Dear Miss Perkins* is an excellent and long-overdue study of Frances Perkins's compassionate and tireless efforts to aid Jewish refugees during one of history's darkest times. Through meticulous research, Graham reveals the little-known battle Perkins fought behind the scenes in FDR's administration, often at great personal cost. The detailed stories of individual refugees who sought her help—those she was able to save and those she couldn't—are both moving and essential reading. This book is an invaluable resource for understanding Perkins's legacy and would have been an indispensable aid in writing my own novel."

—STEPHANIE DRAY, *New York Times* BESTSELLING AUTHOR OF *Becoming Madam Secretary* AND *America's First Daughter*

"Rebecca Brenner Graham's work examines a lesser-known legacy of pathbreaking social justice crusader Frances Perkins: her farsighted, resourceful humanitarian effort to help Jews fleeing the Holocaust find refuge in America. She has crafted a compelling portrait of Secretary Perkins's fearlessness and compassion in the face of misogyny and bigotry."

—SENATOR SHELDON WHITEHOUSE, RHODE ISLAND

"Finally, proper attention is being paid to Frances Perkins and her dogged efforts to aid European Jews during the Holocaust. Rebecca Brenner Graham's expansive and modern telling reminds us that there are historical figures to whom we can—and should—look for inspiration as we continue to face some of the same xenophobic, racist, antisemitic dynamics as Perkins did in the 1930s. You'll emerge from this book with a new hero."

—REBECCA ERBELDING, PhD, HOLOCAUST HISTORIAN AND AUTHOR OF THE NATIONAL JEWISH BOOK AWARD–WINNING *Rescue Board: The Untold Story of America's Efforts to Save the Jews of Europe*

"*Dear Miss Perkins* offers a refreshing millennial perspective on the history of American immigration policy through the actions of Frances Perkins, one of the most underappreciated women of the Roosevelt era. Meticulously researched and detailed, it goes far beyond Miss Perkins's efforts to help Jewish refugees prior to the war. Dr. Graham paints a compelling portrait of a quiet hero who transcended the misogyny of her time, shattered glass ceilings, and rewrote the rules for the huddled masses yearning to breathe free."

—PAUL SPARROW, FORMER DIRECTOR OF THE FRANKLIN D. ROOSEVELT PRESIDENTIAL LIBRARY AND MUSEUM

"This insightful, incisive, singular new study of Frances Perkins's effort to rescue European Jews in the late 1930s is timely. The antisemitism, xenophobia, and sexism Perkins confronted resonate, as America confronts new asylum seekers and another crisis of conscience. Graham's engaging narrative is crisp, capturing characters and action with telling anecdotes and memorable descriptions. Both historians and history fans will enjoy this fast-paced, fact-packed page-turner."

—ELISABETH GRIFFITH, PHD, AUTHOR OF *Formidable: American Women and the Fight for Equality: 1920–2020* AND MEMBER OF THE SOCIETY OF AMERICAN HISTORIANS

"*Dear Miss Perkins* tells the little-known story of how Labor Secretary Frances Perkins fought xenophobia, antisemitism, and intra-cabinet rivalry to champion Jews seeking refuge from the Nazis. The story is little-told in part because Perkins wanted it that way; she downplayed her own efforts to contemporary journalists and later historians. But Rebecca Brenner Graham doesn't let that stand in her way. With deft prose and impeccable research, Graham gives Perkins the history she deserved in this inspiring tale."

—REBECCA BOGGS ROBERTS, AUTHOR OF *Untold Power: The Fascinating Rise and Complex Legacy of First Lady Edith Wilson*

Dear Miss Perkins

A STORY OF FRANCES PERKINS'S EFFORTS TO AID REFUGEES FROM NAZI GERMANY

REBECCA BRENNER GRAHAM

CITADEL PRESS
Kensington Publishing Corp.
kensingtonbooks.com

CITADEL PRESS BOOKS are published by

Kensington Publishing Corp.
900 Third Avenue
New York, NY 10022

Copyright © 2025 by Rebecca Brenner Graham

All rights reserved. No part of this book may be reproduced in any form
or by any means without the prior written consent of the publisher, except-
ing brief quotes used in reviews.

All Kensington titles, imprints, and distributed lines are available at special
quantity discounts for bulk purchases for sales promotions, premiums,
fund-raising, educational, or institutional use. Special book excerpts or
customized printings can also be created to fit specific needs. For details,
write or phone the office of the Kensington sales manager: Kensington
Publishing Corp., 900 Third Avenue, New York, NY 10022, attn Sales
Department; phone 1-800-221-2647.

CITADEL PRESS and the Citadel logo are Reg. U.S. Pat. & TM Off.

10 9 8 7 6 5 4 3 2 1

First Citadel hardcover printing: February 2025

Printed in the United States of America

ISBN: 978-0-8065-4317-8
ISBN: 978-0-8065-4319-2 (e-book)

Library of Congress Control Number: 2024943946

For Brandon

Contents

Introduction

*O*N THE NIGHT OF NOVEMBER 9, 1938, Nazis burned synagogues, looted Jewish homes and businesses, raped Jewish women, and deported Jewish men to concentration camps across Germany and Austria. The Night of Broken Glass, Kristallnacht, made headlines around the world, including in the U.S. For many Jewish people, that night marked the first time that they truly wanted to leave their homes forever. For others, it increased their resolve to seek refuge.

In the U.S., the agency that might be able to help them—the Immigration and Naturalization Service (INS)—was under the Department of Labor, which was headed by the first female cabinet secretary in American history, Frances Perkins. At age fifty-eight, she wore a tricorne hat and pearls. She was a white woman with dark eyes and dark, matronly clothing. Her handbag and heels stood out under the cabinet meeting table surrounded by men's shoes. She slept in a single bed because her husband was in a psychiatric institution, but her personal life was off-limits to anyone outside her minuscule private circle. Perkins habitually felt others' pain as her own, and refugees were no exception.

She had a flurry of ideas, mostly good ones, all of which had been in motion before 1938. The ideal course of action would be expanding U.S. immigration quotas—the numerical caps that dictated how many people born in each country could immigrate per year—but because those numbers were controlled by Congress, that seemed unlikely. She proposed mortgaging quotas, combining both 1939 and 1940 allotments into 1939. She supported adding an additional quota for child refugees to offer children a chance at a safe life. If Congress would not adjust quotas, she suggested a separate quota for the American territory of Alaska to settle Jewish refugees there.

Could the U.S. be a refuge to oppressed people? Did it want to be? Could it overcome its own prejudices to be "the golden door"? All refugees whose lives were in danger counted as immigrants under the same quota laws as other foreigners seeking to relocate. Perkins had helped shepherd radical New Deal legislation—the Social Security Act of 1935, the National Labor Relations Act of 1935, and the Fair Labor Standards Act of 1938—through Congress. Could she do the same with refugee policy? These questions kept her up at night.

The morning after Kristallnacht was the morning before Armistice Day on the twenty-year anniversary of the end of World War I. Americans listened to Kate Smith perform over the radio a new song composed by Irving Berlin to mark the occasion. The original first verse of the song, "God Bless America," was "As the storm clouds gather, far across the sea / Let us swear allegiance to a land that's free /

Let us all be grateful that we're far from there / As we raise our voices in a solemn prayer."[1] Musical tones from the accompanying instruments then bounced into a vivacious "God Bless America." *Let us all be grateful that we're far from there as we raise our voices in a solemn prayer.* As a devout Christian, Perkins was undoubtedly praying. But unlike most of the country and most of the government, she tried to translate those thoughts and prayers into actions.

At what point would rising Nazi atrocities awaken the U.S. from its postwar isolationism? How might Americans care about the welfare of noncitizens, especially while struggling through the poverty and scarcity of the Great Depression? Contemporary myths of immigrants taking American jobs and resources date back to the 1930s, and farther. "I am a ratcatcher in Boston for 20 years. I can show you 500 alleys in Boston with 100 children ages 5 to 8 in these alleys ... These children are in bad need of care. So, take care of kids at home first," an American citizen wrote to Katherine Lenroot, head of the Children's Bureau in Perkins's Department of Labor, in 1939. The question of how to share resources with refugees when citizens lacked resources might have seemed well-meaning enough until he signed off, "Are you taking orders from ... the Rich Jews?"[2]

On November 18, 1938, President Franklin Delano Roosevelt announced via press conference his willingness to extend the tourist visas of 12,000 to 15,000 German-Jewish refugees already in the country. Perkins had the idea for these extensions in 1933.

Following a cabinet meeting in spring 1933, a State Department official journaled about a phone conversation in which the State Department had tried to explain immigration to the Labor Secretary. He wrote that Perkins "quite blew our poor Undersecretary off his end of the phone." Perkins claimed that it was an American tradition to help people seeking asylum. By 1938, however, Perkins's tone had shifted. "A great many people seem to hold the belief that there is some provision in the immigration laws for political refugees or for making this country an asylum for the oppressed of all nations. This is absolutely not the case," she wrote to a correspondent.[3]

Between those two different claims from Perkins, she'd come face-to-face with the antithesis of her highest American ideals when anti–New Dealers in Congress tried to impeach her. For her role in protecting an Australian immigrant and labor organizer, Harry Bridges, Perkins faced an impeachment hearing, hate mail, bad press, and even antisemitic slurs from conspiracy theorists claiming she was Jewish. She handled the accusations of Jewishness with grace, publicizing a letter expressing that she'd be proud of her Jewish heritage if she had it, which she didn't. But overall, the impeachment experience shook her.

Nevertheless, she persisted. Through a combination of relaxing visa requirements, reducing deportation numbers, devising the corporate affidavit for businesses to finance refugees, and collaborating with the German-Jewish Children's Aid Inc. on a robust child refugees' program, Perkins contributed to saving the lives of tens of thousands of refugees from Nazism.

By the time initiatives that she'd set in motion reached Congress, however, any political capital that she once had was in shambles because of the impeachment ordeal. These efforts to accept refugee children and create a German-

Jewish settler colony in Alaska failed in 1939 and 1940, respectively. Both ideas crossed Perkins's mind and materialized in scribbles on notepaper across her desk. The Alaska plan signified a rare instance when American colonization and imperialism could not prevail above all else because the antisemitism toward those who would be settling was too strong.

Perkins navigated an American climate of antisemitism, capitalism, misogyny, xenophobia, and more. Her positionality as a Christian, educated, relatively privileged descendant of English settlers made her encounters even more unsettling and stark. As a historical figure, she's a unique tour guide for contemporary readers interested in the history of the U.S. in the 1930s. As an American governmental official, she offers the lens into American responses to the German-Jewish refugee crisis prior to World War II. President Franklin Delano Roosevelt later moved the INS from Labor to Justice in 1940 ahead of America's entrance into World War II—because Perkins's immigration policies were too progressive.

This story is easy to miss. Myths have persisted to obscure it for too long. Sixty years after her death, Perkins continues to be relatively unknown. Keeping a low profile was partially her own doing, and the men who wrote first and second drafts of history through journalism and scholarship didn't need to be asked twice to downplay her role. Further, ideas about American immigration history are still recovering from the "melting pot" myth of American cohesion and happiness. And that leaves historical memory of Nazism and the Holocaust in the American collective consciousness, which has taken a tumultuous journey all by itself. Uses and abuses of Holocaust memory in fiction, politics, and more are endless. As a result, the first female cabinet secretary—a quirky fun fact—the U.S. as a nation of immigrants, and American moralistic outrage and resolve to "never forget" and "never again" might seem like three separate stands of history. In truth, they converge in a singular story.

CHAPTER ONE

Becoming Frances Perkins

*T*ANGLED UP IN WHITE SHEETS as the rain pours outside, the protagonist and her romantic interest in the drama dance film *Dirty Dancing* (1987) have the following conversation:

> "What's your real name, Baby?"
>
> "Frances, after the first woman in the Cabinet." She giggles.
>
> "That's a real grownup name."

Indeed, Frances Perkins was the first woman to serve in the U.S. Cabinet. As Franklin Delano Roosevelt's (FDR's) Secretary of Labor from 1933 to 1945, she became the longest-serving Labor Secretary in American history. Akin to *Dirty Dancing*'s Baby, Frances was her grownup name.

Growing Up in Massachusetts

Fannie Coralie Perkins was born in the South End of Boston on April 10, 1880. Although she later chose not to correct people who claimed that she was born in the fancier Beacon Hill, Perkins was born at 12 Worcester Square in the South End, where her parents boarded rather than owned their home. Her parents, twenty-nine-year-old Susan and thirty-five-year-old Frederick Perkins, each originated from Maine—Bethel and Newcastle, respectively. Perkins's ancestors had settled in Maine in the 1750s, when the Seven Years' War was about to begin. During wartime, they and their neighbors "periodically sheltered in a garrison house" along the Damariscotta River.[1] In 1811, the Massachusetts legislature provided land deeds to white settlers occupying Maine, anticipating Maine statehood in 1820.

Perkins was a New Englander, a descendent of prerevolutionary settlers in the Massachusetts Bay Colony, and a Christian. Throughout her life, she embodied the "Puritan ethic" through her devout religiosity, socially conscious politics, and above all work ethic. German sociologist Max Weber's *The Protestant Ethic and the Spirit of Capitalism* claims that throughout the nineteenth century, Americans switched from serving callings and vocations to working for profit alone. For better or worse, throughout her career Perkins showed remnants of this sense of vocation from an earlier era.

When Fannie Perkins was two years old, her father moved the family west to central Massachusetts, where he opened a stationery shop. Their new home, Worcester, was an industrial city on the rise. Frederick Perkins found success as his stationery business flourished. The town was prospering, thanks in large part to immigrants who powered the factories and mills, increasing the community's wealth without benefiting as quickly themselves.

Perkins's family was Republican, the kind who voted for Abraham Lincoln and would vote for Theodore Roosevelt. Her grandmother's cousin Oliver Otis Howard lost an arm beating the Confederacy in the Civil War and oversaw the Freedmen's Bureau. Like her cousin's Freedmen's Bureau before her, Perkins's social security programs decades later would combine the best intentions with severely limited results for Black Americans. The Freedmen's Bureau sought to create opportunities for formerly enslaved Americans to provide for themselves. In the 1880s, Perkins's family of Republicans assumed a direct correlation between work ethic and financial well-being. In Worcester, however, the dangerous conditions for immigrant communities working in the factories hinted to wide-eyed Fannie Perkins that poverty wasn't poor people's fault.

The Perkins family assumed that Fannie would attend college, not for any feminist reason, but because of their financial means and social status. Founded by missionary-philanthropist Mary Lyon in 1837, Mount Holyoke is the oldest of the Seven Sisters women's colleges. Located in the town of South Hadley in the bucolic Pioneer Valley of Western Massachusetts, the college takes its name from a nearby mountain that overlooks the towns of Amherst and Northampton. The valley was a bastion of youth and ambition emanating from wealthy and white New Englanders. Future President Calvin Coolidge had graduated from Amherst College three years prior and was building his legal and political career in Northampton.

Mount Holyoke became home to Frances Perkins from 1898 through 1902. Perkins's childhood instilled her with humility, resilience, and a strong work ethic. Mount Holyoke added community, leadership, social consciousness, and womanpower. Her Mount Holyoke years remained formative. At her sixtieth college reunion in 1962, the now-former Labor Secretary asked new graduate Marion Fitch Connell about postgraduation plans. Marion replied that she was joining the newly formed Peace Corps, and Perkins encouraged her that this was an excellent decision.[2]

Though her major was in chemistry with minors in biology and physics, Perkins's most influential professor was perhaps historian Annah May Soule. Well ahead of her time, Professor Soule frequently traveled to speak at national conferences. She required her students to visit local factories and assigned reports on their findings. In class, they read works of Progressives, such as *The Souls of Black Folk* by Soule's friend W. E. B. Du Bois. From studying under Soule, Perkins learned that "the lack of comfort and security in some people was not solely due to the fact that they drank, which had been the prevailing view" from her upbringing.[3] The factory tour and assignment confirmed that factory work conditions needed to change.

"Social Justice Would Be My Vocation" in Chicago, Philadelphia, and Manhattan

Almost all photos of Perkins throughout her life depict her wearing her tricorne hat, which her mother instructed would balance her supposedly wide face. She had a "crisp,

direct" way of speaking, a self-conscious habit developed
from her father's criticism over how often she talked.[4] As
a young adult, she wore her brown hair in a singular braid,
which would have swung slightly as she turned to focus
her dark brown eyes on a dubious working condition or a
new acquaintance. She was of average height with an olive
complexion and a certain charisma. Perkins's 1946 obser-
vation that the late president had a great sense of humor
suggests her own affinity for comedy.[5] *New York Times* col-
umnist David Brooks described her in 2015 as "perky,
though certainly not beautiful," which feels as cringe-
worthy as it is false.[6]

Immediately postgraduation, Perkins worked as a
science teacher at multiple New England schools: Bacon
Academy in Colchester, Connecticut; Leicester Academy
near her hometown of Worcester, Massachusetts; and
Monson Academy in Monson, Massachusetts. In 1904,
she moved halfway across the country for a teaching position at Ferry Hall in Lake Forest, Illinois, outside Chicago.

Her Chicago years brought a new name, a new denom-
ination of Christianity, and a new career objective: Frances,
the Episcopal Church, and increasing social welfare, respectively. The young Fannie had grown up a New England
Congregationalist. But as Frances, Michelle L. Kew writes,
"[She] was drawn to the sense of ritual, ceremony, and dis-
cipline she saw in the Episcopal Church. They gave her
comfort and stability, something she felt [was] lacking in
American life, including political life."[7] Perkins's career
represented part of a broader movement for economic, political, and social reform driven by Protestant religiosity in
the early years of the twentieth century.

Perkins later recalled knowing as early as age twenty-five, when she was volunteering at Hull House in 1905, that "social justice would be my vocation."[8] In 1889, Jane Addams and Ellen Gates had founded the Hull House settlement home in Chicago. Addams gained national prominence as a social worker and pioneer of applied sociology. She was born in 1860 in Illinois to a friend of Republican presidential nominee, Abraham Lincoln, and traveled overseas to receive an elite European education. While there, Addams learned about European settlement houses, such as Toynbee Hall in London. The idea was for recent college graduates to "settle" in impoverished communities and to support them structurally. Duties included "helping the nurse with a sick family, working in a political campaign, joining a picket line, compiling statistics on infant mortality, proofreading the magazine, browbeating employers into paying wages unfairly withheld or raising money to keep the settlement going," according to the original Perkins biographer, George Martin.[9] Hull House had been serving immigrant and impoverished communities in the Chicago area for fifteen years when Perkins arrived as a volunteer on top of her teaching job.

After completing the 1906–1907 academic year in Chicago, Perkins moved back to the East Coast. Her goal of full-time employment in the reform work that she'd experienced at Hull House prompted the move. Following a relaxing summer in Italy in 1907, Perkins accepted a full-time position with a new organization called the Philadelphia Research and Protective Association, which aimed to protect vulnerable immigrant and minority women and girls.

She also began graduate studies in economics and sociology at the Wharton School at the University of Pennsylvania, though she would complete her degree elsewhere.

Two years later, in 1909, Perkins enrolled in an economics and sociology master's program at Columbia University, from which she'd ultimately graduate. Her master's thesis was titled "A Study of Malnutrition in 107 Children from Public School 51," which she researched and wrote while living and volunteering at a New York settlement home. Her education and networks at Columbia helped Perkins to secure employment that she likely viewed as a dream position: Executive Secretary of the New York Consumers' League.

Witnessing the Triangle Shirtwaist Fire

The spring of 1911 witnessed one of the most traumatic catastrophes that Manhattan had ever seen to that point, and Perkins watched it with her own eyes. March 25th was less than a month before she'd celebrate her thirty-first birthday. As Executive Secretary of the New York Consumers' League, Perkins was sipping tea with upper- and middle-class friends—supporters of progressive causes—when the butler informed her group that the Triangle Shirtwaist Factory Building was on fire.[10]

When faced with fire, the human instinct is to resist the fire and smoke, even when atop a great height. Triangle Shirtwaist victims, nine and ten stories off the ground, likely experienced their whole fall until they made impact.

Perkins wove through crowds of horrified, powerless onlookers, watching death. Irreversible, unforgettable, preventable death.

At its heart the fire represented the plight of the American working class. Some victims didn't evacuate immediately because they wanted to retrieve their belongings to log their hours. Only by logging their hours could they earn wages. The layout of the factory itself formed a bottleneck to prevent workers from stealing fabric or other materials. In *The Road to Character*, David Brooks recounts: "One young woman gave a speech before diving, gesticulating passionately, but no one could hear her." Perhaps she blamed the factory owner for the fateful, infamous decision to lock the doors. Brooks continues: "One young man tenderly helped a young woman onto the windowsill. Then he held her out, away from the building, like a ballet dancer, and let her drop. He did the same for a second and a third. Finally, a fourth girl stood on the windowsill; she embraced him, and they shared a long kiss. Then he held her out and dropped her too. Then he himself was in the air."[11] Maybe they were in a committed relationship, or maybe they shared a workplace crush. Either way, these were real people.

The Triangle Shirtwaist Factory fire killed 146 workers—mostly Jewish and Italian immigrant women between ages sixteen and twenty-three—in just forty minutes. Barely a year and a half earlier, in November 1909, the "Uprising of the 20,000" marked the largest strike to date in American women's labor history. The Uprising of the 20,000 consisted of "more than 20,000 Yiddish-speaking immigrants," women who joined forces to carry out a general strike for eleven weeks protesting conditions in the New York shirtwaist industry.[12] The 1911 Triangle Fire's victims represented the same demographic as the Uprising of the 20,000, and it resulted from the same labor conditions that labor activists had begged employers to address.

Massive by the time Perkins saw it, the Triangle Shirtwaist Factory fire began slowly on the eighth floor when a lit cigarette made contact with a piece of fabric. If the factory owner had evacuated workers safely instead of focusing on the fire itself, March 25 could've passed without any casualties in the Triangle Shirtwaist building. If the building had more than two underperforming elevators, sprinklers, or a functional fire escape, then fewer lives would have been lost. Perkins grieved the what-if and undertook the what-now. New Yorkers formed a citizens' Committee on Safety, and Perkins accepted the role of Executive Secretary for this newly formed group. In the aftermath of the fire, this group instigated the creation of—for New York—the most comprehensive set of fire safety codes that the nation had ever seen.

For Perkins, witnessing the tragedy of the Triangle Shirtwaist fire firsthand reinforced her long-standing commitment to her vocation as a champion of the laboring class, which began with her earliest efforts at Hull House.

Paul Wilson and Frances Perkins "On the Switchboard of Contemporary Political History"

For many people, timing affects who they marry, and for Perkins this was especially true. When she met Paul Wilson while they each worked in New York politics, she married him because the timing was right. Born and raised in Chicago, Wilson was from a wealthy family. He had dark hair and enjoyed playing tennis and bridge. He experienced his first mental health struggles as an underclassman at Dartmouth College, transferring to the University of Chicago to recover close to home. In 1910, they both lived in Manhattan, worked in New York politics, and shared several mutual acquaintances from both New York and Chicago. Perkins claimed on multiple occasions that she simply didn't remember how she met her husband. Biographer Kirstin Downey suspects that eventually Perkins might have chosen not to remember because of the episodes of mistreatment and the constant financial burden that came to define their marriage.[13]

Paul Wilson wasn't the only man to court Perkins. Author and "gangly, red-haired journalist" Sinclair Lewis professed his feelings to her, but she didn't reciprocate.[14] Though never romantically involved, Perkins and Lewis remained acquainted. In 1933, Perkins learned the details of the Nazi rise to power firsthand from Lewis's wife, renowned writer Dorothy Thompson, who'd spent the interwar period in Europe until Hitler banished her from Germany for her journalism.

Perkins and her husband shared some nice moments. In late June 1912, Perkins, Wilson, and a third friend traveled by train from New York to Baltimore to attend the Democratic National Convention, where delegates nominated Woodrow Wilson for president. That summer, the couple enjoyed beaches and picnics around New York City, and they met Perkins's parents in Maine.

At the same time, when thirty-year-old Perkins first met Paul Wilson in 1910, she felt torn over whether to marry. Part of her never wanted to marry, a choice that gradually became socially acceptable for a woman with an active, busy, or impressive-enough career. Another part of Perkins, however, wanted children. She married Wilson in 1913, in a tiny ceremony at Grace Church in Lower Manhattan with minimal fanfare. She wrote to her mother-in-law in 1913: "I'm so glad you don't mind me marrying Paul. I'll be good to him, you know. He is a dear and I thank you for all that you have given me in giving him life and health and character and sweetness. I'll not forget."[15] She must have felt romantic love for him then. For 1913 through 1914, they scheduled a honeymoon through Europe, but that didn't happen because World War I broke out instead.

Although her name legally became Frances Perkins Wilson, Perkins continued to use her maiden name professionally. The nuances behind this decision signified that she was already navigating the complexities of being a working woman, particularly a white upper-middle-class one. Perkins was "interested in preserving her sense of identity. More pragmatically, she also had seen that in the career world, single women were viewed more favorably than married women."[16] This would be a reoccurring theme: Perkins observed how her choices were perceived and adjusted accordingly, navigating gender politics pragmatically. She consistently aimed to minimize sexism toward her and maximize the positive results for the people her work sought to help.

Immediately after marrying, Frances and Paul enjoyed an extremely comfortable lifestyle, residing near Washington Square Park. Several German servants worked for them. Paul Wilson was employed by the mayor's office, and Perkins's vocation in labor politics overlapped considerably. Around this time Perkins proudly described her work in domestic labor policy in a Mount Holyoke College alumnae newsletter as "on the switchboard of contemporary history."[17] She seemed happy. Barely two years into their marriage, Paul Wilson became a bit too comfortable. He cheated on Frances Perkins with a woman named Rose in 1915. Not much more remains known of Rose besides her first name and the year of the affair, according to Downey. Perkins signaled that she intended to divorce Paul Wilson. However, she then discovered that she was pregnant. Once they had children, divorce was out of the question.

Acute blood pressure spikes—a complication of gestational preeclampsia—almost killed her during her first pregnancy. She delivered a stillborn son and grieved the loss. On December 30, 1916, she gave birth again, this time to Susanna Perkins Wilson, the couple's only surviving child. Susanna was her mother's pride and joy according to all accounts. Following Susanna's birth, Perkins left the workforce temporarily. She remained involved in charitable efforts on behalf of women who died in childbirth.

Paul Wilson struggled with bipolar disorder, known in the early twentieth century by medical professionals as manic depression, a condition for which there was not yet treatment. Millions of Americans must cope with bipolar disorder every year. In the Perkins story alone, her husband, her daughter, Susanna, and her Solicitor of Labor Charles E. Wyzanski, Jr., struggled with it.[18]

Susanna suffered from bipolar disorder like her father. She was also temperamental and, at times, unstable. Biographer Kirstin Downey wasn't the first who tried, but she was the first ever to interview an elderly Susanna Wilson Coggeshall about what she witnessed between her parents. Susanna recalled: "It was a battleground. They were continually shouting at each other. It wasn't a happy household."[19] Tragically, Paul Wilson became physically violent, and Perkins enlisted other men to restrain her husband physically when necessary.

Mayor John Purroy Mitchel of New York City was a personal and professional mentor to Paul Wilson. Perkins's husband was therefore personally and professionally crushed as Mitchel fell from grace. In 1917, Mitchel lost reelection because of political missteps, offending and losing the support of both Catholic voters and suffragists. When the U.S. entered World War I, the former mayor joined the American forces in Europe, where he died by suicide. Paul Wilson consequently fell into a depression from which he never fully recovered. He drank heavily, spent money recklessly, and essentially lost the battle to his severe bipolar disorder. He invested his family fortune in gold, which became worthless. Perkins would ambiguously call her husband's poor financial decision-making "the accident."[20] Paul Wilson's health continued to worsen, and he became incapable of supporting and taking care of himself. He moved in and out of (but mostly into) psychiatric institutions. Throughout her impressive career, Perkins worked tirelessly at her profession, while still finding ways to care for and financially support her husband and daughter, who struggled because of their mental health conditions.

"Ask the Governor Where He Found That Woman"

In 1919, Governor Al Smith of New York appointed Frances Perkins to the state's Industrial Commission. Perkins sought out renowned labor reformer Florence Kelley's opinion before accepting the new position. Kelley expressed how much it meant to her that someone from her own labor movement would be serving in a position where she could enact real change from a governing vantage point. Perkins and the governor's political advisor Belle Moskowitz were often the only women in the room, and so Al Smith sometimes invited his wife and even his mother to ensure Perkins's and Moskowitz's comfort and respectability.

As a member of the Industrial Commission, Perkins navigated industrial disputes and strikes by mediating among labor organizers, union members, and their employers. In a confrontation between the United Mine Workers and profit-driven employers in Rome, New York, Perkins discovered that the workers were planning to dynamite the building and kill their employers. This wasn't uncommon in the late nineteenth and early twentieth centuries. Perkins inquired how conditions were so dire that the miners considered blowing up their employers and place of employment. When the dispute went to court, Perkins submitted to the judge a letter written by the employer so incendiary with respect to the miners that the court ruled in their favor, allowing them to return to work without charges of conspiracy against a private employer. When his workers returned, one of the employers exclaimed: "Do us a favor and ask the Governor where he found that woman."[21] The profit-driven employers and the dynamite-toting miners had both initially hesitated to negotiate with a woman present. Perkins earned their respect and proved an expert mediator of labor disputes.[22] As a married woman in her thirties with her husband in and out of psychiatric institutions, Perkins found meaning in her professional relationships. When she traveled from Manhattan to Albany, Al Smith and his wife, Catherine, hosted her in the governor's mansion. They sipped beer with dinner, and afterward they all played music and sang. According to Downey, while on the road for work, Perkins might have indulged in an affair with labor reformer John Mitchell, with whom Perkins collaborated on mediating labor disputes across the state.[23] Either way, she found meaning in her work life.

In 1928, Al Smith became the first Catholic presidential nominee for a major party when he accepted the Democratic nomination for president. He sought out FDR to run for Governor of New York, hoping that New York could swing Democratic and that he'd be associated with Roosevelt in the eyes of voters. FDR was as white Anglo-Saxon Protestant as possible, which was useful to Smith, whose Catholicism remained a political liability, especially in upstate New York. Headquartered in a Manhattan hotel room, Perkins listened to Smith on the phone struggling to persuade FDR, who preferred to focus on his health and hydrotherapy treatment at Warm Springs in Georgia. FDR agreed to run for governor because Smith persuaded him that his gubernatorial candidacy was vital for Smith to win New York. On election night, despite FDR's gubernatorial victory, Smith didn't even win New York.

Although he lost to Republican nominee Herbert Hoover in 1928, Smith played a crucial role in the rise of Frances Perkins. In addition to mentoring her and hosting her in his home, by vacating the governorship to run for president, Smith reignited the political career of FDR. Perkins's time as a member of the New York Industrial Commission ended in 1929, when newly elected Governor of New York, FDR, appointed Perkins to be Industrial Commissioner for New York State.

Over a decade earlier, Perkins's first impression of FDR had been negative—that he was a self-important elitist, with "a youthful lack of humility," as she put it.[24] A younger FDR had served in the New York State Legislature from 1911 to 1913, when Perkins was active in state politics in her capacity as Chief Investigator for the New York State Factory Investigating Commission. She lobbied for a fifty-four-hour workweek bill that he neglected to support. FDR later agreed with Perkins's assessment, calling his younger self an "awfully mean cuss."[25] She attributed the humbling of FDR partially to polio. In 1921, FDR's famous, nearly fatal battle with polio "purged the slightly arrogant attitude" in Perkins's words.[26]

FDR served as Assistant Secretary of the Navy during Woodrow Wilson's administration, and he traveled overseas at the end of World War I and watched politicians bungle the Treaty of Versailles. According to Perkins, Assistant Secretary of the Navy Franklin Delano Roosevelt "learned to be a politician" and "began to like people."[27] Less than a year into Hoover's presidential administration and Roosevelt's gubernatorial administration, the stock market crashed in October 1929, triggering severe economic depression. As Secretary of Commerce from 1921 through 1928, Hoover appeared qualified to lead the nation economically. However, Americans suffering in poverty grew impatient with the Hoover administration's moderate efforts. Voters desiring a more activist government looked toward the Roosevelt gubernatorial administration in New York as a model.

As the first female member of the Governor's Cabinet in New York, Perkins managed the largest and likely the most progressive state-level Labor Department in the nation. She advised Governor Roosevelt on industrial and labor policies and recovery plans. Together they established a state Committee for the Stabilization of Industry, which spearheaded jobs programs to curtail unemployment in New York between 1929 and 1932. FDR won the 1932 presidential election in a landslide.

The Original "Madam Secretary"

Perkins had advised FDR on labor issues and was personally and professionally close to the newly elected president. Even more, the Democratic women voters who'd supported his election urged FDR to appoint the first female cabinet secretary. A critical mass of these women called specifically to appoint Frances Perkins. She'd attracted their attention by building a national reputation throughout her work in New York government.

Arguably FDR's greatest hurdle in appointing Perkins was that she genuinely didn't want the job. She felt honored and considered accepting the role yet decided in earnest against it. Her husband's serious health problems were among the top of her considerations. Especially now that Susanna was turning sixteen, Perkins didn't want a spotlight on her family. She declined. At his Manhattan lodging, the president-elect asked what the now-fifty-two-year-old Frances Perkins would need to change her mind and accept the cabinet position. She replied with a pre-made list of her greatest hopes for national labor policy, including a minimum wage, old-age and unemployment insurance, public works, and broader economic relief.

Created in response to Progressive Era labor reform movements in 1913, Labor was the newest cabinet department and included responsibility for the Bureau of Immigration. Previous Labor Secretaries had focused their immigration policy initiatives on deporting undocumented immigrants. In contrast, Perkins's agenda was truly radical. FDR promised to work toward achieving Perkins's policy goals, and that's how she became, in the words of Baby from *Dirty Dancing*, Frances—the first woman in the cabinet.

In March 1933, the newly confirmed secretary and her daughter, Susanna, traveled by train from New York to Washington, D.C. Arriving at Union Station, Perkins recognized several familiar faces of Democrats from New York all heading to the inauguration festivities. She and Susanna stayed at the historic Willard Hotel across from the White House. Perkins was no Washingtonian. She and Susanna struggled hailing cabs to various inauguration events. They hurried by foot from the Willard up to St. John's Episcopal Church for the traditional worship services on the morning of Inauguration Day. She first met the other members of FDR's cabinet there at the church. They were all men, and a few, such as Secretary of State Cordell Hull, had been living in Washington for years and employed private drivers. Perkins later recalled feeling relieved that she reached the inauguration ceremony at the Capitol on time. She stood near the podium as FDR performed the Oath of Office rituals and delivered his first inaugural address. Susanna stood farther away with the wife of another cabinet secretary. Later that day, March 4, 1933, FDR initiated a precedent by swearing in all his cabinet secretaries in a singular ceremony at the White House, rather than individually wherever was convenient. But the precedent that national media focused on was that a woman was now Labor Secretary. Reporters wondered how to address her, so they asked:

"What do we call you?"
"My name is Perkins."
"Yes, but what do we call you? How do we address you?"
"Miss Perkins."
"But we say 'Mr. Secretary' to the Secretary of State and 'Mr. Secretary' to the Secretary of the Interior. What do we say to you?"[28]

The newly elected Speaker of the U.S. House of Representatives, Henry T. Rainey, who identified as an expert on Robert's Rules of Order, interjected: "When the Secretary of Labor is a lady, she should be addressed with the same general formalities as the Secretary of Labor who is a gentleman. You call him 'Mr. Secretary.' You will call her 'Madam Secretary.'"[29] Reporters continued to butcher

Perkins's title in a wide variety of ways, notable among them being "the Madam."[30] Although such reporters annoyed her, Perkins redirected her energy toward the mountains of policy problems that faced her. A banking crisis in particular prevented Perkins from accompanying Susanna home to New York, taking on an extended stay at the Willard while she settled into a historic new role and a new town.

FRANCES PERKINS
ABBREVIATED CURRICULUM VITAE
PRESENTED BY THE AUTHOR

EDUCATION

COLUMBIA UNIVERSITY. Master of Arts in Economics and Sociology. 1909–1910.
Thesis: "A Study of Malnutrition in 107 Children from Public School 51."

UNIVERSITY OF PENNSYLVANIA. Graduate coursework at the Wharton School. 1907–1909.

MOUNT HOLYOKE COLLEGE. Bachelor of Arts in Chemistry with minors in Biology and Physics. 1902. Class President.

EXPERIENCE

U.S. DEPARTMENT OF LABOR. Cabinet Secretary. 1933–1945. First female Cabinet Secretary and longest-serving Labor Secretary in U.S. history. Key architect of New Deal legislation, including social security and the minimum wage. Spearheaded efforts to aid refugees from Nazi Germany between 1933 and 1940.

STATE OF NEW YORK. Industrial Commissioner. 1929–1933. First female member of the governor's cabinet in New York. Advised the governor on industrial and labor policies and managed the largest State Labor Department in the U.S.

STATE OF NEW YORK. Member of the Industrial Commission. 1919–1921; 1923–1929. Mediated disputes among employers, labor organizers, and union members across the state.

NEW YORK STATE FACTORY INVESTIGATING COMMISSION. Chief Investigator. 1912–1915. Executive Secretary of Committee on Safety of the City of New York and New York State Factory Investigating Commission. Investigated factories, lobbied for labor reform legislation, and served as expert witness in the aftermath of the Triangle Shirtwaist Factory fire.

NEW YORK CONSUMERS' LEAGUE. Executive Secretary. 1910–1912. Surveyed businesses and managed a team of volunteers to identify problems and propose regulations. Remained on the Board of Directors following departure.

PHILADELPHIA RESEARCH AND PROTECTIVE ASSOCIATION. 1907–1909. Found facts regarding the exploitation of women and girls from minority communities and devised solutions to help.

HULL HOUSE. VOLUNTEER. 1904–1907. Assisted nurses, political campaigns, research on social problems, and publications, as well as other duties as assigned.

FERRY HALL. TEACHER. 1904–1906. Taught chemistry at all-girls college-preparatory school outside Chicago.

CHAPTER TWO

Becoming American Immigration Law

*O*N THE SUMMER OF 2016, at the height of *Hamilton: An American Musical* on Broadway, Alexander Hamilton (Lin-Manuel Miranda) and Marquis de Lafayette (Daveed Diggs) slapped hands and sang, "Immigrants—we get the job done!" Crowds roared with applause. *Hamilton* audiences expressed their disapproval of the unabashed xenophobia of the 2015–2016 Trump presidential campaign. They wanted the U.S. to be a nation of immigrants, where scrappy revolutionaries can ascend to positions of influence, do work that helps people, and perhaps centuries later, achieve great renown.

On the contrary, restrictionism and xenophobia are trends rather than outliers in U.S. immigration history. U.S. immigration law was explicitly racist from 1882 through 1965.

The Chinese Exclusion Act of 1882 prevented Chinese laborers from immigrating to the U.S. The Immigration Act of 1917 doubled down on that by prohibiting immigrants from all of Asia—except for the Philippines, which the U.S. had colonized—and adding additional restrictions. In 1924, the National Origins Act signified the highpoint of racism and restrictionism in U.S. immigration law, creating a rigid quota system based on national origins that would remain on the books till 1965.

Frances Perkins was born two years before the Chinese Exclusion Act of 1882 and died two months before the Immigration Act of 1965. Throughout her lifetime, American immigration law grew increasingly restrictive to people whom the white masses deemed as outsiders. As Labor Secretary overseeing the Immigration and Naturalization Service (INS) from 1933 to 1940, she actively tried to combat xenophobia.

Between the Immigration Acts of 1917 and 1965, the U.S. slammed the door on countless people from around the world who were seeking asylum or a better life. Perkins, in contrast, tried to open back doors for refugees from Nazi Germany when she could.

When the Daughters of the American Revolution (DAR) lobbied to restrict immigration throughout the 1920s, Perkins could have joined them if she wanted, but instead she chose to spend her energy helping immigrants through labor reforms in New York. Rather than a total outlier, Perkins represented part of a broader movement of progressively minded Protestants who sought to be more inclusive and welcoming to newcomers than their ancestors had been.[1] These Protestant Progressives were exceptions to the rule of restrictionism and xenophobia. Yet overall white Christian nationalism prevailed in the early twentieth century U.S. Enshrining these concepts into policy fell to the officials in the nation's capital following an 1875 Supreme Court ruling that immigration policy was a federal matter.[2] Congress has been a central player in U.S. immigration policy, enacting the restrictionist and xenophobic immigration laws. The executive branch's role in American immigration policy increased throughout the twentieth century, ballooning into the Department of Homeland Security in the twenty-first century. Ultimately, immigration policy is both legislative and executive, with substantial pressure from a wide range of lobbying groups.

The spirit that audiences at *Hamilton* felt when Hamilton and Lafayette—who legally were *not* immigrants—praised immigrants was not the spirit of the history of immigration law in the U.S.[3] However, it was the spirit of Perkins's attitude toward immigrants and potential immigrants throughout her career that had an undeniable influence. Perkins's instincts and strategies deviated from a basic history of U.S. immigration law.

"Free White Persons":
 U.S. Immigration Law Prior to 1882

A world could exist without nations, and a nation could exist without immigration laws. In fact, each of these once existed. Declared independent from England in 1776 and having ratified a new Constitution in 1789, the U.S. passed its first law affecting who could enter the country and become a citizen in 1790. The Naturalization Act of 1790 defined citizens as "free white persons," a phrase that remained on the books until 1952.[4] In 1790, lawmakers wanted propertied white male citizens to outnumber Indigenous people within the country's expanding borders.

Congress doubled down on defining U.S. citizens as free white persons through legislation in both 1795 and 1798. The latter, commonly known as the Alien and Sedition Acts, unleashed powerful backlash during President John Adams's administration because even the propertied white men who could vote rejected political deportations during peacetime.[5]

The Alien and Sedition Acts came from a new political party of Federalists. One member of this party was Alexander Hamilton, who rather than an immigrant was a "British colonial settler in New York and virulently suspicious of 'aliens,'" while he aided "structuring the fiscal-military state, a capitalist state created for war," according to historian Roxanne Dunbar-Ortiz.[6] The Naturalization Act of 1798 stipulated that immigrants must wait fourteen years to naturalize, causing recent arrivals to hurry to naturalize before the law went into effect.[7]

Decreasing the number of voters was a key motivation for the Federalists, as opposed to the Democratic Republicans, whose overrepresentation in Congress due to the notorious Three-Fifths Clause led to the expansion of voting rights to include nonpropertied white men, also known as universal white male suffrage. Rather than an egalitarian impulse, expanding who could vote in the 1820s reflected white America's commitment to settler colonialism. Poor white settlers voted for policies that displaced Indigenous communities. Multiple political parties in the early U.S. therefore exhibited competing strands of the same impulse: restricting who could benefit from American privileges. Antebellum America accepted waves of immigrants from Europe who would now be considered white. White Americans welcomed Irish immigrants, for example, so long as they helped them to outnumber and displace Indigenous Americans while taking on work that more established settlers didn't care to do. Escaping disease and famine from the notorious potato shortage, Irish immigrant laborers built the Erie Canal in upstate New York, using dynamite to move mountains. Even Irish immigrants, however, weren't immune from xenophobic backlash.[8]

The first major Third Party in the U.S. was a xenophobic party, and it emerged largely in reaction against Catholic immigration in the 1850s. The Order of the Star-Spangled Banner (OSSB) became known as the Know Nothing party because if an outsider inquired about their nativist political activity, they were instructed to respond, "I know nothing."[9] Know Nothings advocated for deporting foreigners and increasing the necessary period for naturalization, among other white Protestant endeavors.

While small Jewish communities existed in the U.S. since the nation's founding, the early American republic witnessed the arrival of Jewish immigrants from central Europe, especially Germany. For example, Isaac Leeser was a German-Jewish immigrant who helped to steer the course of American nineteenth-century Jewish history. He edited Jewish newspapers, led services, translated Jewish scriptures into English, and traveled up and down the early U.S., connecting Jewish communities across distances.

During the Civil War, Leeser expressed support for Jewish Americans on both sides, suggesting an early claim of Central European Jewish immigrants to whiteness. Though never fully seen as white in the nineteenth century, at times Jewish immigrants to the U.S. participated in white projects, including colonizing Indigenous land and enslaving people of African descent.[10]

Following the Civil War, the Thirteenth, Fourteenth, and Fifteenth Amendments—collectively known as the Reconstruction Amendments—abolished slavery, prohibited discrimination on account of race or ethnicity, and ensured that all men could vote regardless of race or ethnicity, respectively. Each Reconstruction Amendment remains a work in progress because of mass incarceration, continued discrimination, and voter suppression, respectively. Yet the Fourteenth Amendment had important implications for citizenship: "All persons born or naturalized in the United States . . . are citizens of the United States and of the state wherein they reside. No state shall make or enforce any law which shall abridge the privileges or immunities of citizens of the United States."[11] Constitutionally, white supremacists could no longer deprive non-white Americans of citizenship. They could, however, restrict the immigration of non-white foreigners. And that's what they did.

From the Naturalization Act of 1790 through the ratification of the Fourteenth Amendment in 1868, citizenship legally applied to free white persons. People who were neither Black nor white were often non-Black enough to naturalize and enjoy the rights of citizenship. After all, race is a social construct, though racism and its effects are real. Subsequent decades witnessed a series of increasingly restrictionist immigration legislation, culminating in U.S. immigration laws that would contribute to dooming the masses of Hitler's victims who tried to escape and come to the U.S.

"Not Be Lawful for Any Chinese Laborer to Come": Chinese Exclusion Act of 1882

The Chinese Exclusion Act of 1882 was "technically the first federal immigration law," according to Dunbar-Ortiz, who points out that U.S. immigration law "began in overt, blatant racism."[12] The Act stated that "it shall not be lawful for any Chinese laborer to come," and it met no substantial opposition in Congress.[13]

In the 1850s, people entered the U.S. without documentation, and Americans were usually thrilled to exploit recent arrivals for cheap labor. Chinese immigrants worked mines, railroads, and vineyards. Mining and railroad work were especially dangerous, and Chinese workers received too little pay. Often, they couldn't afford to visit or even correspond with their wives and children overseas.[14]

Chinese immigrants built the Central Pacific Railroad, a key piece of the Transcontinental Railroad connecting the country during the Civil War era. Day after day, they "cleared trees, blasted rocks with explosives, picks, and shovels, carried away debris, and laid tracks."[15] Tragically, building the railroad was a "colonial process of ethnic cleansing, the federal government taking Indigenous lands guaranteed by treaties to hand over to the railroad tycoons."[16] The tycoons relied on working-class, predominantly Chinese immigrant labor, rather than dirty their own hands in dangerous and unpredictable conditions. For a time, white Americans accepted Chinese immigrants if they could exploit them to advance settler-colonialist projects.

After the Fourteenth Amendment, many white law-makers sought to reconstruct racial boundaries. They looked with suspicion toward the Chinese immigrants comprising a third of Idaho, 10% of Montana, and nearly 10% of California by 1870.[17] Many had fled famine or warlike conditions in the late Qing dynasty, in hopes of American prosperity or at least stability.

On May 6, 1882, the Chinese Exclusion Act prohibited the entry of Chinese immigrant workers for the next ten years and allowed only "students, teachers, travelers, merchants, and diplomats" to immigrate.[18] Ten years later, Congress renewed the ban on Chinese laborers from im-migrating. Lawmakers used wide-ranging iterations of anti-Chinese racism and fears of employment competition to justify their actions.

The Chinese Exclusion Act kicked off a series of ex-plicitly racist immigration laws. It also created a category of people present in the U.S. without the rights of citizen-ship, which historian Mae Ngai refers to as "impossible subjects."[19]

Federal institutions expanded to carry out immigration laws and to manage "impossible subjects." In 1891, Con-gress created the Office of Superintendent of Immigration, forerunner to the Bureau of Immigration, in the Depart-ment of the Treasury. In 1903, the Bureau of Immigration transferred to the then-created Department of Commerce and Labor. When the Departments of Commerce and

Labor divided in 1913, the Bureau of Immigration remained in the Labor Department. In 1925, Congress added a Border Patrol unit to the Bureau of Immigration, still in the Labor Department.[20]

Barely a year after the Chinese Exclusion Act of 1882, Jewish-American poet Emma Lazarus contributed a poem, "The New Colossus," to fundraising efforts for the installation of the Statue of Liberty: "Give me your tired, your poor, / Your huddled masses yearning to breathe free, / The wretched refuse of your teeming shore. / Send these, the homeless, tempest-tost to me, / I lift my lamp beside the golden door!"[21] Ellis Island looked brighter to European immigrants on the East Coast than its counterpart Angel Island looked to Asian immigrants on the West Coast.

This xenophobia would eventually expand to reject European Jewish immigrants, too. Xenophobes—usually white and Protestant—tried to control the ethnic, racial, and religious makeup of the country. From 1880 through 1910, millions of Ashkenazi Yiddish-speaking Jewish people escaped violent pogroms in Eastern Europe and Imperial Russia.[22] Immigrants arriving between 1880 and 1915 comprised 15% of the U.S. population. Waves of increasingly restrictive immigration laws—1882, 1917, and 1924—followed these new waves of immigration.

"Persons Likely to Become a Public Charge": Immigration Act of 1917

After the Chinese Exclusion Act of 1882, many restrictionists continued to call for even more anti-immigrant legislation. Many white supremacists—turning pages of Madison Grant's 1916 book *The Passing of the Great Race* and indignantly displaying it on their shelves—wanted to ban immigration from the entirety of Asia. The Immigration Act of 1917 responded to this call.

The Immigration Act of 1917—sometimes called the Barred Zone Act because it barred what it designated the Asiatic Zone—banned people with financial hardship, mental health conditions, and physical disabilities from immigrating to the U.S. In part, the 1917 Act signified a reaction against the wave of immigrants who arrived from Central and Eastern Europe between 1880 and 1910. Progressive Era immigrants, many of whom Perkins had met in the mills of Holyoke and settlement homes of Chicago and New York, had reshaped the ethnic and religious composition of the U.S., threatening other white Protestants.

In addition to expanding the restrictions on East Asia to the Middle East, South Asia, and Southeast Asia, the Immigration Act of 1917 banned an exhaustive list of "public charges." According to the Act itself, public charges included "idiots, imbeciles, feeble-minded persons, epileptics, insane persons: persons who have had one or more attacks of insanity at any time previously; persons of constitutional psychopathic inferiority; persons with chronic alcoholism...persons afflicted with tuberculosis...persons... mentally or physically defective."[23] "Polygamists and anarchists" were also prohibited from entry. A subsequent 1918 Act added funds and mechanisms to deport noncitizens associated with anarchism, enabling the Palmer Raids from 1919 through 1920, in which federal officers arrested and deported thousands of alleged anarchists.

President Woodrow Wilson, by most measurements more racist than his contemporaries, entered D.C. and supported his Postmaster General and Treasury Secretary in segregating their departments. Even Wilson, however, vetoed Congress's bigoted Immigration Act of 1917, partially because its English literacy test was too exclusionary. That wasn't enough to counter its momentum: Congress overrode his veto.

Written by people unable to predict the ascent of a proimmigrant progressive like Perkins, the Immigration Act of 1917 granted the Labor Secretary authority over whose financial hardship constituted a public charge. "In the discretion of the Secretary of Labor, be admitted if in his opinion," they wrote, envisioning a xenophobic man in charge.[24] This oversight would provide some hope from 1933 through 1935. However, first the National Origins Act of 1924 would hand over power—often ad hoc discretion—to State Department consuls overseas in Europe.

"National Origins" and "Quotas": *Immigration Act of 1924*

The Immigration Act of 1924, formally known as the Johnson-Reed Act for the senators who cosponsored it, is informally known as the "National Origins Act" and even the "Quota Act" for the racist, rigid immigration quotas that it established based on national origin. From 1924 through its repeal in 1965, U.S. immigration law allowed only a certain number of people per country to immigrate. It allowed more immigrants from Western Europe, fewer from Central Europe, even fewer from Eastern Europe, and next to none from applicable other regions of the world.

QUOTA NUMBERS DURING THE ROOSEVELT ADMINISTRATION	
Great Britain and Northern Ireland	65,721
Germany	25,957
Irish Free State	17,853
Poland	6,542
Italy	5,802
Sweden	3,314
Netherlands	3,153
France	3,086
Czechoslovakia	2,874
Russia	2,784
Norway	2,377
Switzerland	1,707
Austria	1,413
Belgium	1,304
Denmark	1,181
Hungary	869
Yugoslavia	845
Latvia	236
Turkey	226

Further, the law allotted only a hundred immigrants per year from the following countries: Afghanistan, Albania, Andorra, the Arabian peninsula, Armenia, Australia, Bhutan,

Bulgaria, Cameroon (British Mandate), Cameroon (French Mandate), China, Danzig, Egypt, Ethiopia, Iceland, India, Iraq, Japan, Liberia, Liechtenstein, Monaco, Morocco, Muscat, Nauru, Nepal, New Guinea, New Zealand, Persia, Palestine, Rwanda, San Marino, Siam, South Africa, South West Africa, Tanganyika, Togoland, and Western Samoa.[25]

Lawmakers used 1890 census data to justify reinforcing the racial and religious composition of the nineteenth-century U.S. into the twentieth century. According to Mae Ngai, "Demographic data was to twentieth-century racists what craniometric data had been to race scientists during the nineteenth."[26] Rather than measuring heads, twentieth-century racist pseudoscience involved crunching census data.

Racist pseudoscience was in vogue among white American lawmakers throughout the 1920s. President Calvin Coolidge claimed: "Biological laws tell us that certain divergent people will not mix or blend. The Nordics propagate themselves successfully. With the other races, the outcome shows deterioration on both sides."[27] Rather than question racist myths of "deterioration," Coolidge expressed these beliefs confidently. Xenophobic laws benefited from further support from lobbying groups, including the American Legion and the Daughters of the American Revolution. In 1924, the most comprehensive racist immigration law passed overwhelmingly in both chambers of Congress.

The Immigration Act of 1924 reflected the same widespread isolationist sentiment that five years prior had prevented the U.S. from ratifying the Treaty of Versailles at the end of World War I. From 1919 through World War II, Europe witnessed the rise of Nazism without the U.S. involved in the League of Nations. Isolationism simultaneously kept the U.S. out of European affairs and helped prevent refugees from said European affairs from finding safety.

Nearly two decades later, Germany and Japan would become wartime enemies of the U.S. But in 1924, the contrast between Germany's and Japan's reactions to U.S. immigration law reflected a contrast between American treatment of white Germans and Japanese people of color. Political leaders in Japan expressed being offended by the Immigration Act of 1924.[28] Meanwhile, later that decade Hitler complimented the Quota Act in an unpublished sequel to *Mein Kampf* (*My Struggle*).

The 1924 Act reinforced the existence of "impossible subjects," allowing the focus of American immigration policy to become deportation. Ngai explains that "numerical restriction created a new class of persons within the national body . . . whose inclusion in the nation was at once a social reality and a legal impossibility."[29] Two pillars of the Quota Act were the quotas themselves and deporting people deemed ineligible for citizenship.[30]

Congress established a Quota Board to design and implement the Quota Act. The Quota Board designated racial categories: white, Black, Mulatto, Indian, Chinese, Japanese, and Hindu.[31] If the Quota Board had been intellectually honest, they would have concluded that using national origin to assign immigration quotas was "theoretically suspect and methodologically impossible."[32] In 1929, the Departments of State, Labor, and Commerce expressed support for the Quota Board's pseudoscientific, racist efforts when the secretaries of these departments submitted the Board's report to President Herbert Hoover.

After Congress enacted the law, the implementation fell
to the executive branch. Assigning more authority to State
Department bureaucrats overseas, the Act empowered the
Labor Department to focus on deporting Mexican immigrants from the borderlands. The Labor Department prior
to Perkins's tenure conducted these terrorizing raids with
relentless enthusiasm. "Cowboys" and KKK members pa-
trolled the Southern border, too.[33]

By 1933, Perkins would exert influence over the implementation of immigration policies and create positive
change. But first, the Quota Act marked a watershed moment. As the first "compressive restriction law," it laid out
an "ethnic and racial map based on new categories and hier-
archies of difference."[34] It projected an American worldview
regarding each nation and how desirable its people were
from a Christian nationalist, white supremacist perspective.

What Could a Pro-immigrant Labor Secretary Do?

Congressional legislation is one way to trace the history of
U.S. immigration law and policy. But the executive branch
also plays an imperative role in immigration history. Political scientist Neil V. Hernandez uses an analytical framework that he calls *policy innovation through bureaucratic
reorganization* to analyze the nearly constant interplay
between Congress, lobbyists, and each presidential administration. With some infighting and substantial pressure
from interest groups, each presidential administration has
determined how to implement immigration legislation.

For President Herbert Hoover's administration from 1929 through 1933, implementing the Immigration Act of 1924 meant rounding up immigrants—disproportionately Mexican people—for deportation. During the Hoover administration, the Labor Department's "Section 24" officers "indiscriminately raided places where newcomers assembled." Section 24 "arbitrarily sought mass expulsions. Places where foreigners congregated, such as lodging houses, were raided."[35] The cruelty was completely legal.

Amid the Great Depression, the Hoover administration zeroed in on a clause from the Immigration Act of 1917: "likely to become a public charge." Hoover's 1930 instruction for State Department consular officials abroad to adhere strictly to the "likely to become a public charge" clause meant that the U.S. would turn away tens of thousands of potential immigrants, including German-Jewish refugees throughout the 1930s. By 1932, more people left the country than entered.

Since 1924, the State Department exerted authority over consuls overseas, and once each immigrant entered the U.S., the Labor Department was in charge. During the Coolidge and Hoover administrations, the Labor Department conducted raids and carried out deportations. But Perkins tried to redirect the Labor Department's focus toward supporting immigrant communities and welcoming newcomers.

Acting on Perkins's advice, Roosevelt issued Executive Order 6144 in 1933, merging the Bureaus of Immigration and Naturalization into the INS. The merge enabled Perkins to centralize control. She cracked down on practices that she deemed at best bad policy and at worst inhumane.

For instance, Perkins let two hundred thousand dollars of congressional appropriations for Section 24 run out, and then she laid off those fifty-three officers due to "insufficient funds."[36] Can't influence Congress on immigration? No matter, thought Perkins, as she terminated the xenophobes' employment.

Cutting staff was an administrative tactic for resetting priorities. In her first year, Perkins reduced 571 immigration staff. She couldn't just come in and tell them to stop dramatically conducting raids and deporting people. She had to reduce the resources in the areas where she believed staff were harming, not helping immigrants. Harming immigrants had been so ingrained in the Labor Department that the first pro-immigrant Labor Secretary terminated the employment of everyone who'd served at the Labor Department for more than thirty years. Perkins thought that these employees were "set in their ways and would resist implementing" her initiatives.[37] They were unlikely to take orders from a woman, too.

Together, Perkins and Commissioner of Immigration and Naturalization Daniel MacCormack implemented generosity training, literally training people working on the ground in immigration policy to become more sympathetic. Hernandez calls Perkins and MacCormack "simpatico," explaining: "Should a newcomer be detained for more questioning, inspectors were schooled to apologize for taking such action."[38] Perkins and MacCormack sought to make any necessary detentions as humane as possible. They renovated the spaces where immigrants would spend time on Ellis Island, including larger rooms for social workers to advocate for immigrants.[39]

Perkins interpreted Section 3 of the Immigration Act of 1917, regarding Americans departing the country, to apply to noncitizens. As a result, noncitizens could performatively leave the country only to return quickly throughout the 1930s.[40] Refugees would adopt this strategy.

Perkins and MacCormack temporarily banned arresting immigrants without warrants. Unfortunately, this policy change didn't last very long, because MacCormack died on January 1, 1937, and because Perkins received overwhelming pushback from Congress, interest groups, and other members of the presidential administration.

In their rhetoric, Perkins and MacCormack each emphasized the humanity of people who immigrated, prior to the emergence of human rights as an international legal framework. According to Perkins, "Each one of these fellows who comes in as an immigrant, together with his wife and children, are human beings."[41] This line was representative of the way that she talked about immigrants and immigration policy. From MacCormack's perspective, "Every act and decision affects the lives and welfare of human beings. We must, therefore, ever strive for that most difficult ideal—technical accuracy informed by justice and by humanity."[42] Perkins and MacCormack coordinated with each other explicitly to protect human dignity.

When they allocated authority over immigration policy in the U.S. to the Labor Department in 1917 and 1924, lawmakers didn't anticipate someone like Perkins—not only a woman but also a pro-immigrant progressive—at the helm. Across town, Roosevelt's State Department appointees aligned more closely with the xenophobic Congress. For example, William J. Carr, Assistant Secretary of State from

1924 to 1937, repeatedly used a slur against Jewish people. In the 1930s, a crucial decade for German-Jewish refugees, most U.S. lawmakers and implementers did not view Jewish immigrants as carriers of that elusive whiteness that arbiters of immigration policy sought to protect.

CHAPTER THREE

Becoming Nazi Germany

*A*CROSS THE OCEAN, PEOPLE IN Germany under the
Nazi regime felt change, fear, and shifting power.
They heard the crisp, staccato sounds of Nazi marches in
the early morning, as well as tunes like "When Jewish
Blood Spurts from the Knife." They saw the same cafés,
hotels, and traffic patterns as in the previous regime, the
Weimar Republic, except now they were draped in red,
white, and black swastika flags. People smelled and tasted
the same cigars and coffee—and now blood, if they were
in the wrong place at the wrong time.

To understand how Frances Perkins addressed the German-Jewish refugee crisis requires understanding how and
why the Nazi regime spelled disaster for Jewish Germans.
While many Jewish people chose to stay in Germany, thou-

sands more tried to leave. The rise of Nazi Germany struck terror but also unfolded slowly in ways that seemed so unbelievable that not everyone believed it. Antisemitism—while foundational to the Nazi Party from its inception in 1920—veiled itself with economic desperation and German nationalism from the late 1920s through the appointment of Hitler in 1933.

Mass killings did not occur during the 1930s. That was the decade when the perpetrators accumulated power, then laid the groundwork for war and war crimes. It was a decade that turned Jewish Germans into Jewish refugees.

Nineteenth-Century Roots, World War I, and Its Aftermath

Nineteenth-century Europe witnessed the spread of imperialism, the growth of nationalism, the rise of militarism, and the development of alliances, all of which contributed to the outbreak of World War I—once known as the Great War or the war to end all wars—in 1914.

Callous imperialism, powered by exploitation of labor and plundering of resources, brought immeasurable suffering to people on the African continent and around the world. In 1885, King Leopold II of Belgium colonized the Congo by sending explorers to negotiate with local leaders and slaughtering them when that didn't work. England joined the "scramble for Africa" next, and then Germany, which had recently unified as a nation-state in 1871. In late 1884, the European nation-states of Belgium, England, France, Germany, Portugal, and Spain, as well as a representative from the U.S., convened in Berlin to divide Africa among themselves by drawing maps in a room together. German Chancellor Otto von Bismarck represented Germany at the Berlin Conference. In subsequent decades, the European powers continued to "pillage resources" for "record profits."[1] This age of imperialism effectively advanced technology, such as the telegraph, as well as a racist pseudoscience that Europeans used to justify their theft to themselves. In Africa, Europeans continued to divide and conquer, and when that didn't work, they brought out the guns. Dividing and conquering African territories—as the communities resisted—required strong, unified European nation-states to coordinate and facilitate. Hannah Arendt argued in *The Origins of Totalitarianism* that nineteenth-century imperialism contributed substantially to the strengthening of nation-states, which enabled totalitarianism and the Holocaust.[2]

Nation-states are not automatic, not inevitable, and not timeless, argues Benedict Anderson in *Imagined Communities*.[3] Nationalism, the ideology of loving one's country, contributes to maintaining a nation-state through customs and traditions, culture and language, shared religion, and other nationalistic pursuits. Nineteenth-century French nationalism serves as an important example, creating the context in which the French Minister of War wrongly convicted French artillery officer Alfred Dreyfus of treason, known by many as the Dreyfus Affair from 1894 to 1906. Dreyfus's Jewishness fit uncomfortably within culturally Catholic, predominantly secular French nationalism. Before the rise of Nazi Germany, if you asked someone in any European village which empire would attempt to annihilate

European Jewry, the answer likely would have been either France or Russia. The rise of nationalism within each European power contributed substantially to the start of World War I.

Militarism shaped the late nineteenth and early twentieth centuries, as advancements in weaponry became increasingly profitable to national and international economies. The Industrial Revolution resulted in new rifles, gunpowder, and gasses that killed people with unprecedented efficiency. The competing European powers raced each other to reach the most advanced, most devastating technology, including machine guns on land, submarines at sea, and increasingly capable war machines in the sky.[4]

As imperialism, nationalism, and militarism intensified, so did the rise of alliances aiming to protect those interests. France and Germany had squabbled over the borderlands between the two countries throughout the nineteenth and early twentieth centuries. From 1870 to 1871, the Franco-Prussian War ceded the disputed territory of Alsace-Lorraine from the French Empire to the newly unified Germany. For the next several decades, France built an alliance with England. The German Empire built alliances southeast of Germany with the Austro-Hungarian Empire and the Ottoman Empire. England-France and Germany-Austria-Ottomans each developed further alliances with the people of Eastern Europe. For example, the Serbians aspired to become a nation, Serbia, and to resist Austro-Hungarian imperialism. The Serbian people's alliance with France and Great Britain explains why a Serbian nationalist's assassination of the heir to the throne of Austria-Hungary in June 1914 triggered World

War I (and indefinitely postponed Frances Perkins and Paul Wilson's European honeymoon).

As war ravaged Europe, the entry of Americans on the side of the British and French helped to secure the outcome of the war in their favor. At the Paris Peace Conference in 1917, President Woodrow Wilson attempted to persuade European leaders not to be too vindictive in their treaties. Partially because they found President Wilson to be an elitist snob with a high-and-mighty attitude who thought he knew better than the nations that had contributed most of the fighting and dying, they disregarded his advice. Consequently, the Treaty of Versailles formally blamed Germany for all of World War I and required the Germans to pay for it, plunging Germany into national humiliation and an economic crisis.

The Paris Peace Conference created new nations in Eastern Europe, including Czechoslovakia and Yugoslavia. It broke up the Austro-Hungarian Empire and the Ottoman Empire. The territory that Germany won in the Franco-Prussian War, Alsace-Lorraine, was returned to France. The victors forced the German Empire to become a new German democracy, the Weimar Republic. Saddled with the economic consequences of the Treaty of Versailles and bearing the brunt of a lost war, the new government began in a state of disarray that never recovered.

The Paris Peace Conference also established the League of Nations, which Woodrow Wilson proposed, yet he could not convince the U.S. to join due to widespread isolationism. The same isolationism would tighten restrictions on immigration to the U.S., contributing toward dooming the masses of European Jewry.

As a nation economically decimated and profoundly humiliated, many Germans immediately looked for somewhere to place the blame. Stripped of their militaristic identity and prewar nationalism, many Germans began to define themselves against others, against the French who took their territory and against the Jewish communities who resided in their midst. As the French began to treat French Jewry increasingly well, German Jewry suffered because Germans viewed themselves as antithetical to the French.

In 1919, angered by the humiliation thrust upon Germany, Austrian-born German corporal Adolf Hitler joined the fledgling German Workers' Party. Quickly attracting followers and assuming a leadership role, Hitler renamed it the National Socialist German Workers' Party. In Germany, this was *Nationalsozialistische Deutsche Arbeiterpartei*, with an abbreviation: Nazi.

Becoming the Nazi Party

The 1920 launch of the Nazi Party built on centuries of antisemitism. Difficult to define, antisemitism often operates differently from other global structures of oppression. In *Why?: Explaining the Holocaust*, historian Peter Hayes offers one possible definition for antisemitism: "A categorical impugning of Jews as collectively embodying distasteful and/or destructive traits ... the belief that Jews have common repellent and/or ruinous qualities that set them apart from non-Jews. Descent is determinative; individuality is illusory."[5] Universalizing a negative trait of a singular Jewish person as a Jewish trait has been a common example of antisemitism.

One way that antisemitism operates differently from other global structures of oppression is that it often punches up at people with more resources rather than down. This is a complicated nuance to parse because one antisemitic stereotype associates Jewish people with money, even though most Jewish people in Europe were not wealthy. Still, centuries of systematic discrimination against Jewish people ultimately placed many Jewish workers in positions where they could earn a significant income. Hayes explains that "Jews' initial success in commercial activities represented an extension of the few economic roles previously permitted to them. Moneylenders became bankers; peddlers became shopkeepers . . . and cattle traders became brokers of commodities and stocks."[6] Ironically, a long history of discrimination financially elevated a segment of the population, making them vulnerable to even more discrimination.

Antisemitism is fundamentally irrational, yet real. One of many internal contradictions is that from the perspective of antisemitic ideas, Jewish people both somehow control everything and yet are less worthy than everyone else. This hypocrisy did not bother the Nazis, for whom a consistent, rational ideology was not their priority.[7]

Though small and unpopular at the time of its founding in 1920, the Nazi Party penned a platform that set precedent for the party's future. The Nazi Party Platform stated in 1920: "Only those of German blood, whatever their creed, may be members of the nation. Accordingly, no Jew may be a member of the nation." Consistently, the platform emphasized a better, stronger Germany, while also specifying at whose expense. Although the Nazis remained far from dictating national policy in 1920, if given the opportunity they promised to deny citizenship to Jewish people, classifying them instead as "resident aliens." The platform excluded Jewish people from public office and blocked their immigration into the country: "All non-German immigration must be prevented." It banned Jewish people from publishing any news to share their perspectives and plight: "No non-German newspapers may appear without the express permission of the State," and of course they wouldn't grant that permission.[8]

Antisemitism infiltrated daily life in mainstream German society during the Weimar Republic. Attacks on Jewish Germans occurred with greater frequency throughout the 1920s. But it wasn't always physical. Born in 1906, Hannah Arendt recalled that when her childhood teachers during the 1920s treated Jewish children differently or made antisemitic comments, her mother expected her daughter to stand up calmly, exit the classroom, and walk home.[9]

Although the worldwide Great Depression didn't start until 1929, the economic depression began in Germany as early as 1923. In the mid-1920s, the exchange rate in Germany dropped to as low as 4.2 trillion reichsmarks to the dollar. German currency was worthless.

Not coincidentally, also in 1923, Adolf Hitler and the Nazis attempted to overthrow the government of the Weimar Republic. The coup d'état began in a Munich beer hall and sought to overthrow the government in Berlin. World War I veterans, including commander Erich Ludendorff, led the charge but were quickly confronted by German police, leading to several deaths. The German legal system showed sympathy to Hitler and his cronies, awarding five-year prison sentences rather than deportation to Austria. Hitler served only nine months of his sentence. He used his time in prison—clacking a typewriter "painfully with the hunt-and-peck method"—to write a manifesto.[10]

In 1925, he published an antisemitic diatribe entitled *Mein Kampf*. *Mein Kampf* communicated to the world what Hitler, the leader of the Nazi Party, believed and what he planned to do if given the opportunity to lead. Lawmakers and readers around the world read what the increasingly infamous German lawbreaker had to say. As American elites typically knew multiple European languages, future President Franklin Delano Roosevelt read it in the original German. Today, scholars who have read *Mein Kampf* in both English and German attest that the original German is somehow nastier than the English translation.

How did the Nazi ideology outlined in *Mein Kampf* seek to address economic collapse? Hayes describes Nazism as a "kind of bastardized Marxism that substituted race for class."[11] While Marxist ideology views all history as class struggle and seeks for the proletariat (working class) to overthrow the bourgeoisie (societal elites), Nazism interpreted all history as a race war in which Jewish people represented a parasitic race according to Hitler. The reality that Judaism was an ethno-religion—an ethnicity and a religion—from its earliest days through the late nineteenth century didn't matter to Hitler, who used racist pseudo-science popular at the time to support his claims.

Upon publishing *Mein Kampf*, Hitler once again assumed control of the Nazi Party. He learned from the failed Beer Hall Putsch not to retry an armed uprising to seek power. Instead, he exploited the freedoms of assembly, press, and speech that the democratic Weimar Republic ensured. In 1927, German President Paul von Hindenburg—an eighty-year-old World War I hero—delivered a speech repudiating the Treaty of Versailles, a statement that the Nazi Party agreed with wholeheartedly. In the 1928 elections, however, only 2% of the German population voted for the Nazi Party.

In late October 1929, the New York Stock Exchange crashed in New York. The crash compounded a tanking international economy. In *The Death of Democracy*, historian Benjamin Carter Hett writes that "it was the bull market on Wall Street in 1928, not the crash a year later, that drove Germany into recession. Germany depended heavily on foreign loans ... to meet its reparation payments."[12] In the U.S., the crash itself represented a culmination of more than a decade of Americans buying on credit as if prosperity were limitless and consequences were impossible. The laissez-faire economics of the 1920s, at the federal level, ensured that nothing stood in the way of full economic collapse. When the U.S. plunged into the Great Depression, a plethora of transnational debt networks lingering from World War I dragged down the other countries involved, notably already-struggling Germany.

When Nazism was born from both antisemitism and economic hardship in 1920, it was forthright in its antisemitic claims. Anti-Jewish sentiment remained central to Nazism as an ideology. But in the lead-up to the democratic election of Adolf Hitler in 1933, the Nazi Party strategically downplayed its antisemitism, opting instead to center on economics. For an increasing number of followers of the Nazi Party, the economic desperation caused by the worldwide Great Depression felt real and urgent.

By 1932, more than a third of the German population was unemployed. People who still held jobs watched their wages drop substantially. It was in this context that Hitler, newly a German citizen—the Weimar Republic could have deported him to Austria for trying to overthrow the government in 1923 but didn't—ran for president in 1932.

Nazis and Communists both won increased representation in the Reichstag (German Parliament) in the 1930 election. The Great Depression increased the number of Nazi seats in the Reichstag from 12 to 107. Nazi leaders delivered victorious speeches to packed crowds, featuring military music, uniformed troops, and "swastika-emblazoned flags."[13] Most German elites continued to prefer the radical Right (Nazis) over the radical Left (Communists) because the latter sought to redistribute wealth. Elites would rather sacrifice German Jewry than sacrifice their own wealth and privileges in society.

American journalist Dorothy Thompson covered the story. Thompson's "consternation blazed across the pages . . . scrambling to analyze how the modern, admirably civilized, industrially advanced social democratic Weimar Republic could have made way for the popular rise of the Nazi Party," writes historian Nancy Cott in her book *Fighting Words* about American journalists abroad during the interwar period. In 1932, Thompson personally interviewed the Nazi Party's leader and subsequently published a book, *I Saw Hitler!* Thompson both underestimated Hitler's ability to achieve his aims and warned readers about his negative qualities.[14]

Throughout the Weimar Republic, electoral politics split between conservatives who sought a return to the prewar era and Leftists who wanted a revolution. While unabashedly bigoted, the Nazi Party combined key elements of both: nostalgia for something old combined with hope for something new. Still, Hitler did not win the 1932 election. The conservative incumbent, Paul von Hindenburg, won more votes than Hitler and the Communist candidate. As the leader of the Nazis, however, Hitler controlled a large enough block of votes in Parliament that eighty-five-year-old President von Hindenburg chose forty-four-year-old Adolf Hitler to become chancellor. Fearing the Leftists most of all, a "clique of aristocrats and landowners" persuaded von Hindenburg to appoint Hitler in January 1933.[15] Their priority was to protect their economic status no matter who would be doomed.

Becoming Nazi Germany

The skies were not always gray, and the doom was not always palpable. People continued to eat at cafés, such as Café Josty in Berlin. They drove cars, and Potsdamer Platz remained "one of the busiest intersections in the world," featuring a five-way streetlight, one of the first stoplights in Europe.[16] A five-story nightclub, Haus Vaterland, housed six thousand people in its twelve seating spots. One was a Wild West bar with waiters in cowboy hats emulating the American frontier. After all, Hitler viewed the American removal of Indigenous communities as a model for governance.

"Heil Hitler" salutes were everywhere, used for greetings with a tinge of deference to authority. Hitler's bodyguard unit, the Schutzstaffel (SS), marched around largely for the sake of marching. The Parliamentary Army, the Sturmabteilung (SA), also known as the Storm Troopers, wore swastika bands on their brown uniforms. On January 30, 1933, Nazis celebrated in the streets, which were lined with huge Nazi flags: red background, a white circle, and a black swastika in the center. Joseph Goebbels, who would become Minister of Propaganda in March 1933, organized a parade of twenty thousand Nazis: SS, SA, and German civilians.

In February, the Reichstag burned. As flames curled through the cupola and into the sky, Chancellor Hitler arrived in his black Mercedes limousine to deliver a speech blaming political opponents, especially the Communists. With flames in the background, Hitler yelled from the balcony: "Every Communist official will be shot where he is found!"[17] Goebbels led efforts to circulate rumors that Communists were plotting a coup. "With Nazi storm troopers terrorizing the opposition, civil rights suspended by emergency decree, and the conservative coalition government in control of press and radio, the Nazi Party gained 44% of the March vote," Cott explains.[18] Hitler subsequently locked up Communists. Jails and beating stations sprung up across Germany, the sites of increasing Nazi cruelty. Establishing "impromptu prisons and torture stations in basements, sheds, and other structures," Storm Troopers accosted Jewish Germans and political opponents. On March 31, 1933, the SS dragged three American citizens into a beating station, beat them, left them in the cold overnight, and then beat them again in the morning until they were unconscious, at which point they left them on a street.[19]

On May 10, the Nazi Party conducted a mass burning of books by anyone who disagreed with them, especially Jewish authors. Dorothy Thompson explicitly compared the rise of Nazi Germany to the novel *Brave New World* in her reporting. She detected its dystopian quality. She noted two shared characteristics: that the government controlled all information that was available, and that when anything didn't go according to plan, one group absorbed the blame as a scapegoat.

On Sunday, July 16, an American named Philip Zuckerman and his wife were walking in Leipzig when the Storm Troopers attacked them. The Storm Troopers had trailed off from an SS parade of Nazi flags and salutes across the city. They beat Zuckerman and his pregnant wife so badly that she could never again bear another child. Indeed, these were the Nazi aims: to terrorize and terminate the Jewish population.[20]

German people remained friendly as ever only to the people who shared their status in the Third Reich. Later that summer, Ambassador William Dodd's daughter Martha "felt the press had badly maligned the country," and she "wanted to proclaim the warmth and friendliness of the people, the soft summer night with its fragrance of trees and flowers, the serenity of the streets."[21] American gentiles were not Hitler's targets.

Ambassador Dodd represented U.S. interests in Germany from 1933 through 1937. Dodd was born in North Carolina in 1869, in the former Confederacy, barely four years after the Civil War. With a PhD in History, Ambassador Dodd worked as a professor at the University of Chicago. Dodd was not a full-on Lost Causer and saw himself as a more critical thinker than many. Yet he adored Thomas Jefferson, the subject of his dissertation, and he admired Woodrow Wilson, a foreign policy role model.[22] In short, the man protecting American interests in Nazi Germany revered an enslaver and a man who proactively resegregated the U.S. federal government, respectively. The U.S.'s representative to Germany was no great moral agent amid the rise of Nazism.

Even more, American race law directly influenced and inspired the Nazi methods of oppression. President von Hindenburg, not a young man, died in August 1934. Hitler wasted no time appointing himself the Führer (Supreme Leader) of Germany. In 1935, Hitler's government essentially enacted the Nazi Party Platform in the form of the Nuremberg Laws. Nazi lawmakers drew inspiration from racist American legal codes. "Nazi lawyers were engaged in creating a race law founded on anti-miscegenation law and race-based immigration, naturalization, and second-class citizenship law," writes historian and legal scholar James Q. Whitman in his 2018 book *Hitler's American Model*.[23] Whitman provides two key examples of Nazis seeking to emulate the U.S., the first being miscegenation laws. In Germany, Jewish people could no longer marry people who were not Jewish. In the U.S., it was not until 1967 that the Supreme Court held interracial marriage to be constitutional. The other example was citizenship: only white men had full rights of citizenship for most of U.S. history. Nazis discussed these precedents in June 1934, when they sat down to write the Nuremberg Laws, which were enacted in 1935, turning the platform ideas into law.

There are Jewish perspectives that stand slightly apart from more common narratives. In 1933, Henny Brenner was eight years old and living with her Jewish mother and Protestant father in Dresden, Germany. The Nazis characterized her as a "Mischling," or "half-breed."[24] The Nuremberg Laws barred Henny Brenner from citizenship. School teachers treated her poorly. Her parents lost their home, and the Nazis confiscated her father's movie theater business for refusing to divorce his Jewish wife. With her school closed, Henny was subjected to involuntary labor instead of education. By 1941, wearing the mandatory yellow Jewish star (Judenstern), Henny faced increasingly public stigmatization. Yet her father's status as a German Protestant combined with his love for his family provided adequate protection for Henny Brenner and her parents to survive. When World War II started in 1939, she and her mother could not receive food rations. Her father's status enabled traveling to secure food for his wife and daughter. How was their survival possible? Individual cases often unfolded on an ad hoc basis, sometimes referred case by case to Hitler.

History shows that two contradictory things can be true at the same time. On one hand, the Nazi rise to power occurred slowly. Although their platform communicated their aims as early as 1920, the Nazis decentered antisemitism in their rhetoric between the failed coup of 1923 and the election of 1932. Even as Hitler seized power, American journalists and lawmakers alike vacillated over the extent of the threat that the Third Reich posed. When Nazi

Germany welcomed the world to the Berlin Olympics in August 1936, they removed antisemitic signage, projecting a strong and unified Germany. Swimmers' limbs stroked the water, and runners' feet pounded the pavement. Black American track star Jesse Owens triumphed over both American and German iterations of anti-Black racism. Some Jewish families remained in Germany. Other German-Jewish families, such as the Franks, relocated in 1934 to the Netherlands, where Otto and Edith gifted a diary to their daughter Anne for her thirteenth birthday in 1942.

On the other hand, as poet Maya Angelou advised, "when someone shows you who they are, believe them the first time." Hitler's *Mein Kampf* was as vehemently antisemitic as it was well distributed internationally. Educated Americans such as Franklin Delano Roosevelt read the book in its original German, reportedly more foreboding than the English translation. Nazi leaders barked out antisemitic vitriol into the crowds of seemingly ordinary Germans throughout the 1920s and 1930s. The masses cheered in response. The sizes of the crowds only increased from the publication of a Nazi Party Platform in 1920 through the enactment of the Nuremberg Laws in 1935. Antisemitism was central to the Nazi founding, and though its predominance fluctuated, it was always there, threatening Jewish lives in the Nazi path.

CHAPTER FOUR

Charge Bonds Controversy

*B*ARELY A MONTH AFTER HITLER became Chancellor of Germany, Franklin Delano Roosevelt became President of the United States. FDR delivered his inaugural address, including the famous line "the only thing we have to fear is fear itself," on March 4, 1933.[1] As FDR's message about overcoming fear resonated with the general American public, Hitler increasingly used fear as a weapon to control Germany.

Although the Great Depression was their most pressing concern, Americans also followed Hitler's ascent to power and the deteriorating status of Jewish Germans. On March 28, 1933, *The New York Times* reported that Hitler's Nazi Party smashed windows of Jewish stores, broke streetcars, and assaulted Jewish passersby. On April 1, Nazis and complicit Germans boycotted Jewish businesses.[2] *The Dallas Morning News* reported that the boycott "paralyzed the commercial life of its victims." Only a handful of Jewish businesses remained open, including Jewish medical and law practices. Even Jewish state and municipal employees were "discharged."[3] The following week, Nazis removed Jewish Germans and everyone who opposed Nazism from civil service positions.

On April 18, 1933, less than two months into FDR's presidency, the cabinet convened to discuss a sudden surge in applications for immigration visas from Jewish Germans. The cabinet met on the northeast side of the West Wing in a room with white walls and red curtains, which accentuated four windows overlooking the White House Rose Garden. Cabinet secretaries gathered around an eight-sided mahogany table. As the secretary of the newest department, Frances Perkins took her place to the left of the vice president.[4]

FDR's cabinet wasn't homogenous, and as a group they stood far from poised to protect Jewish Germans. All were college graduates, except for the vice president and the Secretary of State, who each had opted instead for accelerated legal training and a quick launch into politics. A third of the members—Garner, Hull, Swanson, and Roper—were born in the late-nineteenth-century South into families who had been Confederate. Roper's father led the 18th Regiment of North Carolina, fighting to preserve enslavement. Some cabinet secretaries descended from Confederates and grew up with Lost Cause thinking. Politically, the president assembled them intentionally to secure support from the white South, which interpreted Democrat to mean "Confederate"

POSITION	NAME	GENDER	EDUCATION	REGIONAL IDENTITY
President	Franklin Delano Roosevelt	Male	Harvard University, 1903	New Yorker
Vice President	John Nance Garner	Male	Legal training instead of college	Texan
Secretary of State	Cordell Hull	Male	Legal training instead of college	Tennessean
Secretary of the Treasury	William H. Woodin	Male	Columbia University, 1890	New Yorker
Secretary of War	George Dern	Male	Midland University, 1888	Nebraskan
Attorney General	Homer Stiles Cummings	Male	Yale University, ~1898	New Englander
Postmaster General	James Farley	Male	Packard Business College, ~1906	New Yorker
Secretary of the Navy	Claude A. Swanson	Male	Randolph Macon College, 1885	Virginian
Secretary of the Interior	Harold L. Ickes	Male	University of Chicago, 1897	Chicagoan
Secretary of Agriculture	Henry A. Wallace	Male	Iowa State University, 1910	Iowan
Secretary of Commerce	Daniel C. Roper	Male	Duke University, 1888	South Carolinian
Secretary of Labor	Frances Perkins	Female	Mount Holyoke, 1902	New Englander

rather than New Deal. As a result, these people weren't as ideologically dissimilar from the Nazis, who drew inspiration from Americans' treatment of Black Americans throughout American history, as one might have liked.[5]

Perkins was, of course, the only woman in the group. Born in New England, like Attorney General Cummings, she'd lived in New York, like the president, Treasury Secretary, and Postmaster General. She wasn't the only one who "spoke in the upper-crust tones befitting her upbringing... with long flat a's, dropped r's, and rounded vowels, 'to-maahhhto' for 'tomato.'"[6] Perkins more than anyone was "deeply religious, idealistic, and liberal." She'd "forged relationships with immigrants and FDR during her years as a pro-labor activist and official in New York." In contrast, top State Department officials were all "restrictionists," and they upheld antisemitism "in a department rife with such sentiments."[7] Thus, the meeting on April 18 launched a "serious clash between State and Labor," a "most unusual legal battle" between two federal executive departments.[8]

"Arcane Points" of American Immigration Law

April 1933 marked the beginning of what historians Richard Breitman and Allan Lichtman call a "long battle between two departments, having opposite views of the world, over arcane points of immigration laws and regulations."[9]

The Immigration Act of 1917 had banned a wide range of marginalized groups from immigrating to the U.S., including, but not limited to, "idiots, imbeciles, epileptics, alcoholics, poor, criminals, beggars, any person suffering attacks of insanity, those with tuberculosis, and those who have any form of dangerous contagious disease, aliens who have physical disability that will restrict them from earning a living."[10] As chapter three explains in greater detail, restrictionist legislation doubled down on the Chinese Exclusion Act of 1882 and set precedent for the National Origins Act of 1924. The 1917 Act also included the phrase "likely to become a public charge," describing any immigrant with the potential to burden U.S. taxpayers.

In 1930, President Herbert Hoover zeroed in on the phrase "likely to become a public charge." He instructed State Department consular officials overseas to adhere strictly to it. As the Great Depression raged, Hoover thought he was protecting U.S. taxpayers from the burden of aiding immigrants. But in practice, the 1930 instruction embedded xenophobia and restrictionism further into U.S. laws.

Consulates were offices controlled by the U.S. Department of State in foreign countries. In these offices, consuls evaluated potential immigrants' papers, including passports, financial statements, and employment histories, to decide whether to admit them to the U.S. The phrasing within the Immigration Act of 1917, "likely to become a public charge," let consuls decide on a whim who might burden U.S. taxpayers.

In April 1933, the State Department claimed to the president that nobody wanted to leave Germany. Neither the German nor the Austrian quota was filled in any year prior to 1939 because State Department consuls exploited the "public charge" clause, and by the time more people attempted to flee Nazi territory, it was too late.

While we cannot know for sure whether State Department officials even convinced themselves of their erroneous claims in 1933, historians concur that the "public charge" clause, not quota laws, was the primary roadblock before 1938. A formal report from Perkins's Solicitor of Labor confirmed that "the consuls are not known for their sympathy toward immigrants, and particularly toward Jews. The State Department (for fear of general weakening effect upon the restrictive program) may hesitate to issue orders that would correct this attitude."[11] In the early 1930s, the State Department was in the practice of intentionally preventing Jewish immigration to the U.S.

State Department restrictionism stemmed from both World War I, which accelerated isolationism, and the Great Depression, which exacerbated xenophobia. In December 1933, division official Paul C. Fletcher posited that Americans "are apathetic in immigration matters; they are completely occupied with economic problems. Nevertheless, they look to us to protect their rights, and if ships begin to arrive in New York City laden with Jewish immigrants, the predominant Gentile population of the country will claim they have been betrayed through a 'sleeping' State Department."[12] While Perkins looked to protect the human rights of vulnerable refugees, top State Department officials sought to protect Americans' rights not to help. Thus, the State Department refused to "sleep," relentlessly serving a "predominant Gentile population."

White Anglo-Saxon Protestantism remained the State Department's norm. Institutional bigotry rather than individual or personal prejudices shaped refugees' fates.[13] Further, no law existed in 1933 to instruct American support of refugees, people fleeing for their lives, who were legally just immigrants.

Perkins understood that Jewish Germans were suffering, and she wanted to use whatever power the Immigration and Naturalization Service (INS) had to help. She arrived at the April 18 cabinet meeting informed by a firsthand account of Germany from journalist Dorothy Thompson, who was married to Perkins's former suitor and now friend, novelist Sinclair Lewis. Thompson, one of the most famous women in the U.S., offered an invaluable perspective as an eyewitness to Nazi Germany. Perkins had also been conferring with a Roosevelt advisor and future Supreme Court Justice, Felix Frankfurter, who happened to be Jewish and took the initiative to draft potential executive orders for FDR to use. Both orders would have relaxed the quota for immigrants from Germany. One proposal mentioned the "public charge" clause, while the other didn't.[14]

At cabinet meetings, Perkins was an attentive listener and a shrewd observer of social dynamics. On one hand, she generally hesitated to speak unless necessary, mainly due to awareness of how men perceived the only woman in the room. On the other hand, she and Postmaster General Farley were the only individuals at the table who'd worked closely with FDR and earned his trust prior to the administration. So, Perkins subtly mentioned the two executive order drafts at the April 18 meeting. FDR took Perkins's suggestions seriously and asked Hull to discuss them with his department.

Cordell Hull was the kind of man who didn't necessarily hold any egregious opinions. In fact, his wife was descended from an Austrian Jewish family.[15] Yet Hull didn't particularly defend any opinions because he "dreaded controversy" so much that he caved to whoever caused the loudest ruckus.[16] The person making the most noise was not the first female cabinet secretary who needed to tread carefully and navigate gender politics as Vice President Garner at the head of the table next to her looked over judgmentally.

As a former representative and senator, Hull was also a Washington insider who valued isolationism. As the newly appointed Secretary of State, Hull believed that the U.S.'s primary relationship with Germany should be trade, specifically to collect debts incurred during World War I. Harboring refugees from German persecution was not on his priority list.

At no point did Hull or other State Department officials claim to be deliberately persecuting Jewish people, no matter how casually cruel and antisemitic some State Department officials could be. Rather, their priorities lay elsewhere. And a culture of antisemitism prevented concerns about what Perkins often called "human dignity" from rising above the isolationism and xenophobia.

Hull aimed not to upset Assistant Secretary of State Wilbur J. Carr and Under Secretary of State William Phillips. Carr regularly used antisemitic slurs, journaling that Jewish people were "filthy, un-American and often dangerous in their habits." Having secured his job from being a childhood friend of the president's wife, William Phillips had journaled while on vacation: "This place is infested with Jews. In fact, the whole beach scene . . . covered by slightly clothed Jews and Jewesses."[17] But the Assistant Secretary and the Under Secretary were not invited to the meeting of cabinet secretaries, where FDR told Hull to bring Perkins's proposal to the State Department. Perkins did not know Carr or Phillips, and they did not know her.

Under Secretary of State
"Blown Off the End of the Telephone"
by New Energy at Department of Labor

Perkins's most candid form of distance communication was the telephone. Under Secretary of State Phillips called her expecting to talk some sense into her.

Perkins sat in her cockroach-infested office in a boxlike building at the corner of G and 17th Street NW. The Labor Department's year of origin, 1913, was also when the Wilson administration allowed resegregation within the federal government. Black employees weren't allowed to eat in the cafeteria. They had to keep food in their desks, which attracted the pests, until Perkins desegregated a new Labor Department building on Constitution Avenue in late 1934.[18]

Chief of the Western European Division, Jay Pierrepont Moffat, reported that "she quite blew our poor Under Secretary off his end of the telephone."[19] Phillips attempted to explain to Perkins that the State Department wouldn't permit the president to aid refugees. Threatening pressure from Jewish advocates like the American Jewish Committee, Perkins assured him that her department wouldn't sit on the sidelines of immigration policy.

The call marked Perkins's first conflict with the State Department on the question of immigration outside of formal cabinet meetings. Perkins "told [Phillips] in no uncertain terms that the right to asylum was based on American traditions and it was up to her department, not the State Department, to decide whether such admission would adversely affect the economic conditions."[20] While the State Department sought to preserve American restrictionism and xenophobia, Perkins maintained a rosy interpretation of the past, present, and future of American ideals.

Perkins hadn't planned for immigration reform to be a policy priority. Yet the conditions in which Perkins found the Labor Department demanded that she sort out immigration first. Perkins was horrified to find in her first week on the job that five separate men introduced themselves to her as "in charge of immigration."[21] The bureau "suffered from divided command," and even that was an understatement.[22]

Sorting out chaos from her predecessor and anticipating further State Department animosity, Perkins continued to push against the grain. She schemed with Frankfurter and others behind the scenes, recruiting more legal experts to bolster their ranks in preparation for legal battle and cultural war: the charge bonds controversy.

To combat abuse of the "likely to become a public charge" clause from the Immigration Act of 1917, Perkins began considering an often-overlooked provision of the same Act. U.S. federal judge and social reformer Judge Julian Mack directed Perkins's attention to the potential use of the charge bond provision. Regarding charge bonds, the Immigration Act of 1917 stated: "Any alien liable to be excluded because likely to become a public charge [may] nevertheless be admitted in the discretion of the Secretary of Labor upon giving of a suitable and proper bond or undertaking, approved by said Secretary, in such amount and containing such conditions as he may prescribe."[23] She (not "he") found this provision encouraging. Her Solicitor of Labor advised her that the "usual amount for public charge bonds is $500" with "no reason to set the figure any higher for refugees."[24] Accounting for inflation, $500 in 1934 would equal approximately $12,000 in 2024. At the onset of the German-Jewish refugee crisis, charge bonds had the potential to influence refugee policy significantly by shielding refugees from the "public charge" clause and from Hoover's 1930 executive order.

The Labor Department argued that Perkins should be able to accept a charge bond before the immigrant or refugee passed through the consulate. This way, Labor would exercise discretionary authority over the admission of refugees. Rather than the State Department's whims, the Labor Department's whims would bode well or at least better for refugees. State objected that Perkins could accept a charge bond only after their consul approved the immigrant in question. Labor and State were poised for a battle over discretionary authority to determine who might become a public charge as a proxy for whether to admit German-Jewish refugees to the U.S.

The INS hadn't always been part of the Labor Department. In 1891, Congress had voted to exclude courts from immigration decisions by placing immigration under the jurisdiction of the Treasury Department. The result was a strict enforcement of rigid immigration laws without much ad hoc discretion. In 1903, the Department of the Treasury transferred control over the Bureau of Immigration to the newly created Department of Commerce and Labor. When the Departments of Commerce and Labor split into two separate institutions in 1913, Immigration remained with Labor. In 1933, FDR accepted Perkins's recommendation to combine the Bureau of Immigration with the Bureau of Naturalization to increase efficiency and minimize loopholes.

Perkins's predecessors in the Labor Department were as xenophobic—if not more so—as her foes in the State Department. In November 1936, Slovenian immigrant and writer Louis Adamic authored an essay titled "Aliens and Alien-Baiters," published in *Harper's Magazine*, lamenting that Hoover's Labor Secretary William Doak had been a "rabid xenophobe." Doak, according to Adamic, was "infected by the anti-alien virus," deriving a "strange satisfaction out of hounding aliens; raiding homes, wedding parties, and other gatherings in which it was suspected that a foreigner illegally in the country might be present."[25] While Doak delighted in deporting immigrants, social reformers advocated for immigrants "left destitute because their breadwinners, many of them people of good character, had been deported, often for technical irregularities in entry which were not their fault."[26] Perkins, shaped by her volunteer work in settlement homes, believed that immigrants were good for the U.S. economy.

In 1933, Perkins appointed as Commissioner of Immigration Daniel MacCormack, an immigrant himself who'd earned the respect of progressive social reformers. Solicitor of Labor Charles E. Wyzanski, Jr., wrote home to his mother about MacCormack, describing him as "a no-nonsense Mill liberal with a David Hume Scottish temperament and a fine taste in brandies. There was never a man better suited for this post. His record is distinguished."[27] While MacCormack's participation in the U.S. invasion of the Philippines and the U.S. imperialist enterprise in the Panama Canal weakened his stated commitment to "humanize," we can presume that he was an internationalist interventionist and not an isolationist restrictionist.

Perkins's progressive politics brought new energy and concerns to the Department of Labor. The charge bonds controversy was not only a disagreement between two Departments, it was a cultural battle and a turf war.

Cultural Battle and Turf War

The Departments of Labor and State agreed that the Attorney General, Homer Stiles Cummings, would decide the fate of charge bonds. They asked Cummings to rule on three specific points of contention. First, could the Secretary of Labor accept a bond before the immigrant in question arrived on American soil? If so, did the Secretary of Labor need to accept bonds according to the chronological order of applications? Finally, did Perkins possess the legal authority to override the consuls?

The Department of State used Provision 48 from the National Origins Act of 1924 to argue that Perkins did not have the authority to overturn a consul's decision that an applicant for immigration was likely to become a public charge, and thus required a charge bond: "Consular officials are not authorized either to require or to accept bonds in immigration cases. The question of bonds does not, therefore, arise until after an alien has received a visa and arrives at a port of entry to the United States."[28] State Department officials did not want to relinquish discretionary authority, and not to Perkins and the progressives whom she surrounded herself with in the Labor Department. One of whom was Solicitor of Labor Charles E. Wyzanski, Jr.

Born in 1906, Wyzanski was twenty-seven in 1933, when he authored the Labor Department's formal legal opinion on charge bonds for Attorney General Cummings. In addition to writing the opinion, Wyzanski was Jewish, which must have made the German-Jewish refugee crisis even more personal to him. Further, he was young enough that the audience for his detailed personal letters was not his future bride, Jewish immigrant Gisela Warburg—but his mom. Wyzanski described in a letter to his mother that the refugee crisis really bothered Perkins, who hoped to alleviate suffering as much as possible.[29]

Having experienced the charge bonds controversy before his thirtieth birthday, Wyzanski was still alive in the early 1980s when historians Richard Breitman and Alan Kraut were researching *American Refugee Policy and European Jewry, 1933–1945*. Wyzanski wrote to Breitman: "My best recollection is that Miss Perkins had turned over to me the problem of drafting a legal opinion to submit to the president. Judge Mack found me, either working on that memorandum or about to do so. He continued to call on me and offer me suggestions and to re-read my drafts until I had a final opinion for submission to Secretary Perkins."[30]

Wyzanski's formal opinion traced the legal history of charge bonds. Using Section 21 of the Immigration Act of 1917, he argued for the "propriety of accepting bonds" on behalf of immigrants not yet on American soil.[31] His point was that being "likely to become a public charge" didn't justify denying someone a visa, because the Labor Secretary could accept a charge bond to ensure that the immigrant would not become a public charge. Therefore, Perkins should be able to accept a bond for someone who had not yet landed in the U.S.

From the Labor Department's perspective, its discretionary authority over charge bonds was a valid option that the 1917 Immigration Act stipulated. The State Department countered that Perkins was overstepping her authority in a way that threatened national security. State Department officials accused Perkins of defying Congress by diverging from their rigid interpretation of the National Origins Act of 1924.

Cummings decided to side with the Labor Department: Consular officials could not designate immigrants as likely to become public charges if Perkins could accept a charge bond to support them. Cummings explained: "Any alien liable to be excluded because likely to become a public charge or because of physical disability other than tuberculosis in any form or a loathsome or dangerous contagious disease may, if otherwise admissible, nevertheless be admitted in the discretion of the bond or undertaking."[32] The emphasis on disabilities and disease here reflected his focus on the Immigration Act of 1917. Cummings's answer to the first of the three questions was that Perkins could accept a bond before the immigrant in question arrived on U.S. soil.

Cummings's decision granted discretionary authority to Perkins. In response to the second question, Cummings clarified the specifics of how the Secretary of Labor could accept a bond. He used the 1917 Act to explain how a charge bond should work: "Such alien may deposit in cash with the Secretary of Labor such amount as the Secretary of Labor may require, which amount shall be deposited by said Secretary in the United States Postal Savings Bank, a receipt therefore to be given the person furnishing said sum showing the fact and object of its receipt and such other information as said Secretary may deem advisable."[33] Friends or family of the immigrant could offer the required money, and Perkins could deposit it in the U.S. Postal Savings Bank. If the immigrant were to become incapable of supporting themself, public officials could draw on the sum in lieu of providing public assistance. Perkins could decide how much money the bond should ensure and any other details. According to the Attorney General, U.S. law could not stop Perkins from reducing the funds required, enabling more immigrants to arrive.

Cummings's answer to the third question was that Perkins could indeed override consular authority, and he supported his claim with the legislative reasoning behind the Immigration Act of 1917. Cummings wrote: "Running through the whole of the 1917 Act, is the legislative purpose to prevent migration to our shores of aliens not fully qualified to enter. It would require more specific language than is contained ... to justify the conclusion that the discretionary power therein conferred upon you, could not be exercised until the public charge alien ... had migrated to our shores."[34] In other words, just as an immigrant could be unfit to enter the U.S. before reaching American shores, a charge bond could deem them fit to enter the U.S. before reaching American shores.

In January 1934, Labor and State officials agreed that the Department of Labor would draft instructions for State to send to the consuls abroad, in light of Cummings's decision. Dating the letter 1933 when it was actually January 12, 1934, Wyzanski wrote to his mother that "no longer could the consuls abroad turn down, without possibility of appeal, aliens on the real or imaginary ground that they might become a public charge." Wyzanski assured his mother that the "Secretary was most anxious to ask at once. With characteristic feminine generosity and sympathy, she wanted at once to entertain applications from anyone to the full limit of the German quota."[35]

After the Attorney General decided the charge bonds controversy in Perkins's favor, the charge bonds controversy was far from settled. State Department consuls abroad awaited specific instructions to adjust their policies according to the new legal standard. Six months later, however, in summer 1934, the consuls had received no new instructions. By summer 1935, MacCormack claimed that charge bonds were no longer needed because "visa cases were now being resolved favorably."[36] MacCormack implied that visa policy was working in favor of refugees. But due to a confluence of reasons, this could not possibly have been the case.

Despite the Attorney General's ruling, Perkins likely felt restricted from using charge bonds on a wide scale because of the political climate of isolationism and xenophobia far beyond Washington, D.C. The American Federation of Labor (AFL) exerted pressure to support restrictive rather than progressive immigration policies. The AFL was an essential ally of the Roosevelt administration to push New Deal legislation through Congress. During the charge bonds controversy, MacCormack himself depended on AFL backing on a bill to control and curtail deportation cases.[37]

In February 1934, Wyzanski recommended caution and moderation to Perkins regarding charge bonds for the sake of placating the AFL and Congress. The AFL assumed that an influx of immigration would exacerbate unemployment. That same month, Wyzanski penned an essay on immigration and the New Deal, pontificating that "even to those of you who under ordinary conditions might seek to open wider the door into this country, it must be apparent that this is not the time to present your plan. So many millions are now unemployed that wholesale accommodations to additional foreigners are unthinkable."[38] In addition to pressures from the AFL, Wyzanski feared a rise in American antisemitism.

The American public would likely perceive a rise in Jewish immigration as the American government's special treatment of Jewish applicants, which would exacerbate preexisting antisemitism. As a Jewish person, Wyzanski wrote to his mother that he was in an "uncomfortable position" because no matter what he wrote about the German-Jewish refugee crisis, he'd either be enabling or provoking antisemitism.[39] If nothing else, the Labor Department gained leverage through the charge bonds controversy.

This dispute represented the opening scene in the story of Frances Perkins's efforts to aid refugees from Nazi Germany. It demonstrated nearly opposite approaches and instincts from Perkins's Labor Department versus Hull's State Department. Labor gained leverage by prevailing in the legal battle, and Perkins may have used that leverage for continued negotiations. While Perkins emerged as a humanitarian through her efforts, this most unusual legal battle between two cabinet departments began educating Perkins on the limits and nuances of her position.

CHAPTER FIVE

Child Refugees

*H*ERBERT AND JOSEF WECHSLER WERE two among countless German-Jewish children whose parents could no longer protect or provide for them amid Nazi persecution. They were among several hundred children whose survival was possible thanks to a special partnership between Frances Perkins's Labor Department, specifically its Children's Bureau (CB) under Katherine Lenroot, and a new humanitarian organization, the German-Jewish Children's Aid, Inc. (GJCA).

This partnership came with great costs. For the GJCA, the cost was financial, made possible through robust fundraising. For the Labor Department, the cost was continued squabbling with the State Department, other governmental structures, and public opinion. For children like Herbert and Josef, the cost was leaving behind everything they knew and never seeing their parents again. But in 1934, they didn't know that yet.

As Nazism took hold in Germany, Jewish children lost educational opportunities, economic security, and in time, physical safety. Jewish adults lost financial and physical security, too. But children found themselves in a different position: Jewish leaders and their allies noticed that the xenophobic American public might be more sympathetic to immigrant children than to the children's parents. Proponents of welcoming refugees portrayed the immigration as temporary, intending for the "children to return to their parents after the danger subsided in Europe."[1] Of course, the danger didn't subside for over a decade. And thus, we reach the paradox of child refugee policy: a haven for children amid the heartbreaking removal from parents.

From 1934 through 1941, the ninety-one ships carrying a few children each to the U.S. signified one of the most successful efforts by the Labor Department to aid refugees from Nazi Germany. Even so, the experience separated children from their parents under the illusion of temporariness. The frequent reality was permanent separation. Some children sent letters back and forth with their parents for nearly a decade before the Nazis murdered their parents.

In 1933, Jewish organizations began mobilizing administratively, financially, and politically to support Jewish immigration to the U.S. Under the leadership of Cecilia Razovsky, the GJCA supported the immigration of 597 German-Jewish children between 1934 and 1941. This feat wouldn't have happened under previous Labor Secretaries, who prioritized deportations. An early advocate for

German-Jewish refugees within the administration, Perkins remained on the side of children seeking refuge in the U.S.

In 1939, the U.S. Congress considered legislation to accept ten thousand child refugees each year for two years. For Congress, the legislation would have marked a radical change. For twenty thousand children, it would have been life-changing, in many cases lifesaving. For Perkins's Labor Department, it would have been a huge relief and eased the burden. However, the bill never made it to the floor of Congress.

Charge Bonds to Child Refugees, 1934

As early as August 1933, the American Jewish Congress had voted in favor of organizing a movement to bring Jewish child refugees from Germany to the U.S. They believed that such a plan "should be in full compliance with immigration laws and, therefore, have a better chance of being approved by the administration and accepted by the American public."[2] The American Jewish Congress appealed first to the State Department, where Assistant Secretary of State Wilbur J. Carr and Under Secretary of State William Phillips replied that visas for child refugees, as well as "to adult visa applicants," would be no problem.[3] This response struck Jewish organizations with worry, as they knew that the U.S. consuls maintained a pattern of rejecting Jewish adults' visa applications. If the State Department treated Jewish children like Jewish adults, Jewish leaders and organizations had no reason to believe that the U.S. consuls would accept children.

On January 3, 1934, the Joint Council on German Jewish Persecutions—which brought together a wide range of Jewish organizations, including the American Jewish Committee, American Jewish Congress, and B'nai B'rith—consolidated the National Conference of Social Work and the Committee on German-Jewish Immigration Policy to create the GJCA, which entered the world barely a week after the Labor Department won the charge bonds controversy.

The GJCA's administrative structure consisted of a board of directors, an elected chair, and three supportive officers. Based in New York, the national office received applications from a partner organization (called Hilfsverein der Deutschen Juden) in Germany on behalf of individual child refugees. From 1934 through 1941, GJCA staffers translated, studied, and analyzed the applications. They coordinated placements for the individual children across the country. After securing a foster home placement for the child in question, the GJCA sent an affidavit of support to a U.S. consul in Germany.

The GJCA granted corporate affidavits, which was an invention of Perkins's Immigration and Naturalization Service (INS). This meant instead of seeking out individual affidavits for each child, the agencies themselves vouched for them through the corporate affidavit. All the other aspects of the visa program, such as birth certificates and medical exams, still had to be fulfilled, but the corporate affidavit streamlined the process of shepherding these children through the visa approval procedure.

Even then, the job was not done. Once children arrived in New York, GJCA staff accompanied them to temporary homes in New York prior to moving to a foster home elsewhere in the U.S. Finally, the GJCA maintained detailed records and followed up continuously with each refugee child for several years.[4] Overseeing all the above work was the unflappable Executive Director, Cecilia Razovsky.

Cecilia Razovsky was born in 1891 to poor Jewish immigrants in St. Louis. She grew up as a child laborer in a factory that made overalls, and she worked other jobs, too, to help her family make ends meet. These experiences launched Razovsky into a career in social work with a focus on helping Jewish families in need. Unlike Perkins, Razovsky didn't need to volunteer in settlement houses to understand and empathize with immigrants and the working poor: They were her own family. After graduating from the Chicago School of Civics and Philanthropy in 1917, she moved to Washington, D.C., where she worked as an inspector for the CB, which Congress had created in 1912. Julia Lathrop explained in her first report as Chief of the CB that it would "be a center of information useful to all the children of America, to ascertain and to popularize just standards for their life and development."[5] By 1934, the CB would become integral to the life and development of refugee children, too.

Razovsky also understood politics. She became Secretary of the National Council of Jewish Women's Immigrant Aid Department in 1921, the same year that Congress passed a restrictionist precursor to the National Origins Act of 1924. In this position, she learned about "public charge, contract laborer, potential criminal, and other State Department synonyms for 'refugee.'"[6] Razovsky advanced to Director of the National Council of Jewish Women's Immigrant Aid Department in 1932, the same year that Adolf Hitler was running for President of Germany.

In 1933, the new Secretary of Labor Frances Perkins called upon Cecilia Razovsky's unique combination of experiences to advise a committee that would work to improve conditions at Ellis Island and other ports.[7] While advising this committee, Razovsky built relationships with Perkins, Commissioner of Immigration Daniel MacCormack, and other key players on immigration within the Roosevelt administration. In 1934, as Executive Secretary of the GJCA, Razovsky took charge of "all contact with government officials and held several successful conferences with representatives of the State and Labor Departments to discuss individual refugees." Historian Bat-Ami Zucker comments that Perkins and Razovsky "joined forces to fulfill an important moral mission—to save as many Jewish refugees as possible from Nazi Germany and to bring them safely into the United States." "Perkins's concern for refugees and, especially, refugee children," Zucker writes, "brought her into a close and mutually beneficial working relationship with Cecilia Razovsky."[8] As the superstar of efforts to aid child refugees, Razovsky could not have played her role without Perkins backstage.

In March 1934, news of the Labor Department's victory in the charge bonds controversy seemed promising to Jewish-American organizations hoping to support German-Jewish refugees. Max Kohler was a leading Jewish activist and scholar who collaborated with Razovsky until his untimely death from a heart attack in July 1934. In April 1934, Kohler wrote to Perkins and Commissioner of Immigration MacCormack, proposing "legally to incorporate a corporation with responsible officials, with at least $25,000 capital [$567,401.12 in 2023] fully paid up . . . expressly for the purpose of ensuring that none of these children will become public charges."[9] The GJCA explicitly did not want to ask donors for money unless they had the Labor Department's approval: "The group wished approval of their proposal before any attempt to raise funds."[10] Perkins approved and assigned the project to MacCormack, who was eager to help with the small stipulation that child refugees would not arrive until after June 1, 1934.

Since the child refugees would be under sixteen and unaccompanied, the Labor Secretary had authority over this policy according to section 3 of the Immigration Act of 1917: "All children under sixteen years of age, unaccompanied by or not coming to one or both of their parents, except that any such children may, in the discretion of the Secretary of Labor, be admitted if in his opinion they are not likely to become a public charge and are otherwise eligible."[11] Once again, the xenophobic lawmakers behind the Immigration Act of 1917 did not anticipate a Labor Secretary like Frances Perkins. Regardless, the Attorney General's decision in the charge bonds controversy reinforced Perkins's authority here. Legally, Perkins could accept a bond on behalf of a child refugee, and even more, "individual Americans would provide passage money for the children."[12] GJCA women dove into fundraising efforts.

In mid-July 1934, the GJCA and the Labor Department agreed on a nine-point plan. First, they would bring in 250 child refugees between the ages of six and sixteen to settle in cities across the U.S. Second, the GJCA would find the homes, and the CB would approve them. Rather than adopted, the children would be in foster care. Third, the children could not seek employment, for the dual purposes of upholding the CB's ideals for child labor standards and appeasing the anti-immigration lobbyists' concerns about taking American jobs. Fourth, both the Labor Department and the GJCA still expected to use the public charge bond procedure that Perkins and Wyzanski had secured, as described in chapter four. Fifth, the GJCA would keep track of the foster homes. Sixth, private fundraising would cover the children's transatlantic voyage. Seventh, the parents back in Germany delegated in loco parentis status to the American foster parents. Eighth, the children met conditions established by the partner organization in Germany. And finally, the homes were spread across the U.S.[13]

Later that July, Razovsky traveled from hot New York to hotter D.C. for the purpose of meeting with MacCormack. She felt shocked when she learned that he had left town unexpectedly. MacCormack instead sent Deputy Commissioner I. F. Wixon. Brushing aside the plan into which Razovsky had dedicated countless hours, Wixon parroted common anti-immigrant claims: The children would overstay their welcome, they'd take American jobs, and they'd want their parents to join them. Wixon subsequently talked MacCormack into ending point four of the plan: the bonds procedure.[14]

In talks with the Labor Department and the State Department, the GJCA raised several objections against switching the bonding procedure to the issuing of temporary visas. The GJCA had already arranged details with German agencies. Changing the plan again would create resentment among all involved and "cause more damage than the admission of 150 children on permanent visas."[15] Children were waiting, and parents would try to make alternative rescue plans. If they didn't have anywhere to return to, they'd become stateless. One reason why statelessness would be a problem was that American foster families understood that their arrangements were temporary. Changing the plan would require selecting different children, and Jewish organizations in the U.S. would need to restart their series of meetings. Further, funds obtained for specific purposes would need to be returned to the donors and requested again.

The GJCA, the Labor Department, and the State Department all agreed that issuing visitors visas—which would be good for only a few months—to child refugees would be a regrettable decision. With the understanding that some child refugee program would transpire, the State Department did not want to take responsibility for it. Consuls abroad did not want to take responsibility for accepting visa applications for children. Reversing their territorial instinct from the turf war a year earlier, Under Secretary of State William Phillips and George Messersmith, head of the U.S. consulate in Germany, pushed the authority and responsibility back to Perkins.

By August 1934, all parties involved shared a new understanding. First, the children would procure immigration visas—through corporate affidavits of support—without charge bonds. Second, "children will be allocated to homes which have been investigated and found satisfactory; that the children will not become public charges, and that they will attend school until at least 16 years of age." Third, the same rule of no employment before age sixteen with zero exceptions maintained the New Deal–era connection between curtailing decades of damaging child labor and protecting jobs for American adults—not children and especially not foreign children. Fourth, the transatlantic travel cost was still accounted for by private donations and now explicitly separate from the cost of living in the U.S. Fifth, the German partner organization would provide the children's names and the conditions—that their parents could not protect or provide for them—to the INS. The sixth and seventh conditions worked to maximize the State Department's authority and control and to minimize the State Department's liability and responsibility. Sixth, "each individual applicant be found by the examining consular officers to qualify for admission to this country under its immigration laws, due consideration having been given to the information and findings received by him from the Department of Labor," and seventh, the GJCA would be financially responsible if a child refugee was deported or needed to return due to violation of the conditions above.[16]

On September 6, the GJCA, Labor Department, and State Department all formally agreed to these new conditions edited by the State Department. On September 13, the State Department agreed to relay instructions to German consuls. The State Department made clear that their only active role in the planning would be to relay these instructions to their consuls. MacCormack "agreed to alter the requirement from placing bonds in advance to requesting them only upon arrival, if necessary. It was understood that the Department of Labor would recommend granting permanent visas to the children." This solution assured the State Department that "responsibility would fall entirely on the Department of Labor" and that the State Department wouldn't receive criticism on this front.[17] It meant that the GJCA could proceed with facilitating the immigration of hundreds of child refugees, and that Frances Perkins's Labor Department had their backs.

The move to care for foreign children while many American children lacked care—and foreign children lacked American legal rights—was truly brave and radical. The CB took the lead on this endeavor within the Labor Department. As a federal agency since 1912, the CB "served as a center for research, information, and advice, available to parents, public officials, and representatives of private agencies concerned with children."[18] Its staff included "physicians, public-health nurses, a nutritionist, social workers, industrial economists, statisticians, lawyers, and representatives of other professions."[19] Katherine Lenroot, the daughter of former U.S. Senator Irvine Lenroot (R-WI), brought a background in social work, including two decades at the CB before she took over the role of chief in 1934. In a 1939 report on its activities, the CB included a visual map of its position within the Labor Department, placing itself below the Office of the Secretary and branching out to connect with six other federal agencies within the Department. One was the INS, because child immigrants—refugees included—were an "important field of mutual concern."[20] Lenroot and the CB were the point of contact and agency that facilitated collaboration with Razovsky and the GJCA, under Perkins's leadership and in connection with the INS.

Razovsky and the GJCA carried out details and preparations for the children to arrive. Razovsky corresponded frequently with the Hilfsverein der Deutschen Juden, a Jewish organization in Berlin that selected the children and gathered the relevant documents.[21] Hilfsverein provided special consideration to children "living in their own homes, but under extreme pressure from the community, placing their safety in jeopardy," to children "in foster homes or institutions living under conditions of insecurity and instability," to children with American relatives "willing and able to provide adequate care in their own homes immediately upon admission," and to children "from families holding affidavits insufficient for issuance of visas for the whole group and therefore subject to consular rejection."[22] Altogether, children in danger from Nazism, children already in foster care in Germany, children with relatives in the U.S., and poor children whose parents could not afford to immigrate received preference.

Razovsky and the GJCA canvassed Jewish communities across the U.S. to find foster homes, emphasizing hospitality over adoption. While Jewish activist groups asked Jewish foster families to take responsibility for the education and the "maintenance" of the children, they established an understanding that foster family members could not "keep the child permanently" because the children's German parents hoped for the "child's return."[23] Razovsky and her team worked to ensure that the shipping companies would provide kosher kitchens to accommodate any observant Jewish children. They refrained from public advertising to protect potential child refugees from American public opinion, which could stifle the plan amid a perfect storm of political circumstances.

Key players in the GJCA's child refugee program epitomized the claim of Pamela Nadell, a foremost historian of American Jewish women, that "those who excoriate America's Jews for their failure to rescue Europe's Jews ignore what America's Jewish women did accomplish."[24] On November 9, 1934, nine Jewish boys from Germany stepped off the SS *New York* into the city of the same name.

The Child Refugees, 1934–1941

"There is nothing more tragic in the present situation than the word that has come from various sources that many of the German Jews would be glad to send their children away to save them from the degradation that faces them," wrote Fannie Brinn of the National Council for Jewish Women in March 1934. "That these parents are willing to consider parting with their children is a measure of the calamity which has befallen them."[25] Child refugees already understood fear and danger beyond their years. Any relief that they may have felt for a new adventure paired with the grief and trauma of separation from their parents. Their arrival also represented a culmination—depending on when they arrived—of years of political considerations, legal wrangling, and administrative coordination.

Negotiations among the State Department, Labor Department, and the GJCA affected real people—living children unable to stay with their parents—looking for a chance at life. While the GJCA did not want media coverage anywhere near the children, a few local outlets covered the story. The *Jewish Post* of Patterson, New Jersey, listed the names of the first nine children[26]:

Siegfried Goetz
Joachim Abend
Gunther Crober

Heinz Liakowsky
Rudolf Liakowsky
Wolfgang Blum
Wolfgang Joseph
Hans Jurgensen
Herbert Wechsler

Information about Herbert Wechsler is available through his brother's 2010 oral history with the United States Holocaust Memorial Museum (USHMM). Born in Nuremberg in 1921, Herbert had three older brothers: Siegfried, Martin, and Josef. Their parents, Jakob and Flora Goldschmidt Wechsler, owned a small business selling a kind of razor, and the family had household help to clean dishes and the home, which was decorated with mementos, including one commemorating the *Titanic*. The boys attended parochial schools near Nuremberg where most classmates were Jewish.[27]

As Jewish Germans, the Wechsler family's life changed when Hitler became chancellor in January 1933. Jakob Wechsler lost his business as a result of economic discrimination against Jewish people, and the family fell into bankruptcy. The family moved to Berlin, where teachers at the boys' new schools were experts on their subjects because they'd been professors before the Nazis removed Jewish people from university positions. Due to bankruptcy, Herbert and Josef's parents would almost definitely be considered "likely to become a public charge" by U.S. consuls if they attempted to apply for immigration to the U.S.[28]

In 1934, twelve-year-old Herbert sailed with the original nine boys on the SS *New York*, and fourteen-year-old Josef followed two ships behind him. Their two older brothers immigrated to Palestine to become manual laborers. With their boys overseas, Flora and Jakob divorced and moved to Holland separately. Josef remembered his mother as more of an "intellectual" than her husband.[29] In Holland, Flora found work as a help aid for elderly people. Jakob—who'd been proud of his business as the first nonmerchant in his family—took a new course to learn dry cleaning in Amsterdam. Deported when the Nazis reached Holland in 1940, Flora escaped to a village, where she hid until a Nazi turned her in to be arrested. Although Josef does not specify in his oral history exactly what happened to his father, neither parent survived the Holocaust.

Under the GJCA program, a total of ninety-one ships carrying a few German-Jewish children each arrived in the U.S. between November 9, 1934, and U.S. entry into World War II in December 1941. The second ship, the SS *Washington*, brought nine children on November 15, 1934: Gerhart Heymann, Marianne Kaufherr, Reinhard Koch, Richard Lewy, Horst Sternberg, Gretl Sofe Landwehr, Peter Benario, Helga Kassel, and Arnold Durlacher. The third ship, the SS *President Harding*, brought six children on November 28, 1934: Thea Gumpert, Alfred Alexander, Ernst Gutjahr, Thea Kahn, Hilde Hirsch, and Josef Wechsler.[30]

Josef Wechsler—Herbert's older brother—changed his name to Joseph Eaton, the last name of one of his foster families. In 1934, the SS *President Harding* landed in New York on the day before Thanksgiving. The Macy's parade moved through the city as the children moved into new homes, some permanently in New York and others temporarily in New York to await transportation elsewhere.[31]

Josef's first foster home with a wealthy Orthodox family near Central Park didn't work out because Josef wasn't Orthodox, which was ironic because more often too few Orthodox homes were available to settle Orthodox child refugees in the U.S. The second home felt awkward because Josef was more academically outstanding than the family's son. While neither home felt "comfortable," Josef felt grateful to foster families willing to accommodate him.[32] Two years later, Josef graduated from high school at age sixteen and spent a year at City College for free before transferring to Cornell University. Drawing on correspondence with his older brothers, Siegfried and Martin, in Palestine, Josef authored a paper about the kibbutz movement that was published in a well-read academic journal and launched his career in academia and social work.[33]

The fourth ship, the SS *Manhattan*, carried ten children, who together took initiative to write a thank-you note addressed to the General Passenger Agent at United States Lines in New York City. In the letter, they expressed gratitude for conditions on the ship: "The meals at the Kosher table were excellent. The rooms are very clean . . . What we all particularly appreciated was the permission given for our Divine Service last Friday evening and Saturday morning. We all wish your Line the best of success . . . As the leader of the ten Jewish children under the care of the Jewish commission." These ten children on the fourth ship signed their names: Hanns Martin Ledermann, Ruth Michel, Fritz Orth, Herbert Simon, Irene May, Hermann Rothenberg, Siegbert Plaut, Yustin Leitenbach, Edgar Leitenbach, and Werner Simon.[34] Razovsky had coordinated details to enable the kosher kitchen and the Shabbat services. In the worst of circumstances—leaving their parents—the children found comfort in community and ritual. In thank-you notes to people involved in the GJCA, child refugees described academic successes and active social lives full of dates and high school parties. A few thanked Razovsky for sending them theater tickets. On April 27, 1939, the SS *Manhattan* brought one German-Jewish girl, Margot Meyer, and that July, her American uncle Martin Meyer, a medical doctor, expressed thanks by offering to give free health care services to anyone whom Razovsky referred to him. The generosity of his offer reflected how significant the GJCA's child refugee program continued to be as dangers escalated in Europe and immigration to the U.S. seemed unlikely to most refugees.[35]

Razovsky and the GJCA pushed against the grain just as Perkins pushed against the limits of American xenophobia. As Labor Secretary, Perkins had a vitally important but more indirect effect on these people's lives than Razovsky, who had a more direct effect but whose work was not possible without Perkins. Within the Labor Department, the CB served as a reliable point of contact for Razovsky and the GJCA, even as the INS repeatedly clashed with the State Department and with Congress.

Communication between the Labor Department and the GJCA remained consistent throughout seven years of the program. On September 17, 1935, the GJCA asked the INS how to proceed when any child refugees' parents died. The INS replied that the children could be adopted rather than fostered in that case.

In November 1935, a year into the program, the GJCA submitted a formal report to the Labor Department. They reached the original projected number of 250 children the following year, September 1936, and the GJCA asked for the Labor Department's permission to continue. On December 9, 1936, the INS asked the GJCA to continue but with no more than ten children entering the U.S. per month. On November 27, the GJCA asked the INS by "oral request," not in writing, to continue the 1937 plan with the constraint of no more than ten children per month through 1938, and the INS agreed.[36]

In January 1937, Commissioner of Immigration Daniel MacCormack died suddenly of peritonitis—inflammation of the abdominal membrane—while on Capitol Hill for a meeting. *The New York Times* quoted Perkins that the immigration commissioner's death marked a "desperate loss both to the department and to the country," as Mac-Cormack had spearheaded a "remarkable piece of work in reorganizing the service and in humanizing and making it more intelligent."[37] Working alongside Perkins, Mac-Cormack's reorganization of the INS had laid the groundwork to facilitate the immigration of child refugees.

The GJCA's program persisted, in collaboration with the CB and the INS, until the U.S. entered World War II in December 1941. The final ship in the GJCA's records of this program, the SS *Santa Rosa*, arrived on December 19, 1941, carrying one refugee girl, Hilde Hanna Michaelsohn.[38] However, the organization continued, and children continued to come. After this point, though, its name changed to European Jewish Children's Aid. It would continue to work and bring refugee children until the early 1950s.

MacCormack's successor, Commissioner of Immigration James Houghteling, continued much of MacCormack's work and had a good working relationship with Perkins. Historians Richard Breitman and Alan Kraut point out that Houghteling's "main qualification for the job was that his wife was FDR's cousin." Author Barbara McDonald Stewart contrasts MacCormack with Houghteling: "The former Commissioner had tended to do what he thought was right if there was no law forbidding it. The new Commissioner looked for a law to give permission first."[39] In May 1939, Houghteling's wife, Laura Delano Houghteling, sat next to Jay Pierrepont Moffat, chief of the State Department's Division of Western European Affairs, at a social dinner in Washington, D.C., when she uttered a heartless statement that now endures in most writings about legislative efforts to admit Jewish refugee children. According to Moffat's diary, Laura Houghteling stated, "20,000 charming children would all too soon grow up into 20,000 ugly adults."[40] The legislative effort in question was the Wagner-Rogers Bill.

The Rise and Fall of the
Wagner-Rogers Bill, 1938–1939

Following decades of immigration legislation from Congress—the Chinese Exclusion Act of 1882, the Immigration Act of 1917, the National Origins "Quota" Act of 1924—the most progressive forces in the executive branch, notably Perkins's Labor Department, used creative implementation of laws to scramble around restrictive immigration legislation. From 1938 through 1939, however, Congress almost stepped up to loosen immigration restrictions for Jewish refugees.

In 1938, Nazis were on the move through Europe. Germany annexed Austria in March 1938 and invaded and occupied the Sudetenland of Czechoslovakia that September. Conditions worsened not only for Jewish Germans but also for Jewish people in German-occupied areas. On November 9–10, 1938, across Nazi-annexed Austria and Germany, Nazis destroyed 7,500 stores, 29 warehouses, and 171 homes; burned 191 synagogues to the ground and physically demolished 76 more; burned 11 Jewish community centers, cemetery chapels, and more; and arrested thirty thousand Jewish men and sent them to concentration camps. At least 230 Jewish victims died, more than 600 were "permanently maimed," and hundreds more lost their lives in concentration camps in the months immediately following Kristallnacht.[41] This state-sponsored pogrom made headlines across the U.S. and around the world.

The Wagner-Rogers Bill proposed that ten thousand children under fourteen years of age should be admitted in 1939, and then ten thousand more in 1940, all outside of the quotas. The children would "not be permitted to work, thus avoiding labor union charges of unfair competition, and they would be reunited with their parents as soon as safe living conditions were reestablished."[42] Within the Labor Department, the CB would supervise these twenty thousand child refugees from 1939 through 1940. This was a joint bill with bipartisan support; the congressmembers and lobbyists who championed the bill knew that they had the Labor Secretary's full support. While the Wagner-Rogers Bill was not exclusively Perkins's idea, Perkins was one of the individuals who thought of the idea for child refugee legislation after Kristallnacht in 1938. From 1938 through 1939, however, Perkins was politically sidelined on immigration policy due to controversy around a Leftist labor organizer from Australia, Harry Bridges, as explained in chapter six.

Clarence Pickett, a Quaker and the Director of the American Friends Service Committee, was one of the brains behind the Wagner-Rogers initiative. On January 10, 1939, he took notes in his diary on a visit to the Labor Department. Pickett "had a visit with Frances Perkins about the children's quota. She was in a most jovial and affable frame of mind, and we had a good visit. She agreed to support the children's quota legislation if she were asked to do so. We then hurried back to Philadelphia," Pickett journaled.[43] Although the Labor Department never formally sided with Wagner and Rogers, Perkins undoubtedly supported their efforts.

The cosponsors of the Wagner-Rogers Bill were Representative Edith Nourse Rogers (R-MA) and Senator Robert Wagner (D-NY). Though not Jewish, Wagner had emigrated from the German Empire at age eight. He was a key New Deal legislator and the namesake of the 1935 Wagner Act, which legalized unions. Wagner and Rogers collaborated with Clarence Pickett and Marion Kenworthy, a child psychologist, on a plan to support child refugees. On April 24, 1939, the U.S. Congress began hearings on the Wagner-Rogers Bill.

Some of the most unlikely supporters of the Wagner-Rogers Bill included the American Federation of Labor (AFL) and former President Herbert Hoover. A more conservative labor union, the AFL had helped prevent the Labor Department from accepting charge bonds on any wide scale. Like their more progressive predecessors the

Knights of Labor, the AFL had opposed increases in immigration since the nineteenth century. The Congress of Industrial Organizations (CIO), which would later combine with the AFL in 1955, also supported the bill, despite a similar history of opposing immigration. Former President Hoover, who had instructed the State Department in 1930 for U.S. consuls overseas to restrict anyone likely to become a public charge—as one of his flailing attempts to curtail the Great Depression—ultimately became another surprising supporter of the Wagner-Rogers Bill. Together, the AFL, CIO, and Hoover's support suggested changing momentum. But they were not enough: Only 26% of Americans supported the bill.[44]

A slew of xenophobic and self-righteously patriotic organizations lobbied to oppose the Wagner-Rogers Bill. They included the American Legion, American Women Against Communism, Dames of the Loyal Legion, Daughters of the American Revolution, Daughters of the Defenders of the Republic, Society of Mayflower Descendants, Sons of the American Revolution, United Daughters of the Confederacy, and the Veterans of Foreign Wars. John B. Trevor, President of the American Coalition of Patriotic, Civic and Fraternal Societies, and one of the most outspoken lobbyists against the bill, had built his career on advocating for the deportation of immigrants with mental illnesses.[45]

Antisemitism and racism shaped the debates and contributed to the bill's failure in summer 1939. Supporters of the bill strategically emphasized that only half of the child refugees would be Jewish. Even the youngest Jewish immigrants appeared to be foreign and undesirable, unwelcome to xenophobic Americans. Colonel John Thomas Taylor, the leading lobbyist for the xenophobic American Legion, admonished: "If this bill passes, there is no reason why we should not also bring in twenty thousand Chinese children. Certainly, they are being persecuted too." Claiming to represent widows of World War I veterans, Mrs. Agnes of Washington state added: "Thousands of motherless, embittered, persecuted children of undesirable foreigners... potential leaders of a revolt against our American form of government... Why should we give preference to these potential Communists? Already we have too many of their kind in our country trying to overthrow our government."[46]

In late May 1939, the president's cousin, Laura Delano Houghteling, supposedly uttered her notorious statement about Jewish child refugees growing into "ugly adults." Her quotation endures in history books not only for its cruelty, but also because it contrasts the optics and rising support for refugee children against the prevailing antisemitism and xenophobia in Congress. Rather than a congressperson, however, Laura Houghteling was married to the Commissioner of Immigration who oversaw the INS in Perkins's Labor Department.

While the Labor Department formally maintained a neutral stance on the Wagner-Rogers Bill, the Secretary of Labor firmly supported the bill personally. Earlier in 1939, a resolution to impeach Frances Perkins and the drama that ensued around it—as explained in the next chapter— demolished the Labor Secretary's political capital, especially on the issue of immigration.

The CB's Katherine Lenroot, however, testified before the House congressional committee on immigration and naturalization. Describing child refugees as a "blessing" to the

U.S., Lenroot delivered a "strong plea" that they "would not lessen in the slightest degree the care and protection afforded a single American child."[47] She took aim at the common criticism that child refugees would take opportunities and resources from American children still struggling with the Great Depression.

Consequently, opponents took aim at Lenroot. "Dear Madam," wrote one American citizen, H. J. Owen from Manhattan, on June 7, 1939, "too bad you don't live in New York City where you could see a million children that love to be fed and clothed, all Native born and don't know what will become of them when they grow up: It's alright to be sympathetic, but no one wants to put up the money to support 20,000 refugees, all they want to do is talk to get their name in the papers." Walter Campbell doubled down from Boston, sending hate mail to Lenroot: "Dear Miss as a father of three I would say that you are Miss Leading [sic] Immigration Committee and I don't mean maybe. I am a ratcatcher in Boston for 20 years. I can show you 500 alleys in Boston with 100 children ages 5 to 8 in these alleys . . . These children are in bad need of care. So, take care of kids at home first." The message was clear, but just in case it wasn't, the ratcatcher added beneath his name: "Are you taking orders from John Bull or the Rich Jews?"[48]

On June 7, 1939, Senator Robert Reynolds (D-NC) retaliated against the momentum of the Wagner-Rogers Bill by proposing the end of immigration to the U.S., full stop. Descended from Revolutionary War veterans and enslavers, Reynolds co-owned an antisemitic newspaper *The Defender*, shared his postal franking privileges with Nazi sympathizers, and supported the New Deal to reallocate resources and opportunity to poor white North Carolinians. "Let's keep America for our boys and girls," Reynolds admonished. "Let's empty our prisons of alien criminals and send them back to their native lands. Let's deport those alien agitators who are eternally advocating a change in our form of government. Let's do our best to save our country from destruction by alien-enemy forces."[49] To opponents of the bill, German-Jewish children were not only a lower priority than American children, but they also threatened the American government and society.

When Senator Reynolds spearheaded backlash against the Wagner-Rogers Bill by proposing legislation to ban all immigration, Commissioner of Immigration Houghteling and the INS took issue. INS officers who testified before Congress on the Reynolds bill repeatedly told Congress to see the Labor Department position within the Wagner-Rogers testimony, which was neutrality, certainly not banning immigration altogether.[50]

By late June 1939, the Wagner-Rogers Bill retained some popularity. For instance, CB records contain a press release for a radio play entitled *Suffer Little Children*, a "Special Broadcast to Dramatize Plight of Child Refugees on Nationwide Hookup" featuring Katharine Hepburn and Burgess Meredith, "eminent stars of the stage and cinema," and written by Arch Oboler, an "outstanding radio writer." The press release expressed confidence that the radio program would be a "most effective dramatization of the tragedy of these homeless children. It is for this reason that we are most eager to have as many people as possible listen to the broadcast." On Sunday, June 25, 1939, from 10:05 to 10:30 p.m., Hepburn and Meredith performed *Suffer*

Little Children over the radio. Listeners who followed the press release's advice would have had "pen and paper at hand and suggest to the members of your local audience that they write immediately to their own Senators and Congressmen stating that they have heard the broadcast and that it has moved them to write urging favorable action on the Wagner-Rogers Bill."[51] Indeed, the last week of June 1939 proved pivotal for the bill, but not in the way that the performers and writers would have preferred. On June 30, the Senate committee voted to approve the bill with certain amendments.

However, one of the amendments was for the twenty thousand children's visas to count as part of the German quota, not outside the quota. Thus, the Wagner-Rogers Bill became less about adding lifeboats to the sinking ship of German Jewry and more like prioritizing children on already limited lifeboats. Supporters were horrified by the prospect of visas for twenty thousand children becoming "death warrants" for the German adults whom they'd displace. The merged Austrian and German quota included only 27,370 slots total. Senator Wagner explained: "The proposed change would in effect convert the measure from a humane proposal to help children who are in acute distress to a proposal with needlessly cruel consequences for adults in Germany who are in need of succor and are fortunate to obtain visas under the present drastic quota restrictions."[52] He withdrew the legislation, and the bill died in committee before reaching the floor.

The Wagner-Rogers Bill had support from Democrats and Republicans, Jewish Americans, Quakers including Herbert Hoover, representatives and senators, leading trade

unions, and even famous actors. The Department of Labor
would have welcomed the opportunity to implement the law.
On July 22, 1939, INS Commissioner Houghteling and CB
Chief Lenroot reported to Perkins in a joint memo that the
GJCA "under arrangements worked out with the Department of Labor, has demonstrated the possibility of
constructive accomplishment in this field. Approximately
400 children . . . on permits issued by the Secretary of Labor
under Section 3 of the Immigration Act of February 5, 1917;
and assigned for care to accredited child-caring agencies" in
the U.S. Houghteling and Lenroot argued: "Many more children could be cared for in the same way if their admission
were made possible."[53] Indeed, the GJCA program persisted
through 1941. Nevertheless, the fate of the Wagner-Rogers
Bill rejected legislative backing for twenty thousand additional refugee children whom Perkins's Labor Department
would have been thrilled to support.

Looking toward the presidential election of 1940, the
president did not go out of his way to push the issue. According to the First Lady, "Franklin frequently refrained
from supporting causes in which he believed, because of
political realities." She described FDR's stance: "First
things come first, and I can't alienate certain votes I need
for measures that are more important . . . by pushing any
measure that would entail a fight."[54] Although Wagner and
Rogers's bill had some momentum, it would have entailed
too much of a fight, because most Americans remained opposed to aiding refugees.

It wasn't that the U.S. government didn't have the capacity to aid immigrants. The quotas were created by Congress
in the National Origins Act of 1924. The Wagner-Rogers

Bill took a stab at revising that legislation amid the dire circumstances for European Jewry. "The bills now before this
committee are a direct attack on the quota system," John B.
Trevor observed apprehensively but correctly.[55] Alas, the reason that it didn't pass—that it would have taken adults' spots
within the quota, the metaphorical lifeboats—was a limit that
Congress itself had created and didn't want to change.

Child refugee Joseph Eaton recalled at age ninety-one
in 2010: "We all know historically that President Roosevelt
took very little action to help the Jews of Germany. He had
a Congress that was not willing to change the immigration
laws, and within the Department of State, the bureaucracy"
was antisemitic. Perkins's Labor Department, however,
was notably progressive. Tragically, it just could not do
enough. The government bureaucracy that enabled the
GJCA program brought at least 597 German-Jewish children to the U.S. The GJCA child refugee program that the
Labor Department supported epitomized Perkins's limited
but undeniable efforts to aid refugees from Nazism. That
limited success came in the form of German-Jewish children stepping off ships in New York, "clutching a single
suitcase and, for the youngest, perhaps a teddy bear."[56]

The tragedy was that to secure refuge, the children left
their parents, who decided to send their children without
them. That the parents couldn't join was an intentional
decision that the U.S. government made repeatedly
through a combination of inaction and restrictionism.

CHAPTER SIX

Resolution to Impeach Frances Perkins

*O*N 1939, THE FIRST FEMALE cabinet secretary faced the prospect of being only the second cabinet member in U.S. history to be impeached, all over an immigration dispute involving an alleged Communist man from Australia.

That man's name was Harry Bridges, and he spearheaded the successful Longshore Strike in San Francisco in May 1934. Across the country, capitalists, xenophobes, and overlapping groups responded with cries to deport Bridges to Australia. By 1939, almost five years after the Longshore Strike, Congress decried the Secretary of Labor for not deporting this labor agitator. Congress didn't care that even with the Immigration and Naturalization Service (INS) still under her department, Perkins lacked legal reason to deport Bridges. They didn't like him and felt that she shouldn't let Bridges stay in the country. Consequently, the first female cabinet secretary in U.S. history had to endure an impeachment attempt.

Perkins was neither impeached nor convicted. Nevertheless, the saga marked a critical turning point in the story of Perkins's refugee policy. Although Bridges was a Leftist immigrant from Australia, not a Jewish refugee from Nazi territory, the Bridges incident left an indelible imprint on Perkins's experience of politics in Washington.

The Bridges incident taught Perkins about the limits of helping immigrants even within the law. Even more, the 1939 impeachment hearing and the buildup to it decimated Perkins's political capital. She'd entered office with the ear of the president and, in her first year, a legal victory in the charge bonds controversy. After the Bridges incident, however, Perkins became a political liability, at least on the issue of immigration, in the view of a president who arguably valued politics above all else.

"Solidarity": Harry Bridges and the Longshore Strike, 1934

The famed Powell's Books in Portland, Oregon, has displayed a quotation from Harry Bridges, President of the International Longshore and Warehouse Union (ILWU), on its wall: "The most important word in the language of the working class is 'solidarity.'" Bridges gave meaning to the notion of solidarity in 1934, when he led a controversial but successful strike among dockworkers on the West Coast.

Born in Melbourne, Australia, in 1901, Harry Bridges joined the merchant marines at age sixteen. At nineteen, he "jumped ship" in San Francisco, where he paid a legal alien tax and began work as a longshoreman.[1] The term *longshoreman*, derived from the phrase *along the shore*, refers to someone who loads and unloads ships, a backbreaking but crucial role in any maritime trade.

In 1932, the same year when the U.S. elected Franklin Delano Roosevelt (FDR) at the height of the Great Depression, Bridges became a spokesman for a group of West Coast longshoremen seeking unionization. In 1933, the International Longshoremen's Association (ILA) earned a union charter. Their employers, however, refused to bargain, thereby provoking the 1934 strike. Organizing up and down the West Coast, Bridges coordinated a strike of all longshoremen and warehousemen in San Francisco. The workers won: Their employers consented to fewer hours, higher pay, and safer workplace conditions.

Bridges lived until 1990. In 1984, he recalled in an interview: "We showed the world that when working people get together and stick together there's little they can't do." He added: "It was about how people treat each other; it was about human dignity. We forced the employers . . . to sit down and talk to us about the work we do, how we do it, and what we get paid for it."[2] This was the perceived villain whose activism terrified a broad swath of Americans and culminated in a resolution to impeach Frances Perkins.

From Strike in San Francisco to Impeachment Resolution in D.C., 1934–1939

After World War I, a flurry of paranoia about Communism, the First Red Scare, spread through the U.S., persisting throughout the interwar period. Political scientist Robert Justin Goldstein identifies 1938 through 1940 as one of several "little red scares."[3] Anti-Communism remained deeply interwoven with anti-immigrant sentiment and xenophobia during the interwar years.

In September 1937, the District Director of the INS in Seattle applied to arrest Bridges on vague charges of subversive activities. Prior to Perkins's tenure, the District Director wouldn't have needed to apply to arrest an immigrant.[4] This policy change alone angered opponents. Further, Commissioner of Immigration James Houghteling and Solicitor of Labor Gerard Reilly determined that the request included insufficient evidence to arrest Bridges. Contrary to the assumptions of Congress, however, Perkins's team didn't stop there. They sent a small team from the Labor Department to the West Coast to continue investigating Bridges's actions and motives. Next, the investigators traveled to New York to conduct a deposition of Bridges. At this point, Congress took notice.

In early January 1939, Representative J. Parnell Thomas, a Republican from New Jersey, and an indignantly anti-Communist opponent of the New Deal, introduced a resolution to impeach Frances Perkins. He cited Article 11, Section 4 of the U.S. Constitution, which states that "the President, Vice President and all civil officers of the United States, shall be removed from office on impeachment for, and conviction of, treason, bribery, or other high crimes and misdemeanors."[5] The ground for impeachment that he focused on was "treason." Thomas stretched Bridges's alleged Communism to mean overthrowing the government, and he twisted Perkins's hesitance to deport Bridges—who according to Thomas wanted to overthrow the government—as treason.[6]

Representative Martin Dies, a Democrat from Texas, joined forces with Thomas to spearhead congressional efforts to impeach Perkins. Dies represented the Dixiecrats of the Deep South, white descendants of Confederates who belonged to the Democratic Party for reasons different from FDR. Dixiecrats were pro-traditional gender roles and anti-immigrant. While Dies targeted several members of the Roosevelt administration with criticism, his speech at the Plaza Hotel on September 9, 1938, focused on Perkins, specifically her approach to the Bridges deportation case.[7] As a former Chair of the Committee on Immigration, Dies now chaired the newly created Special Committee on Un-American Activities.[8]

Representative Mary Teresa Norton, the first-ever Democrat woman elected to Congress and a women's rights supporter, was as much of an ally as Perkins could expect in Congress. In 1938, Norton had played a central role working with Perkins and FDR to pass the Fair Labor Standards Act, which banned child labor and established a federal minimum wage and overtime pay.[9] Using the rhetoric that was popular at the time, Norton tried to help Perkins by soliciting a statement from her in January 1939: "As you know, communism, fascism, and Nazism are extremely repugnant to me personally and to the political ideals for which I have stood for in my public life. I am, therefore, deeply concerned that charges should be brought that the Department of which you are the head is lax in deporting aliens who carry on propaganda hostile to our democratic institutions."[10] While Norton seems genuinely to have wanted Perkins to have an opportunity to explain herself, it must have been infuriating to hear pro-labor Leftism equated with Nazism. Perkins would have preferred to spend her time and energy aiding refugees from Nazism rather than enduring the drawn-out process of defending her use of due process on behalf of a Leftist labor organizer.

Nevertheless, from her position as Chairman of the Labor Committee, Representative Norton supported her fellow female Democrat by using the facts as Perkins presented them in subsequent debates. "From my contacts with the Secretary of Labor, as Chairman of the Labor Committee, I am forced to the conclusion that she is personally as much opposed to communism as I am," Norton said of Perkins.[11] Even if Norton couldn't kill the impeachment resolution, she was a reasonable person in the room assuming Perkins's best intentions, which was rare in Congress.

On January 21, 1939, Congress received a written statement from Perkins, responding to Norton's invitation to explain her reasoning. The Labor Secretary explained her actions calmly and without room for doubt on her position: "I, of course, cannot agree to any charges that I have been guilty of neglect of duty in enforcing any statute of the United States. It must be remembered, however, that the Secretary of Labor has been given no roving commission by Congress to deport all aliens whose activities happen to be unpopular with many people."[12] She maintained that she followed all laws and her Oath of Office. If Congress legislated that she had to deport anyone with unpopular opinions, Perkins added, then the Labor Department would follow suit. Likewise, if the judicial branch decided that alleged Communism qualified as grounds for deportation, the Labor Secretary would follow the law by deporting Bridges. Joseph George Strecker was the subject of a case seeking to determine whether being an alleged Communist qualified as grounds for deportation in 1939.[13] In February 1938, the U.S. Circuit Court had voted no. The U.S. Supreme Court issued a writ of certiorari, meaning that they were interested in hearing Strecker's case. Since Perkins believed that the only valid charge against Bridges was that he was an alleged Communist, she was waiting on the Supreme Court decision on the Strecker case in 1939.

Both Thomas and Dies dismissed Strecker's series of trials as irrelevant to the Bridges case. Perkins wrote: "The report of the Dies investigating committee has censured the Department for postponing the Bridges hearing until the Strecker case was decided on the ground that the latter case does not have any important bearing on the Bridges proceedings."[14] On the contrary, Perkins awaited the Strecker decision to inform her action on the Bridges case because if the Supreme Court mandated the deportation of immigrants with Leftist politics, she'd follow the law. Perkins's opponents insisted that the cases were unconnected because, if they viewed them together, they'd notice at least one glaring difference: Unlike Strecker, Bridges was not a confirmed Communist.

Circumventing the "alleged" status of Bridges's Communism, the Dies Report maintained Thomas's claim that Bridges was plotting to overthrow the government. Perkins clarified in her written statement that nobody had any evidence for this claim. No one could prove that Bridges was plotting an overthrow, Perkins quipped, because "as a matter of fact, there is no such evidence."[15] Bridges posed no threat to U.S. governmental institutions, only to the employers conspiring to exploit workers' labor.

The Longshore Strike, which lasted through July 1934, preceded the legalization of private sector unions in the U.S. by a year. In July 1935, the National Labor Relations Act (NLRA), the Wagner Act after Robert Wagner, guaranteed the right of private sector employees to join unions, to pursue collective bargaining, and to strike.[16] Part of the impetus to antagonize Perkins was capitalist backlash against the New Deal, especially the legalization of unions.

Bridges didn't receive pushback on his immigration status until he led a successful labor strike. Perkins explained: "It was not until the longshoremen's strike in 1934 that any complaint was made . . . During the strike the Department received letters calling attention to the fact that Bridges was an alien and asking that he be deported."[17] Nobody had a problem with a longshoreman carrying out valuable labor in the U.S. until that longshoreman organized and spearheaded a strike that led to fewer hours, higher pay, and safer conditions. At this point, lawmakers turned to a popular tool at their disposal: xenophobia.

On March 5, 1938, the INS arrested Bridges in Baltimore. His case wound its way through the U.S. legal system. The U.S. Supreme Court acquitted Bridges in

1945, six years after the resolution to impeach Frances Perkins exacted its toll.

"Greetings to the Red Paint": Hate Mail

At the Columbia University Rare Book and Manuscript Library, the archival folder that holds Perkins's hate mail is a fascinating place. From 1938 to 1939, she received a slew of hate mail from people who hated Bridges and her, thought she was a Communist, or some combination of those. Many pieces of hate mail called her Jewish, though she was a practicing Episcopalian.

One commonality in the hate mail was that very few of them got her name right, and most seemed to do so intentionally. Remember that Perkins had carefully chosen her name. As a twentysomething she switched her first name to Frances, like the saint. When she married Paul Wilson in her thirties, she strategically chose to remain Frances Perkins professionally. As the first female cabinet secretary at age fifty-two, she chose to go by "Miss Perkins," or more formally, "Madam Secretary."[18] As usually the only woman in the room, she navigated complicated gender politics for men around her to see her as something other than another man's wife. In the 1930s, she couldn't be fully seen as a professional and Paul Wilson's wife in many colleagues' eyes, so she chose the professional. They needed to see her as a colleague so that Perkins could do the important work that she came to Washington to accomplish.

As if on cue, most of the hate mail called her "Mrs. Perkins," "Mr. Paul Wilson," "Miss or Mrs. Perkins," or other

carelessly construed variations. One letter opened: "Mrs??
Perkins, why do you not go by your married name, or are
you really married in the eyes of God! No wonder you take
the side of the Reds—your low-down child-murderess.
Read the attached, then hang your dirty, immoral head."[19]
The author of this piece of hate mail proceeded to construct
an illogical and unsound argument. He rambled, "If for instance, I want your job, and your possessions, I can go take
same and according to you and Russia's way of thinking,
there is no God, consequently, to whom do I have to give
an accounting." He added that "the quicker we blow your
ass up into bits the better for this Government. Don't say
this is nasty, as there is no such thing as anything being
wrong or right," before pivoting quickly to an argument for
more Christianity in public schools. Essentially, he rambled
that Perkins had no morals, he used his own premise of no
morals to threaten assassination, and then he prescribed a
solution, "religious instruction back into the scholls" [sic].[20]

Carelessly butchering her name due to misogyny,
mean-spirited correspondents repeatedly called Perkins a
Communist. During the interwar years, American anti-
Communism fed into broader paranoia, especially in the
context of capitalist opposition to progressive New Deal
labor policies such as a federal minimum wage and unemployment insurance. Although Perkins's only alleged
crime in the Bridges saga was not rushing to deport a
controversial labor organizer for a successful strike, opponents wouldn't miss an opportunity to paint her as a
Communist. "Greetings to the 'Red Paint,'" one letter
started, "of course you wouldn't go back on Bridges. You
couldn't afford to [let] the communist exposure of your

Frances Perkins, c. 1935–1936.
Courtesy Mount Holyoke College Archives and Special Collections.

Perkins, age four.
Courtesy Mount Holyoke College Archives and Special Collections.

Perkins graduates from
Mount Holyoke, 1902.
Courtesy Mount Holyoke Colleg
Archives and Special Collection

Frances Perkins as a young adult.
Courtesy Mount Holyoke College
Archives and Special Collections.

Anti-immigration editorial cartoon, 1921.
Courtesy Library of Congress
Prints and Photographs Division.

THE ONLY WAY TO HANDLE IT.

...iformed men parade down
...ity street in Duisburg, Germany
...ring a Nazi rally, 1928.
...e Nazi Party received
...s than 3% of the total vote
...he 1928 German election.
...ited States Holocaust Memorial Museum;
...rtesy Dottie Bennett.

German troops march through the streets
carrying military banners during a
Reich Party Day parade, 1937.
By this point, the Nazi Party
had complete control over Germany.
United States Holocaust Memorial Museum;
courtesy Richard Freimark.

Roosevelt's Cabinet, 1933.
Courtesy Franklin D. Roosevelt Presidential Library and Museum, Hyde Park, New York.

Refugee children waving to the Statue of Liberty, 1939.
United States Holocaust Memorial Museum; courtesy Anita Willens.

Dorothy Thompson (right)
discusses refugee children with
Rep. Edith Nourse Rogers, 1939.
*Courtesy Library of Congress
Prints and Photographs Division,
Harris & Ewing Collection.*

Impeachment hearing
for Frances Perkins, 1939.
*Courtesy Library of Congress
Prints and Photographs Division,
Harris & Ewing Collection.*

...an surveys the damage to
...ewish-owned store after
... Kristallnacht pogrom.
*...ited States Holocaust
...morial Museum;
...urtesy National Archives
...d Records Administration,
...llege Park.*

Perkins at her desk, 1938.
*United States Holocaust Memorial Museum;
courtesy National Archives and
Records Administration, College Park.*

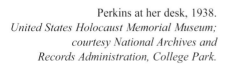

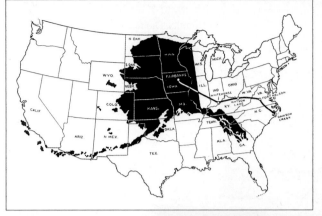

Map of Alaska superimposed over map of continental U.S., 1943.
Courtesy National Archives, RG-30, Records of the Bureau of Public Roads 1892–1972.

James Houghteling becomes the commissioner of the INS, 1937.
Courtesy Library of Congress Prints and Photographs Division, Harris & Ewing Collection.

THE BARON GEORGE VON TRAPP

Baron von Trapp's calling card, 1940.
Courtesy National Archives, RG-174, Subject Files.

Letter from Gertrude Ely to Frances Perkins, about Baron von Trapp, 1940.
Courtesy National Archives, RG-174, Subject Files.

?dication of the United States
?locaust Memorial Museum,
?ril 1993.
?urtesy United States
?locaust Memorial Museum.

?resident Johnson signs
the Immigration and
?ationality Act of 1965.
Yoichi Okamoto;
courtesy LBJ Library.

Elizabeth Warren speaks about Frances Perkins in front of Triangle Shirtwaist Factory building, 2019.
Courtesy Dan Geldon.

Perkins family homestead in Newcastle, Maine.
Courtesy Frances Perkins Center.

quiet world be more than you dare to provoke."[21] Despite confusing sentence structure, this man from Minnesota appears to have called her a Communist.

Conspiracy theorists also alleged that Perkins was a Russian-Jewish immigrant named Mathilda Watsky. They supported their erroneous claim with a court record from Worcester, Massachusetts, documenting the marriage of a younger Mathilda Watsky to a man named Paul Wilson, who simply shared a name with Perkins's husband. Perkins consented to the distribution of a letter to a friend in which she wrote: "There were no Jews in my ancestry. If I were a Jew, I would make no secret of it. On the contrary I would be proud to acknowledge it."[22] Though never Jewish, she certainly took a trip through imagined Jewishness.

In April 1938, a man wrote to her from Los Angeles. "It sure is galling to have to address a being as low as you as Secretary of Labor of this country," he started. The next paragraph simply restated that she didn't deport Bridges because the Supreme Court hadn't yet specified whether political beliefs could be grounds for deportation. He continued, "There is no question but both [the president] and you being Communists," suddenly adding, "Why do you not let the public know that you are a Russian Jew." Once again, she wasn't Jewish. Her opponents both perpetrated antisemitism and viewed it as a tool in their toolbox against a progressive. The same letter continued its vitriol: "There is another name that would fit you very much better, but I will not call you that, as it would be an insult to the female dog. If you want to be a communist, why in hell do you not go over to Russia where you belong and live there with those Devils that are there. Do not worry but there is a day coming when you will get what is coming to you."[23] Misogynistic, bigoted, and threatening.

Not all the hate mail was about Bridges, and not all the antisemitic comments were about immigration, suggesting broader opposition to the New Deal and a more complicated relationship between Perkins and Jewishness. Following is a particularly egregious example:

> Just a few lines to tell you about the Wagner Act. You are a Communist and you know damn well . . . why don't you deport that dirty Harry Bridges I know why because he belongs to the same gang as you, you should be deported if you don't deport him if you ever would go to see Hitler he would know what to do to you and the likes of your Jew or Jewess they destroyed the temple 1938 years ago that truth I am a voter over 50 years and tax payer.[24]

In just a few lines, this correspondent threatened the Labor Secretary that Hitler would "know what to do" with her. Aside from Perkins's devout Episcopalian faith, this man's determination to tie her to Jewishness reflected a deep American antisemitism. It suggested an awareness that Nazis harmed Jewish people in Germany and an acceptance, even enthusiasm for that tragic situation. This letter was written at the end of 1938, a crucial year. Germany annexed Austria in May, and in November, Nazis carried out the Kristallnacht pogrom. In the U.S., a progressive Secretary of Labor still oversaw the INS, and she sought to aid refugees, while backlash escalated around the Bridges affair.

The year 1938, however, did not mark 1938 years since the destruction of the temple, which—contrary to this correspondent's claim—did not occur in the year zero. Most letters were signed from "an American," "true American voters," "an American who practices Americanism," or a similar phrasing around taxpayers and voters. These descriptions were correct. The authors of the hate mail enjoyed the privileges and rights of the same American citizenship that they sought to restrict. They voted for the members of Congress who supported the Immigration Act of 1917, the National Origins Act of 1924, and in early 1939, the resolution to impeach Frances Perkins.

"Ours a Little Nearer Our Conception of the City of God": Perkins's Statement at Her Impeachment Hearing

In February 1939, Frances Perkins had to testify before Congress to defend her handling of the Harry Bridges case, an infuriating use of her time. Aside from immigration, Perkins remained involved in various New Deal legislative matters. Americans were still struggling with the Great Depression. On the issue of immigration, she continuously received letters from loved ones of people trapped in Nazi territory, as explored in the next chapter. Yet congressmen called Perkins to defend the constitutionality of her actions.

The charge was that Perkins, Commissioner of Labor James Houghteling, who took office when MacCormack died, and Solicitor of Labor Gerard Reilly, who replaced Wyzanski when he moved on to the Attorney General's

Office, had conspired against the U.S. government by not deporting Bridges.

On the morning of February 8, 1939, Perkins received visits in her office from several colleagues and employees offering their support and wishing her luck in the impeachment hearing. The hearing itself took place behind closed doors, in a dimly lit "long, narrow room" in which congressmen sat around a "raised mahogany dais, arranged like a horseshoe."[25] Perkins could bring only Solicitor of Labor Gerard "Gerry" Reilly. En route, she whispered to Reilly, "Do you remember the priest that walked beside Joan of Arc when she went to the stake?"[26] Reilly nodded affirmatively.

Perkins read from prepared remarks during her impeachment hearing. The statement had undergone several drafts among her advisors in the Labor Department, with a guest speechwriting appearance from Solicitor of Labor Emeritus Charles E. Wyzanski, Jr., who now lived in Boston. Perkins made the final revisions on the paper that she held in her hands.[27]

Perkins numbered the points that she wanted to make and provided evidence to support each one. First, "there has been no 'conspiracy.'" Perkins added: "The responsibility for the action of the Department of Labor rests directly upon me."[28] While partially a legal strategy, this point of clarification also illuminates Perkins's personal integrity and strong leadership.

Many of the words on the paper from which she delivered her statement are crossed out in pen. For example, she initially included but crossed out the three objectives of her congressional testimony: first, "to state . . . the principles in the light of which I view my duty to enforce the immigration laws"; second, to clarify the facts of the Bridges case; and third, to clarify an additional case, that of Joseph George Strecker, whose immigration led to a case in the U.S. Supreme Court about whether someone should be deported for "subversive" political views.[29] Instead, she focused on what she actually must say.

She clarified that she believes that the U.S. government should act immediately against anyone who offers a "clear and present danger to the Government."[30] She communicated effectively by stating the obvious, upon which everyone could agree, and then moved on to weightier claims.

Perkins clarified that she wasn't a Communist. She was not "in accord with the principles of the Communist Party." Rather, she wanted to fix capitalism by reforming it with progressive legislation and social programs. She explained: "I find in [Communists'] insistence on party authority and their emphasis on class struggle, their conception of a dictatorship of one class and their oft-repeated contempt for religion the negation of that individual liberty and that development of the human personality for which this country and every democracy must stand."[31] She viewed her reluctance to deport Bridges as a defense of freedom of speech in line with democracy and American values.

Then Perkins turned her attention to U.S. immigration law. Her next edit deleted a stage cue—"I turn now from these general remarks to a consideration of the nature of my duties under the immigration laws of this country"—allowing the Labor Secretary to speak directly. She also deleted a rather telling line: "It is not commonly realized that the power which is vested in the Secretary of Labor under the immigration law is in many respects the most serious and the most drastic administrative power vested in any executive officer in our government."[32] Why did they write it, and why did she delete that line seemingly at the last minute? Perkins likely noticed that her next few lines were just as strong and more precise without pointing out how powerful she was while dragged in front of a congressional committee. Further, she strategically downplayed her power as a woman who was already the target of conspiracies and animosity.

Here, testifying before xenophobes in Congress accusing her of Communism and treason, Perkins reiterated her understanding of immigration as an issue of human lives. Calling upon deep reserves of confidence and righteousness, she explained that the Labor Secretary "stands virtually alone among executive officers in his right to restrict personal liberty and freedom of individual action of human beings. The Secretary of Labor has the power, in certain specific situations . . . to order that person to be sent back to the country of his nationality even though he recognizes that in some circumstances this is tantamount to sending an alien to death."[33] Ever aware of the authority that the Labor Secretary still held over immigration policy, Perkins explained the responsibility that she felt to an audience of her staunchest opponents.

In her next point, peeking out from several more crossed-out lines, Perkins commented that even though she exerted authority over immigrants once they reached the U.S., she couldn't ensure their basic human rights. Here she described immigrants as "susceptible . . . without adherence to those elementary standards of due process of law that are at the heart of our Constitution." Considering the context of her rhetoric about the dignity of immigrant lives and the reality that she was being flooded with letters on behalf of refugees from Nazism, we can infer that she felt frustrated with how limited she was to protect immigrants' human rights. The next crossed-out line was a shot at "immigration deportations" by "President Hoover's so-called Wickersham Commission." She contrasted Hoover's administration with her own "due regard for historic safeguards against executive absolutism in all cases where this tremendous power over human liberty and human life is exercised."[34] She viewed previous Labor Departments' active restrictionism as an abuse of executive power.

In her third-to-last point, Perkins clarified why she brought up the Hoover administration's mass deportations. She explained: "I have imposed restraints upon the arbitrary use of this power, and I have sought to build and maintain confidence in our institutions by proceeding in all cases with scrupulous fairness."[35] She meant to contrast her own restraint to deport Bridges against more rash impulses, painting the latter as unconstitutional. However, a critical mass of U.S. lawmakers wasn't interested in protecting the rights of people who weren't citizens.

In her penultimate point, Perkins turned to an unusual topic in her rhetoric: herself. Albeit this line was penned in advance and approved by multiple advisors. "I have spent most of my adult life in the service of the people of my country working to improve their living and laboring conditions and at some sacrifice of personal comfort," she stated. "I have done what I could in time to make this great country of ours a little nearer our conception of the City of God. For eighteen years I have served in public office where my record is an open book. I have consistently favored not only enforcement of law, but also a firm adherence to the basic American standards of fair play."[36] In an earlier draft, these lines had appeared at the end of the whole statement, signaling their importance.

"Ours a little nearer our conception of the City of God" was indeed Perkins's dream, however naïve. At the crux of her impeachment hearing, here was Perkins at her best and worst. The worst: signaling to her beliefs for authority in a way that only Christians can do in America, apparently unaware of the pitfalls of systemic Christian nationalism. The best: pleading to help people for no more complicated a reason than it's the right thing to do.

Perkins spent the next several pages explicating the facts of the case. As Labor Secretary, Perkins could deport Bridges only if Congress commanded her to, if he had entered "unlawfully," if he became a public charge, if he committed a crime of "moral turpitude," or if he attempted to overthrow the government. She could even deport him for joining a formal organization that set out to overthrow the government. But Bridges had committed none of these crimes. Perkins reminded Congress that she couldn't deport him just for disliking him.

Cutting through her accusers' chaos and hypocrisy required emotional energy, mental endurance, patience, and steadiness. She crossed out a line quipping that her accuser knew that the strike occurred in 1934, yet he didn't cry conspiracy until 1937. Between 1934 and 1937, Labor Department employees conducted background research on the labor organizer in question. They concluded that Bridges neither joined the Communist Party nor sought to overthrow the U.S. government.

After explaining more details, Perkins concluded her speech by emphasizing the importance of the democratic method and liberty: how she protected democracy and liberty throughout the Bridges saga, how she would have deported him if he threatened democracy and liberty, and how convicting her would abuse democracy and liberty.

"Good God": The Aftermath

On April 3, 1939, the *Congressional Record* published a "Dismissal of Impeachment Proceedings Against Frances Perkins, Secretary of Labor" in the form of a speech by Representative John A. Martin from Colorado. Martin regretted: "After months of Nation-wide publicizing of unjust and unfounded charges against a public official, the final result is heralded by no blare of trumpets and is scarcely brought to the notice of the public."[37] The impeachment process was so loud, the dismissal proceedings so quiet, and the political ramifications so severe that Perkins continued to feel their effects.

That August, nearly six months after sitting through the impeachment hearings, Perkins penned some words to a staunch opponent: Congressman Dies. She never sent them. Perkins's lettering was almost unreadable, even more so than usual, suggesting that the draft was for her eyes only. My historian friend and I sat in a coffee shop for hours trying to make out the words on the ten notecard pages of scrawl. Perkins also wrote this note upside down on a Labor Department notepad. She often wrote on that notepad, but not upside down, if she intended to send it to someone. These words—the few among them that we could discern—remained unsent.

Thus, I reassemble Perkins's own phrases in the aftermath of impeachment, directed to Congressman Dies, like a poem or a word cloud:

> *Mr. Dies*
> *Integrity*
> *Democracy*
> *U.S.A.*
> *Good God*
> *Volunteer witnesses who are confused*
>   *misinformed*
> *Bound to appear and testify*
> *That they are likely to testify to opinions*
> *Quite as freed on our regard to facts*
> *Malicious regard*
> *Democracy*
> *Of frankness and good will*
> *Fair treatment*
> *Without oppression and false connection*
> *To God and God alone*
> *The oath of office*
> *Conscientiousness*
> *Men of conscience*
> *Of God and His will to man*
> *Poor creature*
> *Labor strike*

Which was notable for all its complete lack of
violence
Not likely to endanger the government[38]

Here is a prose interpretation of that little poem: Perkins valued integrity, democracy, and U.S. governmental institutions. She felt that volunteer witnesses in her impeachment trial were "confused" and "misinformed." She channeled her wrath, "good God," which started a page, to her accuser Congressman Dies. She defended her commitment to the Oath of Office that she'd taken at the White House on March 4, 1933. "Poor creature" likely referred to Bridges himself or immigrants like him, rather than a slight at her political opponent. Ultimately, Perkins maintained that a labor strike was nonviolent and not a threat to the U.S. government, which she valued deeply.[39]

Throughout every step of her career, especially her tenure as Labor Secretary, Perkins worked overtime and made choices that she thought were best for the Americans who were affected. She worked around the clock even while ensuring a forty-hour workweek for most American workers through the Fair Labor Standards Act. She strived to uphold her own values of diligence, empathy, integrity, and selflessness. Critics assumed her worst intentions. They flung illogical reasoning shaped by their own sexist and political biases at her. As a trailblazing woman, she never had the political capital necessary to react as forcefully as anyone in her situation might have liked. And the drama of it all destroyed any sociopolitical capital in Washington that she had.

The case constructed against Perkins relied on essentially no evidence besides "deport him; we don't like him"—a sentiment that aligned with precedents in U.S. immigration law. Prior to Perkins's tenure, the Labor Department deported foreigners for little to no reason all the time. In the views of lawmakers who'd worked on immigration policy in Washington for years, leading a labor strike was more than enough reason to deport someone. And more than enough reason to impeach the woman they felt should have done it.

At times during the Bridges saga, Perkins seemed to forget one important consideration: politics. Maybe she forgot politics, unaware that her position on Bridges would backfire. Maybe she anticipated that it would backfire but remained so confident in the legality of her actions that she'd ride out whatever happened next. Even if she couldn't have done anything differently, and even though she remained in office, she lost this fight.

CHAPTER SEVEN

Dear Miss Perkins

"DEAR MISS PERKINS," WROTE HUNDREDS, perhaps thousands of individuals between 1938 and 1940.[1] Based on the volume of letters from a mixture of acquaintances and loved ones of people trapped in Nazi-occupied territory, Frances Perkins must have received multiple every week.

In 1938, Nazis began expanding their reach across Central Europe, annexing Austria and the Sudetenland. World War II began on September 1, 1939, when the Nazis attacked Poland, the final straw for Britain and the Allied powers. In October 1939, Nazis began isolating Jewish people in their territories into ghettos, where residents had little chance of survival and even slighter prospects of escape.

The impetus for Perkins and the Roosevelt administration's late 1930s efforts to aid refugees from Nazi Germany and other occupied areas was Kristallnacht. On the night of November 9, 1938, through the morning of November 10, Nazis destroyed thousands of businesses and hundreds of homes and synagogues. As the Nazis terrorized individuals and communities and desecrated Jewish cemeteries, not even the dead were safe. The world watched in horror as headlines spread news of Kristallnacht, "Night of Broken Glass," a state-sponsored pogrom.[2]

In conversations with officials in several cabinet departments and with the president himself, Perkins shared ideas for aiding refugees from Nazi Germany. One idea was congressional legislation for increased admittance of child refugees, as discussed in chapter five. Another was a plan to settle German-Jewish refugees in the Alaskan territory, as explored in a subsequent chapter.[3]

Her idea that found the most traction was to extend the visitor visas of German-Jewish refugees already in the U.S. Despite objections from the State Department, the president listened to Perkins this time. Issuing an executive order, the president explained in a press conference: "It would be a cruel and inhumane thing to compel them to leave here in time to get back to Germany . . . I cannot, in any decent humanity, throw them out."[4] Exuding Perkins's influence, this directive alone saved at least five thousand lives, likely more.[5] The executive order extended each visa for six months. Thus, for six months at a time, a refugee could avoid deportation and evade likely death, a high-stakes and high-anxiety situation.

There was no law or directive requiring Perkins to extend the visas further, and frankly, she had a lot on her plate, including a resolution to impeach her. She was exhausted.

But she responded to as many requests as she could, and she intervened repeatedly in their immigration cases to extend their stays with varying degrees of success. The letters poured in from refugees, their American relatives, and their concerned, somewhat random acquaintances. Perkins knew the people writing to her from every stage of her career: Mount Holyoke, Hull House, New York politics, and D.C. society. Some she may have met once or didn't remember. They all asked for her help.

In her responses, Perkins's tone was more measured than when she battled with the State Department in 1933, or even when she supported the GJCA's child refugee program. By 1938, she was an expert in the intricacies of the Immigration and Naturalization Service (INS) that she'd helped to build and rebuild throughout her tenure. One mechanism that she used repeatedly was to extend their time in the U.S. by asking a potential immigrant to obtain a new visa from Canada, Mexico, or another nearby country, with the understanding that they'd use it to enter the U.S. This strategy exemplified creative implementation of laws to work around the rigid quota system. It signified a continuation of her earlier successes in reforming the immigration and naturalization processes by creating the INS, curtailing deportations, and humanizing bureaucratic policies.[6] Even after MacCormack's death in 1937, Perkins pushed the INS in the direction of compassion.

Sometimes she redirected correspondents to the State Department with her word of support. Despite fierce cultural and legal battles, the Departments of Labor and State continued working together, productively and with varying degrees of success, throughout the Roosevelt administration.

Perkins's immigration correspondence between 1938 and 1940, much of it handwritten—some via telegrams punctuated with "STOP" and some accompanied by brief notes between Perkins and her colleagues—is where Perkins's diligence, her humility, her humanity shined. Her undergraduate speech, as President of the Mount Holyoke Class of 1902, had advised her classmates "be ye steadfast," and here was where she took that to heart.[7]

These letters epitomize why the story of Perkins's refugee policy matters. They determined the outcomes for countless individuals, some famous and others unknown. Contrasting the gravity of the circumstances was the modesty of the handwriting as they reached out to her, Dear Miss Perkins.

Endre Varady: Cousin of Perkins's Dentist, 1938

Under the Nazi regime, Austria was rife with antisemitic discrimination and propaganda; red, white, and black flags with swastikas; and the nearly constant feeling of violence looming. Trapped in Austria in 1938, with a decade-long wait for the Hungarian quota, Endre Varady had one advantage in his application: His cousin Eugene Weissmann performed dental work on the Secretary of Labor. Weissmann reached out to Perkins, hoping to secure immigration for Endre Varady and his family. "My dear Miss Perkins: As a person who has had the honor of ministering to your dental needs and as one who had the privileges of learning from such personal contacts the kindly sympathies you feel for those in misery and distress,

I take the liberty of appealing to you to help me save the life of one of Germany's victims of racial and religious persecution."[8] Weissmann described how his cousin Endre Varady could not immigrate under the combined German and Austrian quota because he was born in Hungary, even though he moved to Austria as an infant and had an Austrian wife and child:

> Mr. Endre Varady, a cousin of mine, was born in Hungary, but taken by his parents to Austria when only an infant of a few months; was brought up, educated, engaged in business, and lived there ever since. He is 36 years of age and lives with his wife and ten-year-old daughter in . . . formerly Austria, now Germany. Soon after the occupation of Austria by Germany, he was ousted from his extensive business and deprived of his means of a livelihood. Upon his urgent request, I sent to the U.S. Consul in Vienna an affidavit with all the required papers, including a financial statement . . . for a visa to enable him, his wife and child to emigrate to our country. However, I was informed that, on account of his Hungarian birth, he belongs to the Hungarian quota, which is filled for the coming ten years. His wife and child were born in Austria, and there should be no difficulty for them to obtain visa.[9]

When Nazis annexed Austria in March 1938, thirty-six-year-old Varady, his wife, and their ten-year-old daughter lost their business, the means of their livelihood. Since

Varady was born in Hungary, his national origin was Hungarian according to U.S. immigration law, even though his wife and daughter were born in Austria. Patriarchal as always, the U.S. quota system looked first at the man's national origin. Further, the U.S. explicitly favored Western and Central European immigration—Germany's quota of 25,957 and Austria's quota of 1,413—over Hungary, where the quota was 869, and the waitlist was a decade long.[10]

Weissmann described how Varady's brother, now in Palestine, wrote to him "frantically" urging him to "save the life of his brother Endre Varady who, for no good reason, was given until the coming November 15, to leave Germany upon penalty of imprisonment which usually ends with loss of life."[11] Endre Varady—Hungarian by birth, trapped in Austria in his prime, "deprived of his means of a livelihood" due only to his Jewishness under Nazism—was emblematic of a poor refugee struggling to immigrate to the U.S. Weissmann beseeched Perkins, "I feel that your influence with the proper official in charge may be weighty enough in this case to make it possible for this unfortunate person to escape with his life."[12] However, the affidavit of support and his cousin's personal connection to Perkins proved insufficient.

Less than a week later, on October 20, Perkins replied to Weissmann. Although the State Department had discretion over quota visas, Perkins "asked the legal division" of the Labor Department to "explore the immigration statutes to see whether there was any possibility of rendering some assistance."[13] They concluded that the "statutes which govern his case are very rigid since the Quota Act of 1924 is explicit in basing the place of birth rather than the present nationality of the applicant... Consequently, the consul under the law must wait until there is a vacancy in the quota for Hungary before he can grant him a visa."[14] Perkins could not influence the ten-year waitlist for the Hungarian quota. Kristallnacht happened less than a month later. Nazis sent Jewish men and boys from Austria and Germany to concentration camps, not death camps yet, but the work camps could nonetheless be fatal. Nazis assessed and stole remaining assets that deportees possessed. Endre Varady was one of them.

Unable to immigrate to the U.S., the Varady family fled to New Zealand. Nearly a decade later, Endre Varady became a naturalized citizen of New Zealand under the name Andrew Varadi. He settled with his wife, Paula, and their daughter, Ilse Varadi. Born in 1928, Ilse was eighteen years old by the time she became a naturalized New Zealander in October 1946. On their immigration paperwork, Paula's occupation was listed as "housewife," and her husband was "manufacturer of knitted goods." As a businessman, Varady had not qualified to circumvent the U.S.'s quota waitlist through a non-quota visa. While quota visas remained almost without exception under the State Department, the National Origins Act of 1924 also specified non-quota visas for professors, students, and select professionals.[15]

Norbert Glatzer: Professor and Scholar, 1938

Perkins received a letter from Rabbi Stephen Wise, dated November 1, 1938, about an academic named Norbert Glatzer. After Nazis removed him from his position teaching Hebrew at Goethe University Frankfurt in 1933, Glatzer continued his scholarship. When he applied to immigrate to the U.S., Glatzer's career as a professor carried weight for the Quota Act of 1924, which allowed non-quota visas for professors and select other jobs that would count as separate from the quota system.

When Glatzer applied for a non-quota visa as a professor, however, a U.S. consular official in Toronto objected that Glatzer didn't qualify because he'd been engaged in research rather than teaching for too long. Thus, Rabbi Stephen Wise of the American Jewish Congress reached out to the Secretary of Labor. "Dear Miss Perkins: You know how reluctant I am to tax your time by calling upon you unless there be urgent need for your assistance, but in the following matter I have no other recourse, since only you can decide this case authoritatively." Rabbi Wise explained: "Dr. Norbert Glatzer, one of the outstanding Hebrew scholars of Europe, formerly on the faculty of the University of Frankfurt... is now in Toronto, Canada, seeking a non-quota visa to take up his new duties as director of the School of Jewish Studies for Girls, an affiliate of the Hebrew Theological College of Chicago." Wise told Perkins, "One of the young Vice Consuls in our Consulate General at Toronto has refused Professor Glatzer his non-quota visa on the ground that he is not a professor within the meaning of the Immigration Act, since his leave of absence for Research Work during the last academic year disqualified him." Pivotally, Wise added, "Of course any person with academic experience knows this is absurd."[16] Rabbi Wise was right: Denying a non-quota visa to Norbert Glatzer rested on an absurd definition of the word *professor*.

Perkins sent word to the State Department consul in Toronto. She replied to Rabbi Wise on November 4:

"The Solicitor has reached the conclusion that Dr. Glatzer has been continuously carrying on the vocation of a professor of the past two years and, therefore, falls within the provisions of Sec. 4(d) of the Quota Immigration Act of 1924."[17] Thanks to Perkins's intervention, Glatzer immigrated to the U.S. on a non-quota visa. The State Department consul and the Labor Secretary's contradictory interpretations of the Quota Act's Section 4(d) epitomized their different approaches to the gray area of immigration policy.

Perkins's intervention helped to enable Glatzer's long and distinguished scholarly career in the U.S. From 1946 to 1951, Glatzer served as editor-in-chief of Schocken Books, a Jewish literary imprint. As a Professor of Jewish Philosophy and Ethics, he taught at Brandeis University from 1951 to 1973. Glatzer's 1959 to 1961 Guggenheim Fellowship was only one of many accolades for his pioneering work in Jewish Studies until his death in 1990.

Angelica Balabanoff: Writer, 1939

Angelica Balabanoff was born in Imperial Russia in 1878. She built a career as an author, lecturer, and poet in Austria. On January 1, 1938, *Harper's Magazine* published Balabanoff's memoir, entitled *My Life as a Rebel*. It was well received and widely read, especially in Europe.

In 1939, Balabanoff was living in the U.S., composing poetry and writing a play, when she received a deportation notice from the INS. She'd already renewed her visa once but needed to renew it again. An American contact, Harriet B. Randegg, reached out to Perkins, vouching that "*My Life as a Rebel* had an enthusiastic review and good sale," and that Balabanoff was "one of the five most intellectual women of the world," emphasizing Balabanoff's accomplishments and ability to support herself financially. She added that Balabanoff was a "gentle, great-hearted woman who has suffered for her unselfish ideals and shouldn't mind hardships."[18] Randegg beseeched Perkins, "Where can she go? She has repudiated Communist Russia where she was born, and [she also repudiated] Nazi Germany."[19] Balabanoff was Jewish, not safe in Nazi-occupied territory, and the wrong kind of Leftist for the Soviet Union.

In 1939, extending the visitor visa of a Leftist immigrant was the opposite of politically astute for Perkins. She extended the visitor visa anyway, because she could and because it was the right thing to do.

Angelica Balabanoff remained in the U.S. on a visitor visa to continue a lecturing circuit. She socialized among prominent American socialists in New York City, and she contributed frequently to the *Socialist Review*. After World War II, Balabanoff relocated to Italy, where she published additional books, and died in Rome in 1965.[20] Her story represents a success: Balabanoff was able to outlive the Nazi regime. Survival was, of course, not automatic for refugees.

The Langer Family: Death by Suicide, 1939

In August 1939, Houghteling informed Perkins that a Czech family, the Langers, had died by suicide while on temporary visitor visas in Chicago. Barely five months earlier, Nazi Germany had invaded and occupied parts of Czechoslovakia.[21] The Langer family chose death over deportation to Nazi-occupied territory. While the Langer family technically had the option to extend their visitor visas, the process must have seemed daunting or overwhelming, or maybe they didn't understand how. Perhaps they felt a disorienting homesickness specific to refugees, or something happened to a loved one back home. In their last moments, the Langers saw only death as a viable option. Perkins contacted Adolph J. Sabath, a U.S. congressman who represented Chicago. Sabath had also emigrated from Czech lands many years previously. "The Langer case is indeed distressing," Perkins wrote. "On looking up the record I find they only arrived in New York on July 1, 1939, and had been admitted for a six-month period, which expires on December 5, 1939, and that there had been no indication to them that they could not stay here for the temporary period they were admitted." She didn't stop there. "I can well imagine what strain they must have been under before they arrived here and that they had not opportunity to overcome it."[22] In Chicago, thousands of mourners attended the funeral of Mrs. Langer and her two children. According to Houghteling, multiple attendees of the funeral felt that the "only thing left for them to do is to follow the act of Mrs. Langer."[23] Their suicide was distressing but not unique.

When Perkins checked the status of the Langer family's visitor visas after they died, the fact that they could have extended them highlighted prevailing anxiety, distress, and uncertainty. While delicately maneuvering around immigration restrictions could save lives, and it did, it could not ensure safety or security.

Leopold Prinz: Medical Doctor, 1939

Dr. Leopold Prinz worked as a medical doctor in Germany until the Nazis removed his chance of supporting himself and seized his assets. In May 1939, Florence Harriman—suffragist, social reformer, and cousin by marriage of the late Mary Harriman Rumsey—wrote to Perkins on behalf of Prinz, who had "permission to stay in America" only until August 4, 1939. "Then he must leave—and where shall he go? If he returns to Germany, they will directly put him in a prison or something like that."[24] Wounds fresh from her impeachment hearing, Perkins responded that Dr. Prinz needed a quota number for permanent entry to the U.S.[25]

Harriman was astonished. "Is it really no possibility to save Dr. Leopold Prinz? Cannot exceptions be done I do pray and impose you to help me because I know perfectly well that he is going to take his life if he is obliged to return to Germany," Harriman continued. "Do not be cross with me because I am urging and imploring you to save a very important person, a man who is useful for the community . . . We do live in a bad world and usually too late we do understand and regret the mistakes we have done."[26] Prinz felt hopeless, Harriman felt incredulous, and even in the most powerful position that she achieved, Perkins felt powerless.

Perkins restated that she felt sympathy for Prinz, but that she could not intervene unless Congress passed new immigration legislation. "If it is possible, under existing new laws, to give consideration to Dr. Prinz's situation, you may be sure it will have very careful consideration," Perkins tried to assure Harriman to no avail.[27] Here was Frances Perkins beaten down by the very real limits of American immigration law—antisemitism, restrictionism, rigidity, xenophobia—of which she was previously aware but now understood.

Sometime between 1938 and 1940, in an undated letter to an unclear recipient, Perkins wrote: "A great many people seem to hold the belief that there is some provision in the immigration laws for political refugees or for making this country an asylum for the oppressed of all nations. This is absolutely not the case."[28] Since 1933, Perkins had tried to carve something from nothing. "The immigration laws do not mention political refugees, except in one very minor way. They exempt from deportation as criminals all aliens who prior to entry may have been convicted in other countries of crimes purely political."[29] For example, when the Nazis charged German Jewry with made-up crimes, German-Jewish refugees did not count as criminals in the U.S. immigration system. U.S. lawmakers were more creative in their strategies to keep out refugees: definitions of professor and student that could be absurd for non-quota visas, decades-long quota waitlists, likely to become a public charge.

Felix Weinheber: "Incredible Pearl of a Domestic Servant," 1939–1940

Santa Monica, California, has by most measurements perfect weather in mid-to-late June: ample sunshine with low humidity. I happened to be there while reading a telegram that Dorothy Thompson sent from her Santa Monica hotel to Frances Perkins on June 19, 1939. Thompson stayed at the Miramar, now a historic hotel, which sits across from a beach walk lined with palm trees.

Dorothy Thompson made two earlier appearances in the story of Frances Perkins's efforts to aid refugees from Nazi Germany. In chapter one, she married Sinclair Lewis, who had first proposed to Perkins. In chapter three, Thompson emerged as a pathbreaking American journalist covering the rise of Nazism on the ground in Germany. By 1939, she was living in the U.S. and writing a column, essentially working as a public intellectual and writer.

Thompson sent a telegram to Perkins, received at the Department of Labor in undoubtedly more humid D.C. Thompson's tone was deeply concerned. "Dearest Frances what can I and what can you do for an acquaintance of mine named Felix Weinheber who is here on a visitor's visa which finally expires September 6th," she recounted. "He was the former chauffeur valet and general factotum of a film magnate and was arrested and put in a concentration camp wholly because of his employer ... He got out by getting a visa ... His passport being Austrian is not good."[30] Weinheber, now working in Hollywood on a visitor visa, had spent time in a concentration camp, and he no longer had a valid passport. His circumstances warranted Thompson's tone.

From her oceanside hotel, Thompson assured Perkins that Weinheber would not become a public charge. "There is not the slightest chance of his becoming a public charge because he is an incredible pearl of a domestic servant including secretarial work and has any number of jobs offered him in Hollywood which he cannot take permanently because of his status," Thompson explained frantically. She asked Perkins if Weinheber's domestic service work could qualify for a non-quota visa. The answer was no, as he was not a professor, student, or other qualifying professional. U.S. immigration law was fundamentally classist. Thompson continued: "I cannot bear it that people who are entirely competent to take care of themselves anywhere because of their capability adaptability and willingness to do any sort of work well should be hounded like animals."[31] She signed off with her address at the Miramar.

Perkins responded the next day, June 20, explaining that if Weinheber wanted to apply for permanent residency, he must depart for another country where an American consulate outside of the U.S. could issue working documentation. Both his expired Austrian passport and the waitlist for the German quota posed obstacles. Further, Perkins clarified that a domestic servant could not qualify for a non-quota visa. She concluded that a visitor visa would likely be Weinheber's best option, though she could not promise its approval.[32]

By August, Weinheber was still living and working in Hollywood on a wide variety of jobs. Back on the East Coast, Thompson wrote to Perkins again. She explained how Weinheber was still in need of a visa extension, but that his documentation might be a serious obstacle because he lacked a valid passport. U.S. immigration law intended for visitors to have a home country where they could return. In June, Perkins had suggested that "persons in a similar status sometimes found it possible to make such an arrangement [for a visitor visa] with Mexico or some other country," adding, "Perhaps that is where you can help Mr. Weinheber."[33] Thus, in August, Thompson worried that Weinheber would need to stay many months in Mexico without the means to support himself.

The following spring, Perkins received more correspondence from Thompson regarding Felix Weinheber. The refugee himself had written to Thompson, "Impossible for me to depart now have no country to go in. Kindly write a Letter to Secretary of Labor requesting other extensions at least six months."[34] He seems to have received an extension in summer 1939, and he was anxious about traveling to Mexico to obtain usable documentation.

In spring 1941, however, Felix Weinheber secured a perhaps unlikely visa from Mexico. His file specified immigration from Tijuana, Mexico. Felix Weinheber changed his name to Felix Wayne. In June 1941, he married a Czech immigrant, Elisabeth Glatz, in Las Vegas. They stayed in Los Angeles after World War II and became citizens. Felix Wayne acted in a few movies and has an IMDB page. He died in Los Angeles, California, in 1975, at age seventy-eight.[35]

Dr. Paul Boschan: Insurance Worker, 1940

In early 1940, the Director of Hull House, Charlotte Carr, wrote "My dear Miss Perkins" on Hull House letterhead. She was writing on behalf of an insurance man from Vienna whose immigration status was uncertain due to a physical disability and for whom multiple Hull House reformers were vouching financially. Physical disability, a target for persecution in Nazi Germany, was also an obstacle in U.S. immigration law, according to the Immigration Act of 1917, which barred "idiots, imbeciles, feeble-minded persons, epileptics, insane persons . . . persons of constitutional psy-

chopathic inferiority . . . persons afflicted with tuberculosis . . .
mentally or physically defective," unless the Labor Secretary accepted a charge bond on their behalf.[36] By 1940, the
idea of a charge bond had evolved into the practice of U.S.
citizens offering affidavits of support for potential immigrants. Boschan had the financial backing of multiple
residents at Hull House in Chicago.

Dr. Paul Boschan was trying to board an Italian Line
when the people running the ship doubted whether he was
eligible for immigration to the U.S. On January 27, Perkins
replied to Carr and added that "You are at liberty to ac-
quaint the Italian Line with the contents of this letter." The
contents included the Labor Secretary's reassurance: "I
feel safe in assuring you that this is a case where admission
under the provisions of Section 21 of the Immigration Act
of 1917 . . . will be authorized in retaliation to Dr. Boschan's
physical condition resulting from infantile paralysis," Perkins explained. "Dr. Boschan is stated to have held a fine
actuarial position with a Vienna insurance company and,
because of his profession, his physical condition should not
be a material handicap."[37]

Harvey O'Connor, a Hull House resident funding Boschan's transatlantic passage, thanked Perkins on February
9. "Certainly, I realize you cannot commit yourself before
the case comes under your jurisdiction," O'Connor wrote,
"but you did say enough to make the Line feel safe in recommending his embarkation for other authorities to judge."[38]
Perkins's influence seems to have ensured Boschan's safe
passage out of Nazi Germany. Worth noting here is that
even if the Labor Secretary's authority in the matter seemed
relatively straightforward, Perkins was the only Labor Sec-

retary who regularly prioritized aiding immigrants rather than deporting them.

On February 29, however, Carr asked for Perkins's help again for the same man. This time, Boschan was detained on Ellis Island. Carr rambled to Perkins that Boschan was a "man of superior mental caliber, and has experience in a field that is now expanding—visual statistics," that Boschan "did some work at one time in the Social and Economic Museum at Vienna, and has since helped to plan illustrations for the work of various economic writers, besides his work at the Vienna Insurance . . . There is no chance of his becoming a public charge."[39] Perkins agreed and intervened again, this time at Ellis Island, where her authority was more straightforward. Harvey O'Connor, too, sent cash from Hull House to the National Council of Jewish Women on the ground in New York to ensure that Boschan would not become a public charge. On March 2, 1940, Paul Boschan was admitted to the U.S.[40]

Ilka Gruning: Actress and Theater Teacher, 1940

In April 1940, Perkins's friend Elisabeth Bigelow reached out in hopes of accrediting the new Max Reinhardt Workshop for Stage, Screen and Radio, "recognized as a school to which foreign students may come," under section 19E of the Quota Act. Bigelow described the situation of Miss Ilka Gruning, "now acting as an assistant to one of our teachers, unpaid, because she is here as a visitor. She was a character actress of great distinction in Germany and had a school of her own in Berlin for years."[41] Gruning was in the process of "applying for a non-quota admission as a teacher and actress." The INS in Los Angeles had extended Gruning's temporary visa for two six-month stints since Kristallnacht. Bigelow mentioned that Perkins had already intervened on behalf of another German-Jewish actor, Haussermann, who according to Bigelow secured a visa to continue teaching at the Reinhardt Workshop.

Bigelow added that Gruning's "immediate fear is of going back to Germany in August when her visa expires. She is Jewish."[42] Understandably, Gruning was in tears off and on for months. Bigelow "withstood Miss Gruning's tears for months, telling her that [she] could do nothing whatsoever to hurry the normal course of the school's recognition by the Labor Department."[43]

Perkins checked on the status of the workshop, which it turned out, was not accredited to accept refugees with non-quota visas because the State Department had directed that "dramatic, art, music, and other institutions offering instructions in the beaux-arts" were "not deemed colleges."[44] Nevertheless, the Labor Department found a solution to keep Ilka Gruning in the country. While not the accreditation that Bigelow requested, converting Gruning's visa from a visitor for pleasure to a visitor for business served the same purpose of saving Gruning from returning to Germany. In this case, Perkins worked around the State Department. A Labor Department memo explained:

> Insofar as Miss Gruning is concerned [the] principal and immediate question is to permit her

> to remain here without being required to go
> back to Germany in August [since] she unques-
> tionably is in refugee status . . . We permit aliens
> temporarily here to accept employment if they
> are of the artistic or professional classes. It most
> certainly seems that Miss Gruning's employ-
> ment would be of an artistic nature. In the
> circumstances I would suggest that we consider
> the letter of Miss Bigelow as an application on
> the part of Miss Gruning to have her status
> changed from that of visitor as 3(2) for pleasure
> to visitor 3(2) for business and permit her to
> accept employment for pay with the Max Rein-
> hardt Workshop.[45]

Perkins conveyed the news to her friend Elisabeth Bigelow, who while undoubtedly pleased, likely didn't fully
grasp the limits of what Perkins could control. As war
raged in Europe, the INS would remain in the Labor
Department for only another month. In May 1940, the
president transferred the INS from the Department of
Labor to the Department of Justice, as chapter ten
explains.

Bertolt Brecht: Dramatist, Playwright, and Poet, 1940

Bertolt Brecht was born in Germany in 1898, to a Protestant mother and Catholic father. At age twenty-four, he
found early success with the production of *Trommeln in*

der Nacht (Drums in the Night) in 1922. Two years later, he moved to Berlin, where he worked as a consultant for Max Reinhardt's German Theatre. Opera fans might recognize Brecht's collaboration with Kurt Weill in Berlin from the late 1920s. In the final years of the Weimar Republic, Brecht was reading Marx, criticizing the government in his films and plays, and speaking out against the rising Nazi Party. Brecht fled Germany in 1933. The Nazis included all of Brecht's works up to that point in their book burnings.[46]

A few years older than Brecht, Hamilton Fish Armstrong also found early success in writing in 1922, when he became managing editor of *Foreign Affairs* at age twenty-nine. Armstrong was a veteran of World War I, a graduate of Princeton University, and a direct descendent of Hamilton Fish, President Grant's Secretary of State during unwelcome capitalistic imperialism in East Asia. Hamilton Fish Armstrong followed in his family's tradition of internationalism and interventionism, perhaps with less colonialist aggression. Undoubtedly, he maintained a deep interest and knowledge of international affairs. In 1933, Armstrong published a book entitled *Hitler's Reich: The First Phase.* In 1940, he reached out to his contact Frances Perkins on behalf of Bertolt Brecht.

"Dear Miss Perkins," he wrote on April 17, 1940, "I am venturing to write to inquire what advice I might give the friends of a well-known anti-Nazi German writer who is now in Sweden and whose life will obviously be in danger if, as seems very possible, Germany invades that country." Armstrong described Brecht as "a well-known Bavarian writer . . . a famous enemy of both the Nazis and the

Communists, and he is therefore a marked man if he should come into the power of either." Armstrong told Perkins that Brecht possessed a "contract by a well-known producer in Hollywood."[47] The German American Writers Association sent an additional telegram informing Perkins that Brecht had secured a teaching appointment at the New School for Social Research in New York. With multiple prestigious offers of employment, Brecht needed visas for himself, his wife, and their two children.[48]

Perkins responded to Armstrong that Brecht's best course of action was to apply for visitor visas for himself and his family from the U.S. Consul in Stockholm. If he lectured for two years, he'd have the option of applying for a non-quota visa as a professor, she added. Armstrong communicated the information to the German American Writers Association, which advised Brecht. Bert Brecht and his family relocated from Sweden to Finland, where they awaited American visitor visas that finally arrived a year later in May 1941. In the U.S., Brecht lived in Santa Monica, where he coauthored a Hollywood screenplay, rather than teaching. Criticizing the Nazi regime, the film was well received in the U.S. and supported the Brecht family financially. After World War II, Brecht encountered struggles relating to Communism with the House Un-American Activities Committee (HUAC), and he returned to Europe in 1947. In August 1956, Brecht died of a heart attack at age fifty-eight in East Berlin.

Brecht likely could have escaped the Nazis without Perkins explaining immigration processes to Hamilton Fish Armstrong and the German American Writers Association. However, the immigration story of Bertolt Brecht exemplifies Perkins's willingness to provide clarity and comfort when acquaintances reached out to her. "Dear Miss Perkins: Thank you for your prompt reply . . . I have transmitted the information to his friends, and they join me in warm thanks for your interest and help," Armstrong thanked her.[49] Even more, having the option of visitor visas was a lifeline for refugees from Nazi Germany. Prior to Perkins's tenure, the INS raided visitors. As Labor Secretary, Perkins pushed the president to allow repeated extension of visitor visas with considerable success, especially after Kristallnacht and before World War II. Perkins encouraged refugees to use this option with her characteristic compassion and steadfastness, despite rising congressional disapproval.

Counting the Uncountable, 1940

In early 1940, Congress asked the Labor Department for a precise number of temporary visas in the U.S. The task became the responsibility of Commissioner of Immigration Houghteling, who commented that the "question involved is one of considerable difficulty and cannot be answered very briefly."[50] He was less than prepared to assemble comprehensive records, because local INS districts were accustomed to compiling all their information only once a year, according to Houghteling, to submit an annual report. Yet the Labor Department compiled a chart documenting the number of immigrants on visitor visas in the U.S. from each European country or nationality.

COUNTRY OR NATIONALITY	1938	1939	1940	TOTAL
Total Europe	2,905	9,865	16,344	29,114
Belgium	30	134	221	385
Bulgaria	2	26	29	57
Czechoslovakia	27	106	47	180
Denmark	22	296	346	664
Estonia	7	9	15	31
Finland	12	54	24	90
France	298	576	1,057	1,931
Germany	458	1,457	1,566	3,481
Great Britain	1,127	3,870	8,372	13,369
Greece	40	95	190	325
Hungary	25	152	144	321
Ireland	18	238	723	979
Italy	136	458	403	997
Latvia	6	23	22	51
Lithuania	11	35	30	76
Netherlands	75	367	605	1,047
Norway	20	325	384	729
Poland	71	179	303	553
Portugal	7	40	62	109
Romania	9	70	146	225
Soviet Russia	30	84	37	151
Spain	339	402	393	1,134
Sweden	56	513	756	1,325
Switzerland	67	288	346	701
Yugoslavia	7	60	113	180

The 1940 numbers accounted for only the first seven months of the year.[51] Overall, if under thirty thousand immigrants visited the U.S. from Europe between 1938 and 1940, the years when European Jewry both wanted to leave and, in many cases, still had the required documentation to do so, these numbers seem relatively low. Houghteling likely submitted a conservative estimate both because he wanted to appease Congress and because a comprehensive estimate proved nearly impossible.

Efforts to count—or at least to perform counting for an audience of Congress—the visitors persisted. The Department distinguished between people visiting "legally" and people visiting "illegally" from the countries where refugees were most likely to originate. (For the twenty-first century

COUNTRY OR NATIONALITY	DOC. 1938	UNDOC. 1938	DOC. 1939	UNDOC. 1939	DOC. 1940	UNDOC. 1940
Czechoslovakia	25	18	372	23	318	7
Danzig	2	0	11	0	10	0
Estonia	0	4	11	3	25	1
Finland	2	10	81	9	51	11
Germany	219	161	3,599	253	2,817	49
Hungary	37	11	443	16	338	7
Latvia	1	4	31	5	65	1
Lithuania	8	2	57	6	94	2
Poland	56	19	406	48	693	13
Soviet Russia	33	9	209	8	261	33
Spain	48	70	217	108	589	3

reader, I instead use the terms "documented" versus "undocumented," abbreviated as "doc" and "undoc."[52])

By far, the most visitors originated from Germany, which included Austria, and the next most visitors came from Nazi-occupied Czechoslovakia and Poland. Additional records from Labor Department files reported that of 12,036 people in the U.S. "legally" on visitor visas, 2,573 people were "Hebrew," and 266 of those people originated from Germany. The largest group of visitors, 5,707, originated from Germany but were not classified as "Hebrew." Of the 975 people in the U.S. "illegally" on visitor visas, 188 people were "Hebrew," and 74 of those originated from Germany. The largest group of "illegal" visitors, 382 people, originated from Germany but were not classified as "Hebrew."[53]

Congress's solicitation of this information tells us first and foremost that Congress did not like the Labor Department's policy of extending visitor visas, no matter the president's 1938 directive after Kristallnacht. Barely a year after the resolution to impeach Frances Perkins, Congress was not writing to the Labor Secretary to congratulate her on a job well done.

CHAPTER EIGHT

Alaska

*F*ACED WITH GROWING ODDS AGAINST them, proponents of refugees turned their attention toward a
distant idea—in terms of both practicality and mileage: the
frozen tundra of Alaska.

Frances Perkins supported the idea of a settler colony
for German-Jewish refugees in Alaska. In late 1938, she suggested that Congress open a separate quota for people to
immigrate there. Quotas for immigration from many European countries accrued decade-long waitlists in the
immediate aftermath of Kristallnacht. The Alaska idea was
one among many suggestions, and she was not alone in proposing it.[1] A settler colony of German-Jewish refugees in
Alaska aligned with other U.S. government officials' aims,
economic development of a sparsely populated territory

and militaristic defense of the Aleutian Islands, barely three thousand miles east of the Japanese Empire.

While Perkins proposed several ideas to aid refugees, including issuing charge bonds, prioritizing children, and approving repeated visa extensions, the idea of an Alaskan quota stands out as exceptional. The idea of a German-Jewish colony in Alaska cannot be separate from its imperial context. When these conversations were happening in 1939, Alaska was one of several territories where colonized people lived under U.S. control without full rights as Americans.

By late 1939, Secretary of the Interior Harold Ickes took seriously the possibility of German-Jewish settlement in Alaska, brought the idea to Congress, and collaborated with lawmakers in an attempt at legislation. In these conversations, Perkins-appointee Isador Lubin, head of the Bureau of Labor Statistics, represented the Labor Department alongside the Interior Department and Congress. The resulting legislative entity, the King-Havenner Bill, failed in Congress for the same reasons as the Wagner-Rogers Bill a few months earlier: antisemitism, restrictionism, and xenophobia.

Unlike Wagner-Rogers, the King-Havenner Bill had an additional factor: American imperial control over colonized people. Alaskan newspapers covered it, and some Indigenous Alaskans opposed the idea. Representatives of Alaska testified for the opposition alongside the usual suspects: xenophobes John Thomas Taylor of the American Legion and John B. Trevor of the American Coalition of Patriotic Societies. The rhetoric of both the colonists and the colonized often included an assumption: *Isn't Alaska too cold for the Jews?* In the end, antisemitism, restrictionism, and xenophobia prevailed over the American imperialistic drive to expand, develop, and settle Europeans on Indigenous lands.

Here, the story of Perkins's efforts to aid refugees overlaps with the story of American imperialism in two profound ways at a crucial moment. First, American antisemitism, restrictionism, and xenophobia were so strong that they overpowered even the drive to imperialize. Predominantly white European refugees were still too Jewish or too other to pass as white settlers in the eyes of enough congressmen, interest groups, and voters.

Second, while the primary impetus for Perkins's suggestion to settle refugees in Alaska was undoubtedly an effort to save refugees' lives, Perkins had an imperial mindset. Her earliest American ancestors settled in Massachusetts Bay Colony. She revered her mother's cousin, Oliver Otis Howard, who despite some notable accomplishments, killed Indigenous people.[2] At Mount Holyoke, she learned a progressive labor history ahead of its time, right next to learning colonial history in a colonialist mindset. It's not that Perkins's imperialist mindset itself was somehow evil. Of course, it's misguided, but as historical thinkers, our primary purpose is not to cast judgment. The point is that Perkins seemed truly to believe that the U.S. would aid refugees. In 1933, she entered the charge bonds controversy with the same faith in institutions, patriotism, and progressive zeal that fueled her to reform the Immigration and Naturalization Service (INS) and to serve as a key architect of the New Deal. Her imperialist mindset was intertwined with her belief in American goodness and progress. America as a land of opportunity worked for her ancestors, so why not for the masses of European Jewry?

Perkins was not an opening-credits character in the story of the King-Havenner Bill because, just like during the Wagner-Rogers Bill's time on Capitol Hill, the 1939 resolution to impeach Perkins had decimated her political capital. Nonetheless, while the Alaska idea gained steam, Perkins couldn't see the whole picture.

Alaska: *Aleutian Word for "Mainland"*

In 2019, historian Daniel Immerwahr's pivotal book *How to Hide an Empire* connected with readers hungry for a more accurate view of American imperialism and state-building. The book argues that first, the U.S. is a settler state that violently conquered a continent of Indigenous people, and second, the U.S. has hidden its empire through innovative means such as relinquishing control when advantageous and projecting its nationalism through strategies such as portraying the "logo" map of the continental U.S. with the forty-ninth and fiftieth states as happy add-ons.[3]

Alaska is a fifth of the size of the continental U.S. From the perspective of the Aleuts in the Bering Sea, Alaska is the mainland, which is why *Alaska* is the Aleutian word for "mainland."

Around 15,000 BCE, the first people who migrated to the Americas emerged from the Bering Land Bridge between Asia and North America. Glaciers were melting, sea levels were rising, and Beringia was flooding. The Bering Land Bridge has not existed for millennia. In the *Wilderness at Dawn*, author Ted Morgan explains that "during the evacuation, as catastrophic as anything in human experience, hundreds, perhaps thousands of people fled the plain, as biting winds blew down from the glaciers, darkening the sky with volcanic grit. Imagine families separated and children lost, a scene of confused alarm and desperate flight as the tide broke through the straits."[4] The first people Indigenous to the American continents were, Morgan writes, "not explorers seeking a new world, but panic-stricken" climate refugees.[5] They migrated all over what is now North and South America.

Alaska is not and has never been a monolith. Aleuts inhabit the Alaskan Peninsula on the North Pacific Coast and the Aleutian Islands in the Bering Sea. The Inuit, Yupik, and other groups inhabit the Arctic coast. The Tlingit people live on the coast of the southeastern strip that borders British Columbia.[6] Indigenous Alaskans are diverse and widespread.

Russian fur traders colonized Alaska by settling there throughout the eighteenth century. They hunted sea otters and traded them at markets along Russia's border with China. Russian imperial presence on the American West Coast stretched from Alaska down to Northern California. In 1799, the Russian empire incorporated a Russian American Company to "administer and more effectively exploit Russian America," as historian Ned Blackhawk explains. It was an "extractive, violent form of colonization," where Russian fur traders required Indigenous people to hunt and process a certain number of furs per year, and if they did not pay forward enough furs, the penalty was death.[7]

In 1867, the U.S. annexed the Alaskan territory by purchasing it from Russia. American leaders viewed the Aleutian

Islands as "steppingstones to Asia," where they hoped to expand international trade.[8]

Missionary schools were a frequent tactic of American imperialism, and Alaska was no exception. In 1884, Congress established a territorial government in Alaska and authorized the Interior Department to oversee schooling for Alaskan children. The education included English language acquisition and other means to spread American culture. The first American school in Alaska was on the southeastern strip, where the Tlingit people lived historically. Funded by Congregational, Episcopal, and Presbyterian churches, the schools expanded north and west to reach Inuit and Aleut children, respectively.[9]

Under American colonial rule, Indigenous Alaskans lived under a system of racial segregation. Their schools and theaters were separate from white settlers. Hotels and restaurants displayed "No Natives Allowed" signs.[10]

In 1924, postwar isolationism and xenophobia and a racist resurgence culminated in the National Origins Act of 1924, an explicitly racist quota system. During an overlapping, related conversation to decide who should count as American, Congress extended citizenship to Indigenous people in all American states. The law did not include Alaska, Hawai'i, or other territories, which were intentionally excluded. The 1924 immigration legislation used the 1890 census to determine its quotas, and the U.S. Census did not even count Alaskans until 1900. In practice and in theory, U.S. citizenship and immigration laws kept Alaskans separate from the U.S. In the 1930s, Perkins's idea of adding a separate Alaskan quota for refugees would maintain this ideological and practical separation.

By the 1930s, the U.S. Census counted seventy-five thousand people in Alaska, half Indigenous and half settlers. Their economy revolved around fishing. Though still in proximity to unfriendly empires, the American colony of Alaska during the interwar period had a tiny air force, no navy, and no road connecting it to the continental U.S. Prior to World War II, Congress allocated minimal funding to Alaska.[11]

The 1930s marked a time of change amid the Great Depression. The Roosevelt administration brought new energy and fresh ideas, and Indigenous affairs were no exception. The ideas were by no means anti-imperialist. As global trades collapsed, the U.S. sought a more active economic relationship with Alaska. In 1936, Congress extended the Indian Reorganization Act to Alaska, inviting an Alaska Native Industries Cooperative (ANICA) to borrow from a revolving loan fund. Although a critical mass of Americans had long found Alaska "too remote for any imaginative economic planning," by the 1930s, that assumption was beginning to change.[12] Within this context of imagining economic potential, Perkins and others looked to Alaska as a possible territory for German-Jewish refugee resettlement.

Alaska: Too Cold for the Jews?

Throughout the 1930s, the U.S. began reconsidering its relationship to the Alaskan territory, at the same time as Perkins sought to help refugees. In November 1938, Kristallnacht accelerated the need to aid refugees, and sending them to Alaska was one of Perkins's ideas in the immediate aftermath.

Simultaneously, child refugee policy was another idea on the move. When the Wagner-Rogers Bill failed in summer 1939, Perkins, Jewish refugees' advocates in Congress, and the Department of the Interior looked seriously toward Alaska. "Recognizing Congress would not permit increased immigration into the forty-eight states," historian David Wyman writes, "various people turned their attention toward the sparsely settled territory of Alaska as a possible haven."[13]

The Labor Secretary and the Commissioner of Immigration looked toward Alaska as early as January 1935. At that time, the GJCA child refugee program had been in operation for two months. In the U.S., New Dealers focused on the National Labor Relations Act of July 1935 and the Social Security Act of August 1935. While in Germany, Nazis were planning the Nuremberg Race Laws, which they'd pass that September.

Antonin Fokrovsky, who signed his name "Rt. Rev. Antonin, Bishop of Alaska," sent a letter to Perkins in January 1935, recapping a recent in-person conversation with her and Commissioner of Immigration MacCormack. An "aged bishop" of Alaska, Fokrovsky's personal story had made *The New York Times* in March 1933, recounting how the divine saved him from a shipwreck off the coast of the Aleutian Islands, in a tale about how Indigenous Alaskans clearly, in the bishop's own words, "held me to their warm bodies while a fire was built. They heated rocks and laid them against me. For three days and three nights they rubbed my arms and legs," he told the *Times*. While "natives plodded across frozen rocks to rescue him," the bishop recalled, "my deliverance is to be attributed to a conscious act of God."[14]

The bishop's letter to Perkins epitomizes key themes of settler colonialism. He referenced the counting of Indigenous people and white people—and wanted to see more of the latter. The bishop addressed the Labor Secretary: "Your Excellency: In addition to my personal report and conversation with you and Hon. Colonel [MacCormack], I consider it [useful] to present you the same in the written form," he wrote, "the vast area of Alaska . . . is very sparsely populated as you know." He referenced the Russian American Company's 1844 census: 20,000 to 25,000 thousand Indigenous people and 8,587 white settlers. The bishop added that in 1930, "there are now 59,278" people in Alaska, "out of which 10,180 only are whites," adding "if we exclude all temporary residents as Government employees and the rest, hardly 4,000 will be left for the permanent settlers."[15] In addition to his desire to settle Alaska with more white people, the bishop demonstrated what historian Immerwahr calls *how to hide an empire* by considering the white governing officials as an inherent presence but not part of the community.

Christianity was long part of American colonization efforts, and the bishop's attitude of dismissiveness toward Indigenous people was no exception. The letter continued: "As a characteristic for Alaska natives we have to admit that they are, as a general rule, a good-natured people but very easy-going ones and not industrious at all." He continued, "Moreover, some tribes are dying out," as if this development happened on its own. The bishop urged, "In case the Government of the U.S. will find and move up to Alaska 40,000 (10,000 families) white farmers, who will stay there, the further development of the territory into the self-supporting and prosperous state will be guaranteed during the few coming years." The bishop recommended "the Russian people" as the "new settlers for Alaska."[16]

Perkins seems not to have responded directly to him, likely considering their in-person conversation to be sufficient, as well as the ideas that she pulled from his letter. On February 7, 1935, Perkins wrote to the Secretary of the Interior: "My dear Mr. Ickes: Please find herewith copy of a letter from the Right Reverend Antonin, Bishop of Alaska, with reference to a proposal to encourage the immigration to Alaska of Russian refugees now in Europe. I would be glad to have your views as to the practicability and desirability of the project."[17] Though both were in motion, neither Alaskan development nor refugee crises topped American headlines or political priorities in early 1935. By late 1938, however, both had changed amid a geopolitical landscape on the brink of World War II.

On December 3, 1938, Perkins wrote to Secretary of the Interior Harold Ickes with a newfound sense of urgency about the Alaska idea in the aftermath of Kristallnacht. Even in the weeks leading up to Kristallnacht, some Jewish advocates for Jewish refugees on the President's Advisory Committee on Political Refugees were already recommending "a plan to solve the refugee problem by settling Catholic, Protestant, and Jewish refugees in Alaska."[18] Between Kristallnacht and Perkins's letter to Ickes, Democratic Congressman Charles A. Buckley of New York suggested the Alaska idea to the president, who dismissed it as "obviously out of the question."[19] The Labor Department and Interior Department persisted regardless.

Ickes, a self-described "curmudgeon" who didn't get along with his wife or many of his subordinates, got along with Perkins as much as he got along with anyone. Author Derek Leebaert suggests that they connected over a deep sadness. Ickes was an "abused son of an alcoholic" who built a career in Chicago for "causes such as the newly founded American Civil Liberties Union and the city's Indian Rights Association, which he organized."[20] An unlikely choice for Secretary of the Interior and not the first choice, Harold L. Ickes was nevertheless one of the few cabinet secretaries who served throughout twelve years of the Roosevelt administration alongside Perkins. Ickes and Perkins met for the first time at the Roosevelts' Manhattan home in February 1933. Perkins recalled that she "liked Ickes almost from the start."[21]

Perkins sent to Ickes details from the Commissioner of Labor Statistics, Isador Lubin, regarding the "admission of refugees to Alaska."[22] With a PhD in Economics, Commissioner of the Bureau of Labor Statistics Isador Lubin was appointed by Perkins and worked under the Labor Department, but he had an office in the West Wing to advise the president directly on measuring the labor market. Perkins asked Ickes what he thought of the details that Lubin had compiled. Representatives from both Departments convened the following month.

On January 14, 1939, a group of ten people met in Lubin's office. They included Lubin, Felix Cohen from the Department of the Interior, a representative from B'nai B'rith, and Cecilia Razovsky. Cohen delivered a report arguing that increasing immigration would bolster American economic growth in Alaska, and that increasing the population in the territory would support national defense. Specifically, he reported that the "fishing, wood pulp, timber,

[and] oil" industries had room for growth and development. "It is important to have people in Alaska in great numbers," Cohen added.[23] Subsequent discussion culminated in an understanding that the governmental officials and immigration advocates present should draft legislation for Congress.

The idea of settling refugees—both Jewish and not Jewish—in Alaska was taking more concrete shape. Legislation would grant "concessions to six or seven non-profit making corporations" to develop Alaska, and the nonprofits would employ immigrant labor to do so.[24] Clearing each acre would cost $50 to $75 and settling each immigrant family would require $5,000 to $7,000. "Each would have to have a minimum of 40 acres," Razovsky wrote down, "with stock home equipment, machinery."[25] The process would take three to five years.

If the idea became a reality, immigrants would not be permitted to leave Alaska. They could not apply for U.S. citizenship unless Alaska became a state—which in 1939 was two decades away.

Unfortunately, the Colonial Governor of Alaska from 1939 through the postwar era had a rivalry with the Secretary of the Interior. From 1934 to 1939, Ernest Gruening served as Director of the Territories and Island Possessions within the Department of the Interior. He was of German-Jewish ancestry himself. With a small office and little more than lobbying influence, Gruening's role was to supervise American colonial possessions. Regarding Gruening's relationship to Secretary of the Interior Harold Ickes, Daniel Immerwahr writes: "Their politics didn't differ much, but the pair nevertheless clashed with all the passion and pointlessness of two apparatchiks in the Soviet bureaucracy.

Like any good Kremlin rivalry, it ended with exile in Siberia. Or, in this case, with Ernest Gruening being removed
from Washington and sent to Alaska in 1939."[26]

Immerwahr's comparison between Alaska and Siberia
has greater significance than banishment of a political rival
to a frigid climate. While the U.S. began to consider using
German-Jewish refugees as contract laborers to develop
Alaska, Joseph Stalin sent Jewish refugees to Siberia for
forced labor.[27]

In August 1939, the Interior Department published a report entitled *The Problem of Alaskan Development*, also
known as the Slattery Report. While Felix Cohen wrote it
and Under Secretary Harry Slattery signed an introductory
note, the Slattery Plan "sounded better than" the Cohen
Plan, historians Richard Breitman and Allan Lichtman
quipped.[28] *The Problem of Alaskan Development* proposed
moving fifty thousand settlers into Alaska, ten thousand
each year from 1940 to 1944.[29]

In October 1939, Gruening expressed positivity about
his gubernatorial appointment and sympathy toward the
possibility of settling refugee populations. Gruening wrote:
"I am very sympathetic with the refugee problem and
should be glad indeed to have the right type of refugee
come to Alaska. By 'right type' I mean persons who are
physically and mentally equipped to adapt themselves to
an environment and a mode of life which is very, very different from anything they have hitherto experienced."
Gruening added, "Alaska has opportunities for people who
are willing to work hard and are willing to endure a certain
amount of hardship and privation; it is still a frontier and
it needs the pioneer type."[30] Gruening speculated that East-

ern Europeans, especially Czech immigrants, might be better fit than Central Europeans for Alaska, joining a chorus of government officials speculating which national origins would be most adaptable to the cold.[31]

Reacting to the Slattery Report, however, Gruening wrote to Ickes expressing his opposition to the plan. Gruening accusatorily argued that the claims of economic development and military defense aimed to disguise the primary intent: aiding refugees. Ickes snapped back that helping refugees was precisely their intent, and therefore Gruening's point was inconsequential.[32]

Ickes felt that the most reputable opposition to the plan came from Indigenous Alaskans who, according to historian David Wyman, "feared that a population increase would endanger their control of the territory's resources." Wyman contends that the Alaskans' disapproval "centered on the refugee aspect of the measure." An *Alaska Weekly* editorial described, "Colonizing Alaska with refugees, financed by private capital. That it is Jewish capital and that the refugees to be poured into Alaska if this bill is passed will be Jewish is obvious."[33] Here the editorialist tapped into antisemitic tropes of monetary greed and inhuman levels of control.

While they had good reason to resist that settler-colonialist expansion, some Indigenous Alaskans employed antisemitic tropes in their efforts. People are complicated. This story is complicated. The same *Alaska Weekly* editorial continued: "Consensus of opinion . . . that Jews would be the least desirable of immigrants because of being the least adaptable." The supposed physical weakness of Jewish people is another antisemitic trope.[34] Indigenous Alaskans resisted colonization with the tools at their disposal, and casual antisemitism was a socially acceptable rhetorical tool. Alas, Indigenous Alaskans were not the only ones expressing that Alaska might be too cold for Jewish people. Present in Perkins's files is a miscellaneous "Resolution on Political Exiles of Germany," authored and signed by the United Fishermen's Union, the Copper River & Prince William Sound Fishermen's Union, and the Alaska Fishermen's Union. The Alaska Fishermen's Union included branches in Washington state, Oregon, California, and Alaska. The Alaskan branches were in Anchorage and Ketchikan. Predominantly white, these workers included cooks, deckhands, dock workers, waiters, and waitresses.[35] Their resolution assumed that the U.S. was "founded by oppressed people of many diverse races and nationalities," adding that "another great race, the Jewish people, is now faced with mass extinction by the brutal fascist oppressors of Nazi Germany." They proposed "welcoming the oppressed Jewish people to the United States, and that we make this nation their haven, as it has always been for oppressed peoples." They wanted the U.S. to welcome oppressed European Jewry and for the refugees to "contribute to the cultural and technological growth" of the U.S. Ultimately, the three Northwest-based fishers' unions proposed for refugees to settle in the continental U.S., "not be shipped off to Alaska [as] has been suggested," on the grounds that "these people are not adapted to making a living in the Territory due to its climatic and geographic conditions."[36] From their perspective and that of many others, Alaska was too cold for refugee settlement. The phrasing "these people" and "not adapted" fell under the *Alaska's too cold for the Jews* trope, which seemed popular among everyone except for the Jewish refugees themselves.

Jewish refugees expressed eagerness to move to any place where they could live safely. "Neither coldness nor other nature-forces shall prevent us to do our duty . . . give us not charity, but assistance that will be the very thing for us Alaska new-pioneers," wrote refugee Bruno Rosenthal from Neustadt, Germany.[37] Indeed, the Interior Department received pleas from refugees begging "upon my knees to send the permission to entry into Alaska" throughout 1939.[38] The Labor Department, of course, received various correspondence relating to a wide range of refugees, but on the issue of Alaska, Perkins was more likely to hear from American workers.

The fishermen's unions sent copies of their resolution to the press, the president, the Secretary of the Interior, and the Secretary of Labor. A union writing the administration would always include the Department of Labor because especially after the Wagner Act, it was the department of precisely that—labor. Further, Perkins's progressive immigration policy and sympathy for refugees were well-known.

The Rise and Fall of the
King-Havenner Bill, 1940

The King-Havenner Bill was named for its cosponsors: Senator William H. King (D-UT) and Representative Franck Havenner (D-CA). On March 13, 1940, Senator Robert Wagner introduced it to the Senate on behalf of

King because Wagner was a political face of progressive immigration legislation in 1930s Congress. While the Wagner-Rogers Bill had shown initial signs of popularity because the refugees were children, the King-Havenner Bill showed initial signs of popularity because the refugees would not be entering the U.S.

The King-Havenner Bill proposed a plan that was structured around jobs to develop Alaska only in certain industries. Refugees between the ages of sixteen and forty-five could participate only if they qualified for these jobs. If they did, they could bring their wives and children. If these refugees wanted U.S. citizenship, they'd need to apply from their country of origin and count toward the quota system from 1924. The bill specified that the jobs themselves would be open to American citizens first, aiming to counter opposition from the Wagner-Rogers debates about refugees taking American jobs.[39]

The Senate Committee on Territories and Insular Affairs heard testimony regarding the proposal. In his testimony in support of the bill, Ickes reiterated the Interior Department's points about economic development and military defense. "If a proposition is good for business, and good for the national defense, and good for the American people," Ickes testified, "we ought not to turn it down merely because it has some humanitarian byproducts."[40]

Four individual witnesses expressed opposition. Two represented Alaska: Don Carlos Brownell, Mayor of Seward and Senator-elect of the Alaska Legislature, and Anthony J. Dimond, delegate from Alaska to the U.S. Congress. Born in New York and not Indigenous to Alaska, Dimond claimed that any immigrants to Alaska outside of the U.S. quota were "opposed by practically every one of the present residents of the Territory," Indigenous and settlers alike. Dimond himself was sympathetic to further economic development and population growth, just not by immigrants who were not permitted in the continental U.S. He instead recommended improving infrastructure to bring in American settlers.[41]

Dimond agreed with Brownell that Alaskans did not want refugee settlers. Neither distinguished much between Indigenous Alaskans and white settlers. People in Alaska, however, distinguished between settlers and immigrants. In many of their views, settlers increased Alaska's chances of statehood and the accompanying rights of citizenship, whereas an immigrant population on the rise in Alaska would compound Alaska's sense of otherness. By 1940, Gruening firmly sided with the opponents, looking out for his own popularity in the territory where he governed.[42]

The other two opponents who testified were practiced advocates of American xenophobia: Colonel John Thomas Taylor of the American Legion and John B. Trevor of the American Coalition of Patriotic Societies. Taylor and Trevor pulled considerable weight in American politics. The Wagner-Rogers Bill had died in committee the previous summer following their opposition, and King-Havenner met a similar fate.

By June 1940, the Committee on Territories and Insular Affairs decided that the bill would not reach the floor. Historian David Wyman attributes the bill's failure to "nativism, antisemitism, and economic insecurity" characteristic of the late 1930s and early 1940s.[43] The plan to welcome Jewish refugees to Alaska had reached a dead end.

Groups weighing in on the King-Havenner Bill had complex motivations. Indigenous Alaskans split between those who resisted any settlement and those who wanted the settlement to be white Americans so that they were more likely to gain the rights of U.S. citizenship, rather than being outsiders alongside Jewish refugees. White settlers in Alaska likewise sought additional white Christian Americans, not refugee settlements. The archetypal xenophobes—the American Coalition of Patriotic Societies and the American Legion—opposed the entrance of any foreigners to either the American territory of Alaska or the U.S. Ultimately, the government officials who wanted to develop Alaska and save refugees in the process—Cohen, Ickes, Gruening, Slattery, Lubin, Perkins, and even Roosevelt, though he was unwilling to intervene on this issue during a presidential election year—attained only the imperialist development that they wanted.

The victors in this Alaska saga were those who wanted development and those who wanted to keep the settlement as white, Christian, and American as possible. Following American entrance into World War II, the U.S. built a road to connect with Alaska, and Congress funded a new military presence in the territory. Alaska became a state in 1959. But Jewish refugees never settled in Alaska.

"Jewlaska"

Historians typically do not engage in counterfactuals, cases of *what if this thing had happened?* In the case of a German-Jewish settler colony in Alaska, however, renowned Jewish writer Michael Chabon takes a stab at speculation for us in his 2007 book *The Yiddish Policemen's Union*. In the novel, Jewish refugees settled in Alaska with the stipulation that they could not move or leave because the "Act could not be forced up the American body politic without a certain amount of muscle and grease, and restrictions on Jewish movement were part of the deal." Chabon presents an alternative timeline in which, in August 1948, "the defense of Jerusalem collapsed and the outnumbered Jews of the three-month-old republic of Israel were routed, massacred, and driven into the sea." More of the Jewish diaspora migrated to the settler colony in Alaska. On this alternative timeline, in 1959, "candidacy for separate statehood was explicitly ruled out." Lawmakers promised, "No Jewlaska."[44]

In the context of the Alaska idea that Perkins supported and the rise and fall of the King-Havenner Bill in real life, Chabon's term *Jewlaska* is striking. Jewlaska: half Jews and half "laska." Half a refugee people looking for somewhere to live without being murdered and half an Indigenous population colonized and terrorized first by Russian fur traders and then by the American empire.

The xenophobes—Taylor, Trevor, and the groups they represented—won. American lawmakers did not take Indigenous Alaskans seriously, except American imperialist politicians like Gruening, Dimond, and Brownell used Indigenous editorials and opinions as evidence for the claims that they wanted to make regardless. Both xenophobia and imperialism prevailed by using Indigenous Alaskans' words against their fellow oppressed people.

Perkins built a career on trying to alleviate suffering. But once again, she found her influence most limited at the peak of her career. Chabon's term *Jewlaska* captures an ostracized colony of otherness that could have emerged if the King-Havenner Bill had passed. In the novel, it lacked statehood and the accompanying citizenship. Serious divisions persisted between the Indigenous Alaskans and the Jewish refugee settlers.

Perkins viewed them both just as people. Here was her compassion and her shortcoming. An American empire was not her motivation, but it was her blind spot. As Daniel Immerwahr enlightens readers, the U.S. knows how to hide an empire.

CHAPTER NINE

The Transfer of the INS from the Labor Department to the Justice Department

$\mathcal{A}$ S WORLD WAR II ESCALATED and political concerns intensified in the spring of 1940, the president was considering the transfer of the Immigration and Naturalization Service (INS) from the Labor Department to the Justice Department. "I didn't feel that the criticisms of Frances Perkins, and her handling of the Labor Department were justified," Attorney General Robert Jackson later recalled telling the president. "I had complete confidence in her loyalty and a feeling that the fact that she was not getting a fair deal from the public, the press, and Congress for what she was trying to do."[1]

By loyalty, Jackson did not mean the personal sort. He was referencing how some members of Congress had accused Perkins of disloyalty to the U.S. government in early

1939. Referring to what she was trying to do, he likely meant humanizing and reforming the implementation of U.S. immigration law. Alas, mid-year 1940 marked the end of Perkins's authority over immigration. Was transferring the INS a heartless move by a politically calculating president? Or did it signify part of a broader restructuring of government agencies to prepare for war? As always, two things can be true at the same time. The transfer of the INS from Labor to Justice was about much more than Frances Perkins as Labor Secretary. It signified American reactions to the outbreak of World War II in Europe, a broader executive reorganization plan, and the president's political agenda in an election year. However, at the same time, it was thoroughly about Perkins's leadership over the INS. It was a blow to people who'd worked tirelessly on immigration reform—policies that enabled refugees from Nazi Germany to immigrate to the U.S.

"Immigration Is a Civil Function": Broader Executive Reorganization and Department of Labor Reflections

In the final years of the INS's home in the Labor Department, active reforming of U.S. immigration processes backslid and, in some ways, discontinued. Commissioner of Immigration James Houghteling was not the progressive reformer that his predecessor Daniel MacCormack had been. Further, INS employees in a wide range of locations requested more autonomy, more decentralization. Perkins obliged, in part resulting from diminished political capital amid the resolution to impeach her for not deporting immigrant labor organizer Harry Bridges.[2]

In April 1939, while Perkins was recovering from a resolution to impeach her barely two months earlier, Roosevelt set in motion a broader reorganization plan. The Reorganization Act of 1939 authorized the president to restructure the executive branch. Part I placed the Social Security Board under a newly created Federal Security Agency. Part II created the Executive Office of the president and added within it the Bureau of the Budget. The following year, Part III made changes to the structures of the Treasury Department, Interior Department, Agricultural Department, Labor Department, and more. For Perkins's Labor Department, Roosevelt's Reorganization Plan No. III of 1940 abolished offices of the Commissioner of Immigration at several ports and consolidated their authority under the Labor Secretary.[3]

Amid broader reorganization, in July 1939, Perkins and her colleagues were working on a written justification for the INS to remain in the Labor Department. "The relation of the Immigration and Naturalization Service to the Department of Labor" progressed through several drafts.[4]

Their reasons were threefold. First, immigration was "looked upon" as related to job wages. Second, exclusion and expulsion functions belonged together as much as immigration and naturalization, which Perkins consolidated in 1933. Third, and most important, immigration was a "civil function and hence should be administered where it is at present instead of being identified with criminal investigation and prosecution."[5] Perkins viewed immigration as finding a new way to support oneself and seeking a life in a new country, not something to criminalize. It was legal in the sense that laws governed immigration, but for Perkins, conditions out of the person's control should not be punishable.

The document reviewed a brief history of American immigration law, including legislation to exclude Chinese laborers in 1882, culminating in the National Origins Act of 1924. Labor was originally part of the Department of Commerce and Labor, which split in 1913. Immigration was in the Department of Labor. Naturalization was in the Department of Labor. In Perkins's own words: "The naturalization function is concerned with the transition of the status of a person from that of a resident alien to that of a citizen of the United States. The immigration function deals with the admission of persons as aliens into the United States for residence."[6] She combined them in 1933, reforming Department policies through innovative implementation of law. The Brookings Institute reported that combining Immigration with Naturalization "resulted in an evident increase in effectiveness as well as a substantial reduction of personnel and of expenditure."[7]

Crucially, "The relation of the Immigration and Naturalization Service to the Department of Labor" noted that some of the Acts in between 1882 and 1924, such as the Immigration Act of 1917, addressed the "physical, mental and moral qualifications of immigrants which affect their status as laborers as well as the broader social and political life of the American people," and therefore the Labor Department was the best fit.[8] For half a century, many xenophobes tended to use the economy as an excuse to bar immigration.

By doing so, the Labor Department argued, they inscribed an inseparable connection between immigration and labor. For this reason, they argued, the INS should remain in the Labor Department.

"Fifth Column" Fears Amid the Escalation of World War II

Although the U.S. did not enter World War II until December 1941, the president began preparing as soon as the war began in Europe on September 1, 1939. He added 150 new agents to the FBI to oversee domestic espionage investigations. Although the FBI had identified only one Nazi spy in Manhattan in 1938, the incident loomed large in American imaginations.

The term "fifth column," which originally labeled "individuals in Madrid who aided and supported Francisco Franco against the Spanish Republic," during the Spanish Civil War between 1936 and 1939, now "applied more generally to all those whose behavior aroused suspicions of disloyalty."[9] As war broke out in Europe, the American public increasingly projected their fifth-column fears onto European immigrants and refugees.

Due to widespread fifth-column fears among American voters in an election year, the president began considering the fingerprinting of immigrants as early as January 1940. Perkins outright opposed the fingerprinting procedure. Making immigrants feel like criminals and outsiders contradicted her values and interfered with the tone that she worked for seven years to set for the Labor Department and the INS. The Attorney General was more likely to support fingerprinting in the event of a transfer.[10]

American isolationist sentiment lingering from World War I prevailed through 1940 into 1941. Yet, as historian Deborah Lipstadt describes, "The public's mood was grim. It did not want to go to war, but it needed someone to fight."[11] Immigrants and refugees provided an easy, albeit unfortunate, target.

Under Secretary of State Sumner Welles long supported transferring the INS from Labor to Justice. In 1936, he had replaced Perkins's foe William Phillips as Under Secretary of State. In 1940, Welles recommended the transfer to the president due to Labor's purported "duality of interest" regarding immigration enforcement and labor markets.[12] Welles was a longtime friend of the president with greater influence than his predecessor Phillips or even Secretary of State Cordell Hull.

By late May 1940, as Germany was actively taking over France, Roosevelt brought up fifth-column fears during a cabinet meeting. Historians Richard Breitman and Alan Kraut explain some of the questions that were on the table: "How could a consul tell a frightened Jewish refugee from a spy trained to conceal his identity? And what of these refugees forced into becoming subversives through coercion? How could American officials prevent their entry?"[13]

These fears heightened the following month. On June 22, Nazis occupied Paris and all its glamor, fame, and expatriates. Germany occupied the northern part of France, and Vichy France refers to the unoccupied area in the south. Vichy France set up a puppet government that propped up Nazism through bureaucratizing and legalizing Nazi governance.[14] The collapse of a powerful Western nation shocked the American public. And because the French defeat was widely "attributed to its having been betrayed by those to whom it had offered refuge," this provided another reason for the Roosevelt administration to increase its suspicions of a fifth column in the U.S.[15]

"To Increase Efficiency": The President's Message to Congress

In late May 1940, the president introduced a plan to transfer INS from Labor to Justice, which Congress approved days later in June. With both an election and a war on the horizon, Roosevelt's calculations prompted him to remove the INS from the Labor Department. Considering Perkins's impeachment ordeal of 1939, her adversaries in Congress were not going to stand in Roosevelt's way.

Congressman John Taber (R-NY), for example, spat: "We are going to vote for this reorganization plan because the president has not the patriotism nor the courage to remove the Secretary of Labor, a notorious incompetent, and one who for the last seven years has steadily and steadfastly failed and refused to enforce the Immigration Law, and continuously admitted and kept here those who were not entitled to stay."[16] Taber's comment was emblematic of Congress's overwhelming sympathy with the xenophobia of the American voters. Ironically, his complaint provides further evidence that Perkins went out of her way to help those seeking refuge in the U.S.

On the night of May 21, 1940, the president called the Labor Secretary on the phone. Out of courtesy, he gave her a heads-up about what would be happening the following day. Perkins reiterated to Roosevelt that her problem with the move was not that she was dead set on keeping the INS. She wasn't. On one hand, she had channeled tremendous energy and reform efforts into it, with mostly positive results except in circumstances outside her control. But what most upset Perkins about the transfer was the principle of shifting the implementation of immigration law from a civil context to a criminal one. Tightening legal procedures, such as fingerprinting, around immigration would criminalize moving to the U.S. and prosecute people for seeking a better life, in some cases for trying to save their lives.[17]

On May 22, 1940, the president sent the plan to Congress. "The Immigration and Naturalization Service of the Department of Labor (including the Office of the Commissioner of Immigration and Naturalization) and its functions are transferred to the Department of Justice and shall be administered under the direction and supervision of the Attorney General," Roosevelt submitted to Congress. "All functions and powers of the Secretary of Labor relating to the administration of the Immigration and Naturalization Service and its functions or to the administration of the immigration and naturalization laws are transferring to the Attorney General." The plan transferred all "records, property, and personnel," including office equipment.[18]

The president added a personal message to Congress. He noted that while he had submitted Reorganization Plan IV earlier that year, he did not at that time anticipate further reorganization. He specified that war conditions in

Europe necessitated the transfer. The president explained, "I had considered such an interdepartmental transfer for some time but did not include it in the previous reorganization plans since much can be said for the retention of these functions in the Department of Labor during normal times"; however, "under existing conditions the immigration and naturalization activities can best contribute to the national well-being only if they are closely integrated with the activities of the Department of Justice."[19]

The president was considering transferring the INS around the same time that the impeachment resolution ended in spring 1939. He decided not to do it then. Perhaps Perkins's report was convincing in the summer of 1939, arguing that immigration was a fundamentally civil matter, not criminal or prosecutorial. She effectively used the rhetoric that immigration necessitated who was taking what jobs. By 1940, however, circumstances changed. Europe was at war.

Historians cannot examine counterfactuals, and thus we cannot know whether Roosevelt would have initiated the transfer if not for a presidential election. What we do know is that the political pressures of the presidential election of 1940 shaped his thinking. Roosevelt consistently operated with political concerns front and center. His relentless politicking enabled much of his successful leadership. Nobody had won a third term as president before; he intended to be the first, and he won the election that November.[20]

Roosevelt's May 1940 message explicated five reasons for the transfer: first, "to reduce expenditures"; second, "to increase efficiency"; third, "to consolidate agencies according to major purposes"; fourth, "to reduce the number of agencies by consolidating those having similar functions and by abolishing such as may not be necessary"; and fifth, "to eliminate overlapping and duplication of effort." Each reason presented a different wording of "efficiency."[21]

A government agency can be efficient only if its functions align with its objective. From the president's view, the Justice Department's functions aligned more closely with what he now saw as the primary objective of the INS: not to shepherd in immigrants, but instead to protect national security from them during wartime. The president signed this message, "Franklin D. Roosevelt, from the White House, dated May 22, 1940."

Congress swiftly passed Reorganization Plan No. V on June 4. It became law on June 15, 1940.

"Mal-administration of the Law": Mixed Reactions to the Transfer

Attorney General Robert Jackson did not even want to oversee the INS as late as spring 1940. Born in Pennsylvania and raised in New York, Jackson started a law practice and became active in Democratic politics in New York, where he crossed paths with Franklin Delano Roosevelt. In 1932, he chaired Democratic Lawyers for Roosevelt. The president appointed him U.S. Solicitor General in 1938, U.S. Attorney General in 1940, and an associate justice of the U.S. Supreme Court in 1941. As of 2023, Jackson remains the only person in U.S. history to hold all three of those offices.

While Attorney General for barely a year, Jackson received the INS from the transfer. In 1940, Jackson worried that with the INS under the Justice Department, immigration cases would lack independent legal reviews, which had previously tried to prevent the same people from acting essentially as both judge and jury.[22] From an anti-immigrant view, however, housing the INS within the Justice Department promised a stricter "control of the privilege of entering this country."[23]

Jackson had a good working relationship with Perkins. Roosevelt teased Jackson: "Bob, you're the only man in the government that isn't coming to me asking for more employees, more power, and a bigger department."[24] When pressed, he admitted to Roosevelt that he believed that criticisms of Perkins's handling of the INS were baseless, that her impeachment ordeal was unjustified, and that transferring the INS was unfair.[25]

The transfer of the INS received some pushback. Housed in Perkins's own records, a Midwest-based attorney named Sylvan Bruner wrote to President Roosevelt on June 5, 1940. "I must most sincerely protest the adoption of Government Reorganization Plan No. V," she wrote, predicting that the transfer would "eventually result in severe mal-administration of the law applying to immigrants and aliens and result in needless persecution and discrimination against that part of our population which has given as much as any of our population to the betterment of our country with the least reward."[26] Perkins agreed that she conducted administrative procedures fairly, and that immigration made the country better not worse.

Labor Department Reactions to the Transfer

On June 13, 1940, the Labor Department authored a press release, tracing the progress that took place when the INS was in the Labor Department. The day after the press release, June 14, the INS officially transferred from the Labor Department to the Justice Department. The night before the press release, Perkins "was the guest of Service officials at a farewell dinner."[27] INS officials honored her at the Mayflower Hotel in Washington, D.C.

From the perspective of the INS officials at the celebratory dinner, Perkins was a beloved boss. She reformed the INS into a "genuine career system."[28] Under Perkins's leadership, the INS trained employees in both immigration and naturalization. They held lectures to educate INS employees on relevant topics ranging from best practices to world languages.

On June 30, 1940, Perkins's team compiled an additional document, entitled "Notes for Annual Report on the Transfer of the Immigration and Naturalization Service to the Justice Department."[29] This document reiterated that the INS transferred for the "period of the national defense emergency," and it sought to review what changes the Labor Department had made during the first seven years of the INS. The notes were from Perkins's first-person perspective.

Prior to Perkins's tenure, both the Immigration Bureau and the Naturalization Bureau resorted to what Perkins called "extralegal methods." These included raids on groups of people, "exorbitant bail bonds," unnecessary deportation, letting the same person serve multiple roles in the process such as arresting and then judging an immigrant, unnecessary rigidity, inconsistency, unreasonable standards, and a culture of miscommunication within the services.[30] In short, it had been a disaster.

She appointed Commissioner of Immigration Daniel MacCormack, whom she held in the highest esteem. She assembled an Ellis Island Commission, including Cecilia Razovsky, the Jewish woman activist who spearheaded the German-Jewish Children's Aid child refugee program in collaboration with Perkins's Labor Department. "The most immediate reform undertaken was the elimination of the oppressive practices which had made the Service notorious," Perkins reflected.[31] Her team curtailed the disaster, and in the process, they cut costs.

Perkins expressed in the document that "conflicting views entertained in Congress" stood in the way of further progress, specifically "avoiding the deportation of refugees or aliens of good character who were deportable on no other grounds than the manner of their entry."[32] For Perkins, the Department shouldn't squander time, energy, and cost by deporting people who did nothing wrong besides enter, and who might not have anywhere safe to return. In 1939, Congress did grant amnesty to people in the U.S. since 1924, Perkins noted.

During the move in 1940, Congress transferred funds that it annually allocated to the Labor Department and instead allocated it to the Justice Department to house the INS. They transferred the expenses of salaries at many levels, as well as services like printing and binding. They passed along descriptions of the responsibilities of various jobs. A wide variety of positions moved from Labor to Justice. For example, the telephone operator "approx-imately 30% of the telephones of the Department of Labor. It is believed the salary of one operator should be trans-ferred to this Department." A library assistant "does not use the facilities of the main library to any large extent, nev-ertheless in view of the comparatively large library force of the Department of Labor, it is believed that the salary of at least one library assistant should be transferred."[33] While common, the transfer of an executive agency requires work; it is no small undertaking.

Once located in the Justice Department, the first major task of the INS was to register 4.7 million foreigners in the U.S. without U.S. citizenship and to fingerprint them. Per-kins had opposed fingerprinting immigrants, and Attorney General Jackson was less than enthusiastic about it. However, Roosevelt soon appointed Jackson to the U.S. Supreme Court, and his successor Francis Biddle took ownership over the fingerprinting procedure.[34] Biddle's perspective was not too far off from the Under Secretary of State. Under Secretary Welles exclaimed: "Thank God!...Fran-cis Biddle is going to have a real job with that outfit."[35] Welles implied that he disapproved of how the Labor De-partment ran the INS, and that Biddle would oversee the INS closer to his liking.

In *The Roosevelt I Knew*, Perkins claims to have reques-ted repeatedly to transfer the INS out of the Labor Department. The agency consumed a significant amount of both mental and physical space within the Labor Depart-ment. However, Perkins produced a report in summer 1939 outlining reasons why immigration belonged in Labor. Further, biographer Kirstin Downey interprets the transfer

as a "public humiliation" for Perkins.[36] All things considered, Perkins's claim to have wanted the transfer while it
was happening seems like trying to control the narrative and
reclaim a sense of autonomy in the years immediately following the Roosevelt administration.

"No Longer Under the Supervision of the Department of Labor. Very Truly Yours"

Perkins continued to receive letters on behalf of refugees
beginning "Dear Miss Perkins..." She answered them in
some variation of the following: "Your letter has been for-
warded to the Immigration and Naturalization Service which
is now located in the Department of Justice and is no longer
under the supervision of the Department of Labor. Very
truly yours."[37] "The Immigration and Naturalization Service
is no longer in the Department of Labor. Several months ago,
this Service was transferred to the Department of Justice."[38]
"I am replying so that you will know that the Immigration and
Naturalization Service is no longer in the Department of
Labor. This Service was transferred some months ago to the
Department of Justice."[39] "Your letter was immediately sent
to the Department of Justice... I requested that it be given
special consideration. The [INS] was transferred from the
Department of Labor to the Department of Justice several
months ago."[40] Another one—to U.S. Senator George W.
Norris—"This correspondence and the attached application
were at once sent over to the Department of Justice, where
the [INS] is now located. Very sincerely yours,"[41] Perkins explained to correspondents repeatedly.

These letters are only a sample, not all the ones that she sent communicating the exact same message repeatedly. The typed documents in close succession convey a blend of monotony, formality, and exhaustion. Perkins's network was accustomed to addressing her with immigration and refugee-related concerns. Now she was no longer in charge of these. Seemingly endless immigration-related correspondence addressed to her, from 1940 through 1941, continued to remind Perkins and her office of the transfer. She gritted her teeth and redirected them straightforwardly, with the occasionally exhausted *several months ago.*

From the Nazi ascent to power in Germany in early 1933 through the transfer of the INS in mid-1940, the person in charge of the department that oversaw the implementation of U.S. immigration policy was a foremost advocate for aiding refugees. While the power of her office was severely limited, she used it innovatively and compassionately.

With the notable exceptions of the Children's Bureau helping to facilitate the immigration of child refugees, as well as Perkins passing along occasional recommendations to the INS in the Justice Department—such as an example in chapter ten—the transfer of the INS from Labor to Justice marked the end of the story of Perkins's chance to aid refugees.

CHAPTER TEN

The Trapp Family Singers

*Y*OU MIGHT RECOGNIZE A FAMILY of professional singers who escaped the Nazis from *The Sound of Music,* which won five Academy Awards in 1965. That year witnessed the death of eighty-five-year-old Frances Perkins in May, the Hart-Celler Immigration Act that abolished the quota system in August, and a critical mass of Americans beginning to form ideas about the incomprehensible horrors of the Holocaust. In the movie, which won the Best Picture Oscar, seven adorable white Christian children, their esteemed father, and their jovial stepmother escaped Nazi-annexed Austria by first singing, then hiding in the abbey where their stepmother once entered the novitiate, and finally hiking to Switzerland. Their real-life story shared key elements. They sang. They were not Jewish. They escaped successfully in 1938, and they lived the rest of their lives in the U.S.

Missing from the movie was the fact that Frances Perkins aided this family of singers. They shared a mutual contact: reformer and suffragist Gertrude Ely of Pennsylvania. Perkins expedited their visitor visas once in spring 1940, and then again in fall 1940. She paid attention to their case both before and after the Immigration and Naturalization Service (INS) transferred to the Justice Department. She also might have put in a word to relieve their detainment at Ellis Island in October 1939, after an INS employee worried that the Trapp family would overstay their visitor visas. Perkins's refugee policy, however, was structured precisely for refugees to overstay their visitor visas. The Trapps' immigration story sits on the most successful end of the spectrum of Perkins's efforts.

Their non-Jewishness, their non-otherness, their whiteness, their musical career, and their father's birthplace—in a region that changed nationalities but ended up in Italy—enabled the family's relatively smooth immigration process. Even a brief detention and multiple letters to the Labor Secretary constituted a relatively smooth immigration story during that time.

The Trapp family represents an archetype for the people that the U.S. could help. In 1965, when the hills came alive and *The Sound of Music* delighted viewers across the U.S., that's all that Americans were ready to see.

Trapp Family Singers
"Leaving Europe and Our Old Life Behind!"

The film takes creative liberties with the family's circumstances. While Agathe von Trapp was the oldest child in the family, her life did not play out as portrayed by the character Liesl. She did not date a Nazi named Rolf, and she did not call out "Rolf, please!" while hiding in an abbey. She was not sixteen going on seventeen. To the contrary, Agathe, born in 1913, was twenty-five in 1938, when the family arrived in the U.S. In the early 2000s, Agathe authored a memoir entitled *Memories Before and After the Sound of Music*.

Like all memoirists, she has remembered what fits into her narrative, including celebration of her father's heroism beginning with a movie star–like description of his physical appearance. She affectionately recalls her father, "tall with a slender, well-proportioned build. Distinguished in appearance, he had dark hair, a mustache, and brown eyes that commanded attention in a gentle manner. His hands were strong, well-shaped, and accentuated by his engagement and wedding rings. Attentive and sensitive to his surroundings, Papa . . . looked good in whatever he wore."[1] While not Christopher Plummer, he seems well enough cast. Prior to World War I, Georg von Trapp operated submarines in the Austro-Hungarian navy. His first wife, Agathe Whitehead, was a granddaughter of the inventor of the torpedo. He played the guitar and mandolin, and she played the violin.

Georg became an Austrian naval hero in World War I. Agathe describes how "on April 27, 1915, Georg von Trapp took a double risk in a maneuver that was beyond the call of duty . . . However risky this maneuver was, the risk was modified by his carefully considered tactics and his full trust in his crew who, in turn, fully trusted him." The enemy vessel "disappeared in the waves within nine minutes," and as a result, "the enemy refrained from sending more battleships into that area of the Mediterranean; it was assumed that Austria had a far superior submarine fleet than [was] the case. Instantly Georg von Trapp became a hero by the standards of the Austrian Navy. The title of baron also came with the award."[2]

Following defeat in World War I, the Austro-Hungarian Empire in 1918, in Agathe's words, was "left in shambles."[3] Even aristocratic families like theirs experienced hardship and poverty. She recalled the paradox of retaining household help and a cook but lacking access to food to prepare. In 1922, the Trapp family experienced another disorienting tragedy when their matriarch, Agathe Whitehead, died from scarlet fever. The family moved to Salzburg, Austria, after their mother's death.

The Trapp children's real-life stepmother, Maria, really did arrive with guitar in hand. Named Maria August Kutschera, she joined the Trapp home in Salzburg in 1926, primarily as a tutor for Agathe's sister, also named Maria. Their soon-to-be stepmother "wore a dark blue summer dress with an unusual neckline, and a leather hat. In one hand she held a briefcase, and in the other hand, a guitar."[4] She came from an abbey and was no aristocrat. Agathe recalls that her stepmother was shocked to experience kindness and generosity among the Austrian elite.

In 1933, the Trapps lost their mother Agathe's family money in a bank failure. As a result, they let go most of their servants, and to start earning money, they began renting out rooms. As a national hero, Baron von Trapp delivered an occasional lecture about his World War I service to earn money.

Slowly, the family embraced a new adventure: singing professionally. According to Agathe, "Our family had just the right voices to sing four- and five-part music. We had two first sopranos . . . two second sopranos . . . two altos . . . one tenor . . . and one bass . . . Imagine our delight at this discovery!" Their first performance outside of church was for "an elaborate governmental affair in Vienna in the Belvedere Palace" in the mid-1930s. The group's name evolved: Trapp Family Sings, Trapp Family Choir, Choir Concert by the Family Von Trapp-Salzburg, Salzburg Chamber Choir Trapp, Chamber Choir Trapp, Salzburg Trapp Choir, Trapp Family Choir, and finally—the one that stuck—Trapp Family Singers.[5]

On the evening of March 11, 1938, the family crowded around their radio. Chancellor Kurt von Schuschnigg of Austria announced, "The German army is at our border with tanks and troops ready to invade Austria . . . Austria does not have enough capability to avert the German invasion. Resistance would accomplish nothing. It would only cause a terrible bloodbath." Agathe remembered that Schubert's "Unfinished Symphony" followed on the radio. Then the "sounds of Nazi marches with fifes and drums came through the radio."[6] Nazi Germany officially annexed Austria the following day.

In spring 1938, Nazi emissaries, "teenagers on motorcycles," demanded that the Trapps fly a Nazi flag like the other families in Austria. Baron von Trapp retorted that "if they wanted to see the house decorated, we could hang a few . . . carpets out the windows!" Soon the Nazis ordered Baron von Trapp to command a Nazi submarine. Again, he refused to take part. Subsequently, Rupert Trapp—the eldest son, having just completed medical school—declined an offer to become chief physician in a Viennese hospital, where he would have replaced Jewish doctors. Finally, the "Trapp Family was invited to sing over the Munich radio on the occasion of Hitler's birthday," on April 20, 1938. Agathe proudly recalled, "We refused in unison."[7] From Agathe's recollection, they felt safe temporarily, owing to Italian citizenship status thanks to their father's birthplace.

However, in August 1938, they received a warning from a former butler who was now a member of the Nazi Party that "Austrian borders would soon be closed." Italian citizenship could not protect them from what might transpire if they could not leave. So, after "accepting and signing the contract... for concerts in America," they left for Italy. Nazis occupied the family home in Salzburg, which became Heinrich Himmler's headquarters during World War II.[8]

The family took the train to Northern Italy, and then they sailed to the U.S. on a ship named *American Farmer*. Each member of the family carried one backpack and one suitcase. They "did not climb over a mountain," Agathe von Trapp recalled, just "crossed the railroad tracks behind [their] property." On October 7, 1938, they set sail for the U.S. carrying a contract, passports, and visas, which they understood would expire six months later in March 1939. Despite the temporary status of the visas, Agathe felt that "we were leaving Europe and our old life behind!"[9]

Between Salzburg and New York, the Trapps added "a case containing a spinet, a different case for the four legs of the spinet, five violas da gamba, one suitcase for the recorders," and an additional suitcase to their luggage.[10] They prioritized their instruments, their means of work.

The Trapps stayed at the Hotel Wellington, a frequent home base for European musicians. Their first concert was in Eaton, Pennsylvania, and they traveled the country in a chartered bus. A staple of their set was "Ave Maria," in which a line translates to "*Pray, pray for us sinners / now and in the hour of death.*"

In the U.S. in 1939, their stepmother Maria gave birth to their third half-sibling, Johannes, a birthright U.S. citizen. In March of that year, the Trapps sailed back to Europe for a Northern European tour. But when World War II officially began in September 1939, the Trapps accelerated their plans for another concert tour in the U.S. They arrived in New York on October 7, 1939.

Upon arrival, Maria von Trapp made an otherwise harmless comment that cost the family several days in an unpleasant detention facility, reflecting the precarity of the system of extending visitor visas. She commented that she wanted to stay in the U.S. forever, overheard by an INS official. The INS detained the family, except for Rupert, who had a permanent visa. Agathe never forgot how the INS officials had "an attitude toward newcomers that was stern, strict, and professional. They fired a list of direct and unexpected questions at the newcomers. If people did not answer to their satisfaction, they had the authority to take these individuals into custody."

By this point, it was a different reality for the political leadership of the INS. In 1939, Frances Perkins was post-impeachment resolution hearing. Daniel MacCormack was dead. A stricter enforcer than MacCormack, James Houghteling was less committed to reforming the INS. "The faces of the officials and wardens were taciturn," Agathe remembered. "And we could not detect even a hidden smile or the smallest sign of compassion. Everything was done in a cold and serious manner."[11]

While his family endured detention at Ellis Island, Rupert reached out to contacts from their tour the previous year. Perhaps one was Gertrude Ely, who would have contacted Perkins. The Labor Secretary still had influence over the INS in October 1939, even without political capital to spare. In the off chance that Perkins was not involved in Rupert's efforts, her visitor visa policy remained crucial for the Trapps' immigration. Agathe was aware that "one country after another fell under Hitler's steamroller, and refugees from those countries had permission to remain" in the U.S.[12]

Following successful release from detention for commenting that they wanted to stay forever, the Trapps did exactly that. Ironic, but consistent with Perkins's creative use of the policy. First, however, she needed to intervene to extend their visas repeatedly.

Perkins's "Efforts on Behalf of the Entire Delightful Singing Family"

On March 12, 1940, Frances Perkins received a letter from her friend, Gertrude Ely, who lived in Pennsylvania. Ely was born and raised in Pennsylvania in the late 1800s, educated at Bryn Mawr College, and was active in predominantly white upper-middle-class women's organizations such as the Junior League and the League of Women Voters. In addition to Perkins, Ely's personal friends included First Lady Eleanor Roosevelt, journalist

Dorothy Thompson, and—perhaps more surprisingly—
Baron von Trapp.

"I am sending this note with the sheaf of forms made out
by Baron von Trapp for his singing family," Ely wrote to
Perkins, "making the request that their visitors' visas may
be extended for six months." As Ely wrote, the Trapps had
approximately a month remaining in the U.S. before their
visas expired. They did not have anywhere to return safely.
The Trapps had secured visitors visas based on business as
esteemed performers. "The Trapps have signed a very
good contract with the Columbia Broadcasting people
which starts in the Fall and a record of the income which
they made during the last few months is included in the applications," Ely wrote, signaling the Trapps' professional
success and financial security.[13]

On March 18, Perkins replied to Ely that the Trapps'
"cases were considered, and extensions were granted to October 16, 1940."[14] Perkins's administrative secretary
followed up with Ely on April 9, reassuring her "there is
nothing for them to be concerned about." By "them," she
meant the Trapps; the Baron's secretary, Martha Zoech-
bauer; and their musical conductor, Franz Wasner.[15]

Ely's later letter to Perkins to introduce her to Baron
von Trapp included "written at a party!" in the top right
corner. On March 19, 1940, Ely wrote in elegant, happy-
looking script, "Dear Frances—Baron von Trapp is to be
in Washington tomorrow on some business and he may try
to see you for a moment if you have it—to thank you for
your efforts on behalf of the entire delightful singing
family."[16] Ely underlined "singing." The next record in the
archival files is Baron von Trapp's business card, crisp and

rectangular with the words "The Baron Georg von Trapp" stenciled in the center.

In March and April 1940, the INS was still under the Labor Department before it transferred to the Justice Department in May 1940. Nevertheless, Perkins continued following the Trapps' case even after it was effectively outside her purview. Perkins and her administrative secretary, Frances Jerkowitz, corresponded with Edward J. Shaughnessy, Deputy Commissioner of the INS, who previously worked beside them at Labor but was now on the Justice Department payroll. A September 24 letter from Jerkowitz to Shaughnessy reaffirms a reason behind Perkins's attention to the Trapps' case: their mutual friend Gertrude Ely. Jerkowitz wrote, "Miss Gertrude Ely, who is one of the friends listed, is a very close friend of Miss Perkins. Miss Perkins would like very much to have this application receive very careful attention."[17]

By September 1940, how much weight a request from Perkins would pull was uncertain. The hearing on the resolution to impeach her was over a year ago, yet it undoubtedly continued to affect her clout within the administration. Perkins added in a note to Ely: "I . . . have been glad to pass on the request for the von Trapp family and ask that it have attention. I think in addition to this it would be a good idea for you to write to Francis Biddle yourself."[18] Francis Biddle, U.S. Solicitor General from 1940 to 1941, became U.S. Attorney General from 1941 to 1945.

On September 27, 1940, a Justice Department official who did not know Perkins well—as evidenced by his address to her, "Dear *Mr.* Secretary"—followed up via letter. The Special Assistant to the Attorney General—not an INS guy but now with oversight over the INS—informed the Labor Secretary "regarding [her] interest in the von Trapp family, who desire to prolong their visit to the United States." This letter confirmed that "the aliens have been granted an extension of temporary stay until April 14, 1941."[19] He passed along the same information in a separate letter to Ely.[20]

Earlier that month, Ely had written to Perkins again, affectionately chiding her for missing a social gathering and exclaiming, "I feel lost in the new Immigration set-up!" Indeed, the transfer of the INS from Labor to Justice was weighty not only for governmental employees—and of course the immigrants themselves—but also for individuals like Ely trying to navigate federal institutions on behalf of people in desperate circumstances.[21]

The Trapps lived on repeatedly extended visitor visas in the U.S., until America's entrance into World War II, in which Rupert and Werner von Trapp enlisted. The two older boys became naturalized citizens by joining the U.S. Army, and the youngest boy Johannes was already a citizen because he was born in the U.S. From 1942 to 1944, Maria von Trapp and her five stepdaughters began the process of seeking U.S. citizenship. It required reentering the country, in this case at Niagara Falls on the Canada side. Reentrance produced the first required document, a certificate of arrival, closely followed by a declaration of intent. By 1948, Maria and her five stepdaughters—Agathe, Hedwig, Johanna, Maria, and Martina—became U.S. citizens. Maria's two biological daughters became citizens once their mother's citizenship changed. Baron von Trapp, who in 1947 died of lung cancer—because of the air quality during his submarine days—never became a U.S. citizen.[22]

Historical Memory and The Sound of Music

As the next three chapters explore, the phrase *historical memory* describes the complex relationship between history and memory. Individual memory, collective memory, and official memory each play a key role in how we understand the past. Differences between the Trapps' real-life immigration story and the portrayal of it in the film reveal what Americans were able and willing to understand in the 1960s. Because of the movie's overwhelming popularity, it has continued to shape historical memory.

In *The Sound of Music,* Nazis chased the Trapp family out of Austria. First, the family sang "Do Re Mi," "Edelweiss," and "So Long, Farewell" at an Austrian festival. *Small and white, clean and bright / You look happy to meet me,* Maria, played by actress Julie Andrews, lovingly filled in for the captain as his voice broke, overcome with emotion upon departing Austria. "So Long, Farewell" provided the rhythm for staggered departure so they wouldn't look suspicious all leaving the festival at once. The award that they won for the performance provided extra time for the family to escape to the abbey, delaying the Nazi men who chased them. A musical score for a chase scene played in the background. After outrunning the Nazis against a backdrop of an abbey, the Trapps hiked the mountains to Switzerland. In the final scene of the movie, Baron von Trapp carries his youngest daughter on his back, and Maria holds the second-to-youngest daughter's hand as they climb every mountain.

To the contrary, no dramatic diversion took place in real life. "We left by train, pretending nothing," the daughter Maria later told *Opera Magazine.*[23] They boarded a train to Italy, rather than climbing the mountains to Switzerland. Obtaining visas in Italy was relatively straightforward because Baron von Trapp had Italian citizenship. He was born in Zadar—now Croatia—which was part of the Austro-Hungarian empire when he was born in 1880, but it became part of Italy in 1920.

U.S. immigration papers proved more challenging. Rather than providing a diversion to escape Nazis on foot, the Trapp Family Singers' music enabled their visitor visas to the U.S. Music tours as grounds for visitor visas both maintained the illusion that entrance was temporary and provided ample possibilities for extension for more performances. Perkins's immigration correspondence provides several examples of keeping refugee musicians in the U.S. through repeated extension of visitor visas.

As a Jewish child growing up in the 1990s watching *The Sound of Music*, I assumed that the Trapps were Jewish because the Nazis were chasing them. Author and Jewish educator Samantha Vinokor-Meinrath describes many Jewish children's perceptions of Nazism when antisemitism was relatively dormant in much of the U.S. in the 1990s. "Growing up, like most kids I found my friends based on a few key factors . . . most important, if I, as a Jewish girl, needed to go into hiding, would they provide a safe haven?" She writes, "Why was this necessary for a girl from a loving family, living a comfortable and privileged life in suburban Long Island in the 1990s? Obviously, it was because of the Nazis."[24] Vinokor-Meinrath recalls the thought process of countless Jewish children in 1990s America: "Without any broader historical context, it seemed only logical that I, as a Jewish girl, should be ready to run from the Nazis. Because who wanted to be taken by surprise if it ever happened?"[25] She added in a personal conversation with me that she, too, assumed that the Trapps were Jewish. As a child, she imagined the Trapps meeting her own Jewish refugee grandmother on her way out of Nazi Germany. While a looming presence of real or imaginary Nazis shaped Jewish-American children's identity and worldview in the 1990s, those same children projected imaginary Jewishness onto the Trapp family whom they identified with in *The Sound of Music*. "I understood [the movie] as history like I thought all of that really happened," recalls Sarah Margulies, now a Labor Department attorney whose Jewish grandfather escaped Austria in 1938, the same year as the Trapps. "I remember it really scared me—whenever I pictured bad guys hiding in my closet or something it was either Nazis or Fruma Sarah from the *Fiddler* movie," remembers my cousin Talia Brenner, adding that she "thought that [the Trapps] were targeted by the Nazis for being allies to Jews."[26]

The fact that they were not Jewish enabled their real-life escape, and hiding this fact obscures the realities of antisemitism and xenophobia in the 1930s, which 1960s white Americans were not ready to grasp, and 1990s white Americans consumed the fictional narratives of the past. Any mention of Jewish people or Jewishness is curiously absent from Nazi annexation of Austria in *The Sound of Music*. Nazi boots pounded the pavement, and Baron von Trapp dramatically split a Nazi flag into multiple pieces. The film, however, omitted that Rupert von Trapp received an offer to replace Jewish medical doctors at an Austrian hospital. *The Sound of Music* left out an awareness of greater threats to Jewish people.

The real-life Trapps' immigration story was fundamentally not a Jewish one. Not being Jewish helped the Trapps to immigrate. It was not as overt as the antisemitic biases of consular officials. It was more nuanced and subtle. Their music, which originated in church, achieved widespread popularity across the culturally Christian U.S. The singing family and their music presented as Anglo, Christian, and white. Between their 1938 tour and their 1939 tour, the Trapps returned to Europe with relative comfort and ease. Some of the children even returned to Austria briefly in summer 1939. Their freedom of movement, albeit limited, increased their chances at immigration to a country where the immigration laws privileged people with somewhere to return. While Nazis looted Jewish homes while they were still present, the Nazis did not strip the Trapps of their property until after they left Austria. While undoubtedly political refugees, the Trapps' circumstances were less dire because they were not Jewish.

A successful immigration story from Nazi-annexed Austria to the U.S., *The Sound of Music* perpetuated an illusion of leaving American antisemitism in the 1930s and burying it away from collective consciousness. This distortion persisted through the late twentieth century, as even Jewish children identified with the Trapps escaping Nazis in a mountainous, whitewashed world. The distortion of historical memory allowed the U.S. to seem safe and not antisemitic to such children, while the historical reality differed considerably.

Families like the Trapps' were exactly who the American immigration system was structured to help. Their immigration was not representative of the stories of most refugees trying to leave Europe. Applicants for immigration to the U.S. could hope for a quota visa from an overtly racist system, a rare non-quota visa, or a visitor visa. Visitor visas for people traveling for pleasure or especially for business had opportunities to extend, and to extend repeatedly, thanks to Perkins. Though never legislation, her interpretation of existing law enabled the trend of extending visitor visas. Her policy diverged from the norm. In most cases, however, antisemitism, restrictionism, and xenophobia barred refugees. Congress, the public, and parts of the Roosevelt administration perpetuated these norms.

The Trapps all had visitor visas, except for Rupert, because of their style of performance in which they all sang together. They secured the visas to the U.S. from Italy—where Baron von Trapp was born—not Austria, where thousands would perish in the morass of years-long quota waits. Their concerts, including Christian music, were well received across the U.S. Although the public had the backs of the popular singing Christian family, it did not support the immigration of European Jewry to the U.S. The Wagner-Rogers Bill died in committee during their first American singing tour in summer 1939, and the King-Havenner Bill met the same fate during their second cross-country tour in 1940. When the family endured detention at Ellis Island in 1939, "reporters and photographers came to Ellis Island and published articles about the Trapp family being held in detention."[27] While the Trapp adults and children sang across the country, average Americans wrote to Katherine Lenroot at the Children's Bureau in the Labor Department offering to adopt an explicitly "tiny" British or French refugee child or two, explicitly "not Jewish."[28] The Trapps' popularity and success story likely could not have unfolded in the way that they did if they were Jewish refugees.

The Sound of Music fuses fiction and nonfiction, perpetuates myths, and shapes viewers' sense of the past for better or worse, giving us beloved scenes and songs in the process. The iconic lyrics from the Reverend Mother's "Climb Every Mountain" song echoed while the Trapps crossed the mountains into Switzerland, leaving viewers with a sense of freedom, hope, and possibility. But being the Labor Secretary who oversaw the INS was not "A dream that will need all the love you can give / Every day of your life for as long as you live." Instead, the role was sobering. Between 1933 and 1940, Perkins learned that the U.S. was not a haven for the oppressed people of the world. While she intervened when she could, and the policy of extending visitor visas repeatedly was her invention, Perkins could not help all—or even most—people in need. Rather, the Trapps were emblematic of the type of refugee whom she could help.

CHAPTER ELEVEN

Remembering the Holocaust in the U.S.

"*T*HAT'S WHY WE FOUGHT THE Nazis, so you could have a mojito bar!" Adam Sandler screams at his daughter—played by his real-life daughter—in the 2023 movie *You Are So Not Invited to My Bat Mitzvah*. Viewers witness the conversation from the perspective of family members downstairs overhearing the hyperbolic screaming match. That line almost automatically draws laughs from audiences. How did we get from ambiguity around Holocaust narratives immediately post–World War II, to the erasure of Jewishness from the Nazi plot line in *The Sound of Music*, to the leading role of Holocaust memory in American culture and Jewishness today?

Remembering the Holocaust has a complex history in the U.S. "There was not one single moment when Americans became aware of the Holocaust," writes historian Barry Trachtenberg, but "there was a gradual unfolding awareness that was punctuated by . . . events that seemed to 'introduce' the Holocaust to American audiences, time and time again."[1]

In 1999, historian Peter Novick's book *The Holocaust in American Life* traced the history of Holocaust memory in the U.S. How does one measure "distinctions among varieties of awareness, consciousness, belief, attention?" Novick asked.[2] Imprecisely at best. No matter how immeasurable, the evolution of perceptions of historical events matters, considering how they appear to us differently from how events looked to people at the time.

Throughout the story of Frances Perkins's efforts to aid refugees from Nazi Germany, the Holocaust was not an entity. Chronologically, what we now know as the Holocaust had not occurred yet. But even further, as Novick explains, the Holocaust "as we speak of it today, was largely a retrospective construction, something that would not have been recognizable to most people at the time."[3]

A critical mass of American lawmakers and their constituents met the rise of Nazism and the resulting refugee crisis with inaction and indifference. Perkins's approach marked an exception, not a rule. She diverged from the norm because she was pro-immigrant generally; she drew inspiration from a religious, moral imperative; and she was by nature a workhorse—a creative and determined one.

The historical forces that motivated Perkins's adversaries and opponents—antisemitism, nationalism, xenophobia, and more—are not too far off from the social forces behind the journey of Holocaust memory in American life. Sometimes these forces implanted Holocaust memory so prominently that it might be repulsive or upsetting to survivors and their descendants. In some instances, they might resent that personal family trauma is a staple of broader culture. That culture, however, builds from a plethora of influences. Citing the scholarship of French sociologist Maurice Halbwachs, who died in a Nazi concentration camp, Novick explains that collective memory involves the "ways in which present concerns determine what of the past we remember and how we remember it."[4] Bigotry and national identity did not stop when World War II ended, and they continue to be players in the narrative.

At the same time, however, remembering itself can be sacred. Esther Safran Foer is a prominent Jewish Washingtonian who published her memoir, *I Want You to Know We're Still Here*, in 2020. Foer's parents each survived the Holocaust, married and gave birth to her in a displaced persons camp, and together the young and traumatized family moved to the U.S.

Her father—whose first wife and young daughter had been murdered by Nazis while he was on work detail—died by suicide. Extremely complex posttraumatic stress disorder killed him. "There is no word in the Hebrew language that precisely connotes history," Foer writes. "*Zikaron* and *zakhor*, used in its stead, translate to 'memory.'"[5] The Hebrew language conveys an essential truth here: History and memory are irrevocably interwoven. Foer also quoted a line from her son's novel: "Jews have six senses. Touch, taste, sight, smell, hearing... memory. The Jew is pricked by a pin and remembers other pins... When a Jew encounters a pin, he asks: What does it remember like?"[6] While feeling history and feeling memory are not limited to Jewish people, this quotation reaffirms that these senses of feeling them are real.

The history of memory and the memory of history are intertwined and invaluable. How the memory itself—and what we *think* we knew—evolved is necessary for understanding what happened.

"The Things I Saw Beggar Description," 1940s

"The things I saw beggar description . . . The visual evidence and the verbal testimony of starvation, cruelty and bestiality were . . . overpowering as to leave me a bit sick. I made the visit deliberately," remarked Supreme Allied Commander of the Allied Expeditionary Force in Europe, General Dwight D. Eisenhower, in April 1945, "to give firsthand evidence of these things."[7] For Eisenhower, remembering was deliberate.

However, American leaders' sympathy toward Jewish victims pushed up against limits, including antisemitism. Commander of the Seventh Army, General George Patton, misinterpreted the displaced persons and Holocaust survivors by viewing them through an antisemitic lens. Patton described the "Jewish type of Displaced Person . . . a sub-human species without any of the cultural or social refinements of our time."[8] He neglected to factor in the hellish context and experience that they'd endured. Any appearance of sub-humanness was a proportional response and reflection of inhumane treatment. While Patton's comment was on the more overt end of mainstream antisemitism in the U.S., his phrasing epitomized how the horrors of the

Holocaust did not halt American antisemitism. Indeed, American responses to refugees from Nazi Germany did not transcend prior positions when the war concluded in 1945.

Contrary to a common misconception that Americans did not pay attention to Nazi atrocities in the mid-to-late 1940s, Jewish-American communities remembered, mourned, and began educating. One place where active remembering took place was Jewish summer camps. Jewish communities formed summer camps to carry on the American tradition of summer camp while cultivating Jewish identity and meaning. The Jewish day of mourning for atrocities suffered throughout history usually falls in early August, embedding itself within the camp calendar and culture. "Remembering those who died in one kind of 'camp' inflected the lives of Jews within a wholly different one in the decades immediately following the end of the Holocaust," writes Sandra Fox, author of *The Jews of Summer* and scholar of Yiddish and Jewish-American culture.[9]

Despite the "myth that Jews in the Holocaust's aftermath did not speak about the recent tragedy," Fox writes, "the generations in postwar camps reference, talked about, memorialized, and mourned the Holocaust openly and frequently."[10] At summer camps, Tisha B'Av rituals included sitting on the floor in "candlelit spaces" with "somber song," refraining from regular activities, and reciting poems from the Book of Lamentations about the destruction of Jerusalem in ancient times.[11] In 1944, some summer camps integrated education around what we now recognize as the Holocaust into these observances. Fox explains how although one ceremony referenced a "Jewish extermination center in Poland," Americans "did not yet have the vocabulary or the information to go into the kind of detail about the Holocaust that [they] would as the postwar period progressed, when more research and testimony made such detail possible."[12] Indeed, education and knowledge progressed throughout the 1940s.

Back in Europe, and symbolically a decade after the Nuremberg Laws of 1935, the Nuremberg trials served as a major international prosecution of Nazi defendants starting in 1945. The city had been the site of "annual extravagant Nazi Party rallies."[13] Now international communities rallied against the Nazis on trial in the same city. For the Nuremberg trials, the U.S. sent a chief prosecutor: Supreme Court Associate Justice and former U.S. Attorney General Robert Jackson—the same Bob Jackson who'd felt bad when President Roosevelt transferred the Immigration and Naturalization Service (INS) from Perkins to him.

The Nuremberg trials—which convicted over a hundred high-level Nazis and sentenced thirty-seven to death—had an irrevocable effect on broader understanding of the Holocaust. They included film images of the death camps. The audience was shocked, and judges needed a break for the rest of the day. "The most savage and numerous crimes planned and committed by the Nazis," Robert Jackson observed, "were those against the Jews."[14] Following the Nuremberg trials, however, many Americans erased Jewishness from their understanding of the Holocaust, and the U.S. almost completely lost interest in punishing Germans in any formal capacity as mass attention turned to the perceived threat of encroaching Communism.

The Cold War geopolitical context was transformative. Novick explains: "Talk of the Holocaust was something of an embarrassment in American public life, [not] because of any shame or guilt on the part of Americans concerning their response." Rather, "It was a consequence of revolutionary changes in world alignments . . . after which talk of the Holocaust was not just unhelpful but actively obstructive."[15] The U.S. allied with Germany, specifically West Germany, against the Soviet Union. An immeasurable, imagined threat of Communism linked Nazis and the Soviet Union together in American consciousness, obscuring the Holocaust. Further, many Jewish Americans worried about the Communist Jewish stereotype.

Commemorations, however, continued in Jewish spaces, including newspapers, summer camps, and more. After 1948, celebrating Israel often played a role to balance tragedy with resiliency. Zionists "leaned even more heavily on the establishment of the State of Israel as a counterbalance to the heaviness" of Tisha B'Av.[16]

In the immediate aftermath of the Holocaust throughout the 1940s, from Eisenhower's shock and sympathy to Americans grouping Nazism with the Soviet Union in defense of West Germany, Americans' collective memory of the atrocities was already beginning to evolve.

In 1946, Perkins briefly commented on the Nazi era in her memoir, *The Roosevelt I Knew*. Like the rest of the book, she kept the focus tightly on the president and his actions, portraying him in an unflinchingly positive light in the year following his death. "The aggressions against the Jewish people in Germany filled him with horror," she wrote in the immediate aftermath of the Holocaust. "He saw that it was Evil rampant."[17] She repeatedly attributed her progressive refugee policies to the president who oversaw them or at least didn't stop them. "Roosevelt moved to make it possible to bring over people who had relatives here to guarantee their support," she wrote. "He endorsed a program to bring over orphaned and handicapped children who had no relatives."[18]

The only moment when she gave credit to herself was when she commented that the president knew that Perkins predicted the fall of France before it happened and that the State Department had disagreed with her. Though cabinet secretary of a domestically focused department, she demonstrated a keen awareness and intuitive grasp of international affairs. Without mentioning the death camps, Perkins's reflection in *The Roosevelt I Knew* characterized the Nazis as evil and specified that the victims were Jewish, a detail that subsequent narratives of the World War II era would often erase.

"In Spite of Everything," 1950s

Annelies (Anne) Frank and Johanna (Hannah) Arendt were quite different, at least on the surface. They shared German-Jewish ancestry, a life-or-death situation under the Nazis, and a propensity for writing. *The Diary of a Young Girl* and *The Origins of Totalitarianism*—by Frank and Arendt, respectively—each shaped Holocaust memory in the U.S. throughout the 1950s. *Origins* offered an academic attempt at understanding Nazism, theorizing it as "totalitarianism," an umbrella under which Arendt placed the Soviet Union, too. Anne Frank posthumously served a Holocaust narrative literally hidden from the horrors of concentration camps. White Christian readers in 1950s America could read her diary as Jewish as they wanted her to be and as white as they wanted her to be, which was not too Jewish and very white. Meanwhile, Arendt reached the U.S. in 1941, published *Origins* in 1951, and shaped American understandings of Nazism for her remaining life.

Hannah Arendt was born in Germany in 1906 to a secular Jewish family. She was educated in the tradition of classical German philosophy. An early sign of trouble came in 1933, when the Gestapo arrested her on the grounds that they believed her philosophy notes in the Greek language were a secret code. Arendt fled to France in 1933, where she built a new life but lived in nearly constant fear. In 1941, a visa facilitated by Varian Fry's Emergency Rescue Committee enabled Arendt's immigration to the U.S., where she taught at various American universities and emerged as a prolific thinker and writer.[19]

The Origins of Totalitarianism—a "strange hybrid of history, intellectual history, and political theory," according to historian Richard King—marked the first academic attempt at making sense of Nazi atrocities, emphasizing Nazi perpetrators of the murder of European Jewry rather than broader Nazi governance.[20]

Albeit unintentionally, Arendt's first published book indulged the American public's desire to group together the horrors of Nazism with a new enemy: the U.S.S.R. through the label "totalitarianism." Indeed, "Theorizing about totalitarianism itself served to marginalize the Holocaust," Peter Novick writes. "The ruthless persecution of political opponents in concentration camps and slave labor camps was an important link connecting Nazi Germany and

Soviet Russia under the rubric of totalitarianism."[21] *The Origins of Totalitarianism* was so ideologically consistent with animosity toward the Soviet Union and the American zeitgeist of the 1950s that as American social movements and resistance to the status quo exploded during the 1960s, the book's popularity gradually decreased.

The Origins of Totalitarianism also posed zero threat to an important American social force, especially during the Cold War: the myth of American exceptionalism. "By neglecting the ways that American racial politics and warfare tracked the same European phenomenon," Richard King writes, "*Origins* undoubtedly helped confirm the notion of American exceptionalism, particularly when contemplating the horrors of recent European history."[22] From Arendt's perspective, America was exceptional in that it was the only place where she'd experienced living safely and securely. She was safe in the U.S. because she came across as white, a status that Jewish Americans could increasingly reach in the post–World War II era.

At the same time, Arendt recentered Judaism, Jewishness, and antisemitism in discussions on the origins of the Nazi regime. She analyzed antisemitism in its modern form, situating it alongside imperialism as a root of the Nazis' ascent. Arendt distinguished among definitions of "Jewishness as a cluster of characteristics," "Judaism as a theological entity," and "Judaism as an institutional entity."[23] She framed it as an ethno-religion, which is now a useful lens to view the trajectory of Jewish Americans in the mid-twentieth century.

When Frances Perkins received letters on behalf of Jewish refugees, the immigrants in question did not fully have white privilege yet. As evidenced by all the pushback that Perkins, Katherine Lenroot, and others received, anti-semitism separated Jewishness from whiteness in the 1930s. Throughout the twentieth century, however, such separation became increasingly ambiguous.

In the 1950s, white Christian America partnered with corporate America to build a capitalistic, Christian nationalist society. White American society reached out to include white-passing Jewish Americans into power and privilege through increased usage of the term *Judeo-Christian*. "American Jews were increasingly counted as charter members of the culture as reflected in the popularity of the rubric 'Judeo-Christian,'" King writes. "Being Jewish as an ethnic or racial fact was deemphasized, while the religious-culture significance of Judaism was played up. Racially, Jews had become 'white.'"[24]

To American audiences, Anne Frank was no exception. In 1952, an English translation of *The Diary of a Young Girl*—originally published in Dutch in 1947—arrived in the U.S. In 1944, Frank had started revising her diary for public consumption after hearing a Dutch broadcast say that people should record their wartime experiences.[25] By 1945, Anne's father lost his whole family and decided to honor his younger daughter's wishes by editing and seeking publication for the diary. Despite initial rejections for publication, it became "one of the most widely read books in the world," as Trachtenberg describes, the "basis of two Hollywood films, a Broadway play, television and radio dramas, documentaries, memorials, and a museum, and has been the subject of several thousand books. There are two separate foundations in Europe as well as a center in the

United States whose mission is to promote the spirit and message."[26] The diary continues to shape American understandings of the Holocaust.

Frank's diary, crucially, does not directly engage the atrocities and horrors that the Frank family would experience directly post-capture. Trachtenberg explains: "The shocking images that first identified the Holocaust for Americans—the pictures of camps like Buchenwald with its starving prisoners—were replaced by the beatific face of Anne, whose death was understood but never portrayed."[27] In her 2021 book *People Love Dead Jews*, Dara Horn points out that Anne Frank's most often quoted words are "I still believe, in spite of everything, that people are truly good at heart."[28] Frank wrote these words prior to what she witnessed in the death camps. Horn describes: "They flatter us. They make us feel forgiven."[29]

When *The Diary of a Young Girl* was published in the U.S. in 1952, *The New York Times* reviewed it twice, and Eleanor Roosevelt wrote an introduction. From Eleanor Roosevelt's introduction alone, Anne Frank might have still been alive. She did not mention why the Frank family was in hiding or any mass murder of Jewish people.[30] Many Americans would not learn until the 2022 documentary *The U.S. and the Holocaust* that Anne Frank's family wanted to immigrate to the U.S. The consulate closed before they could submit their papers.

Anne Frank's time in the secret annex became the basis for a Broadway play in 1955, and it became a movie in 1959. Both were met with widespread popularity. American portrayals of Anne Frank "successfully validated Jewish suffering in the Holocaust without threatening

American Jewry's move into the white middle class."[31] The initial film and play made Frank seem less Jewish and more American. Indeed, film and television increasingly depicted the Holocaust as a separate strand of World War II. While in real life the expansion of territory and murder of Jewish people were the Nazis' intertwined objectives, Hollywood productions shied "away from overtly Jewish subjects."[32] The plight of Anne Frank was not the only example of whitening Jewish Europeans, just the most beloved and popular one.

For a critical mass of Americans, by the late 1950s, Nazi atrocities were counterbalanced by Anne Frank's faith in humanity, just as animosity toward the Soviet Union was counterbalanced by none other than faith in West Germany.

"The Banality of Evil," 1960s

While Anne Frank's diary found a place in American consciousness, a young survivor named Elie Wiesel was seeking publication for his account of what he endured. His original Yiddish draft of what would become *Night* was entitled *And the World Remained Silent* and was full of righteous anger and resentment, a proportional response to what transpired. However, Wiesel needed to cut several hundred pages to find a publisher. *Night* arrived in the U.S. in 1961. It gradually became the second-most widely read Holocaust primary source after Frank's diary. Dara Horn comments that *Night* "could be thought of as a continuation of Frank's diary, recounting the tortures of a fifteen-year-old imprisoned in Auschwitz."[33]

Collapsing wide-ranging Holocaust experiences into a singular narrative, Americans who read the two books in succession might think of them chronologically, like Wiesel's book describes what Frank witnessed in the camps following her capture from the secret annex. Harrowing, literary, and under two hundred pages, *Night* appeared at a moment when Holocaust consciousness was on the rise in the U.S.

Leon Uris's 1958 novel *Exodus* premiered as a film in the U.S. in 1960. The protagonist of *Exodus* survived the Holocaust, moved to Israel, and died in Israeli-Palestinian violence. The actress playing her was blond-haired, blue-eyed, and young, likely to invoke ideas of benevolence and whiteness to white American audiences forming their ideas of Jewish Holocaust survivors in Israel. This character helped to cement Jewish Europeans as white in the perceptions of white Americans, obscuring the antisemitism and racism that had barred most European Jewry from entering the U.S. throughout the Nazi regime.

While Americans read or watched some combination of *Night*, *Exodus*, or *Diary of a Young Girl*, the defining event for American memory of the Holocaust in the 1960s was the widely broadcast and discussed trial of Adolf Eichmann in Jerusalem from 1961 to 1962.

In May 1960, the Israeli secret service received a tip from a German prosecutor that Adolf Eichmann was hiding under the name Ricardo Klement in Argentina. The Israeli secret service captured Eichmann outside his home in Buenos Aires, "interrogated him, and smuggled him out of the country on an Israeli airline" for trial in Jerusalem.[34] Every day of the trial, Israel sent footage to New York via plane.

Hannah Arendt found herself at the center of the story. Arendt applied for a Rockefeller Foundation grant to support her travel to Jerusalem to cover the trial for *The New Yorker*. "I missed the Nuremberg Trials," Arendt wrote. "To attend this trial is somehow, I feel, an obligation to my past."[35] And so she went.

Arendt's reporting on the trial and the controversy around it marked a crucial moment for Holocaust memory in the U.S. She saw through the bumbling mediocrity of the Nazi bureaucrat who repeatedly insisted that he was just following orders. In 1963, she published in *The New Yorker* a series of essays, "A Reporter at Large: Eichmann in Jerusalem," conceptualizing a new framework of the "banality of evil." "However monstrous the deeds were," Arendt wrote, "it was the most banal motives, not especially wicked ones. . . which made Eichmann such a frightful evil doer."[36] The essays soon became a book, *Eichmann in Jerusalem*.

Arendt's argument sparked controversy for a myriad of reasons. Above all, it would be deeply "comforting" if "a deep and long-standing hatred" were "a necessary precondition for mass murder," writes Novick.[37] If evil was banal and mediocre, then most people could become perpetrators of a Holocaust, an unsettling pill to swallow. Further, Arendt "challenged the conventional wisdom that Western governments and societies had failed to take cognizance of what was going on in the death and concentration camps during the war. Instead, she insisted, the scandal was the failure of any of these governments to act on the knowledge they possessed."[38] Arendt's bluntness diverged from what was comfortable or normal for many of her readers, for whom the interpretations of Nazis were still forming throughout the 1960s. The Nazi era was formative to Arendt's life story, and yet most Jewish immigrants with similar experiences wanted to believe that the Nazi horrors were exceptional and radical in human history and that they were safe in their new homes.

Both Eichmann's widely publicized trial and Arendt's highly controversial writing about it proved formative for Americans remembering the Holocaust. They helped separate the Holocaust from broader Nazi barbarism in American consciousness. According to Novick, Eichmann marked the "first time that what we now call the Holocaust was presented to the American public as an entity... distinct from Nazi barbarism in general."[39] Richard King concurs that *Eichmann in Jerusalem* was "crucial in shaping the contours of understanding of (and disagreements about) the Holocaust from the moment of its appearance until now."[40] Condemned to death by three German-Jewish refugees, Adolf Eichmann was executed on June 1, 1962. Historically, Eichmann's trial had more significance for learning and understanding about the Holocaust than for justice itself.[41]

Academic scholarship progressed alongside the American public as it absorbed, debated, and interpreted the Eichmann trial. Throughout the 1950s, a Holocaust survivor named Raul Hilberg from Vienna, Austria, grappled with sources from the perpetrators' perspectives to complete his dissertation in political science. In 1961, Hilberg published *The Destruction of European Jews*, introducing the language of "bystander," "perpetrator," and "victim," and launched Holocaust Studies as an academic field.[42] This first wave of historiography—how historians tell history—

prioritized how the Nazis carried out the murders over the experiences of Jewish people themselves. William L. Shirer's 1960 *The Rise and Fall of the Third Reich* offered a traditional political history of the Nazi regime. Although barely 3% of the book mentioned the Holocaust, it treated the Holocaust as distinct from other war atrocities.[43] Trachtenberg attributes the relevant silence of academic scholarship on the Holocaust from 1945 to 1960 to the "immediacy and enormity of the murder, the scale of devastation to the Jewish community, and the lack of organized archives."[44] By the late 1960s, that had changed.

In 1968, two major books on American responses to the Holocaust were published. Writer Arthur D. Morse's *While Six Million Died: A Chronicle of American Apathy* provided a readable account of U.S. government officials' varying responses to refugees from Nazism throughout the Nazi regime. His detailed narrative offered glimpses of Frances Perkins, Cecilia Razovsky, and their work together on behalf of child refugees. That same year, historian David Wyman's *Paper Walls: America and the Refugee Crisis, 1938–1941*, analyzed government records as evidence of American apathy. Administrative procedures, bureaucracies, and government structures blocked humanitarian efforts. Wyman's thorough research included a whole chapter on the Alaska plan, including the King-Havenner Bill, though his analysis omitted the imperialist context.

Meanwhile, Jewish-American summer camps continued ritual, poignant commemoration of the Holocaust on Tisha B'Av. In summer 1968, a complicated stretch for American politics and the world, one camper reflected simply:

Today was a sad and quiet day,
Not much for laughing or bouncing around,
A Day to remember the dead six million,
To remember the ghettos that they put us in,
Dying of hunger, of illness, of frost,
And we hope that nothing as terrible will ever
*   happen*
As what happened to our people then.[45]

Holocaust memory could be as loud as the Eichmann trial, as intellectual as the origins of Holocaust historiography, and as quiet and humble as campers sitting on the floor, praying.

"Should Have Been Unbearable," 1970s–1980s

Mourning the Holocaust at Jewish-American summer camp could be especially emotional for children of survivors. One camper, a second-generation survivor, recalled: "Learning of [the resistance] was a powerful antidote to the humiliation and shame I felt about my father's travails."[46] This was 1971. Throughout the 1970s, an era of activism empowered Americans, including Holocaust survivors and their children, to relearn history and to restore justice.

The 1970s and 1980s witnessed a few competing trends in historical memory of the Holocaust. The Black civil rights movement emphasized learning and restorative justice throughout the 1970s. People wanted to learn Jewish history from a new NBC *Holocaust* miniseries like they relearned Black history from other programs, like *Roots*.[47] In 1978, over a hundred million Americans watched *Holocaust* on NBC, depicting concentration camps, exterminations, forced deportations, Kristallnacht, mass shootings, and sexual violence.[48] While Elie Wiesel characterized the miniseries as "untrue, offensive, cheap," and perhaps most searingly, "an insult to those who perished and to those who survived," critics agreed that NBC transformed American collective memory of the Holocaust.[49]

The Cold War had also advanced so that the U.S. seemed to be winning as a superpower, compounding ideas of American exceptionalism. Because the 1980s were so empowering to many, some Americans looked back and falsely applied that state of mind to the 1930s and 1940s. For example, if World War II–era Americans had wanted to aid refugees, then 1980s Americans believed that they could have. One example was a report published in 1981 by the American Jewish Commission on the Holocaust, comprised of a few dozen Jewish Americans. The report concluded: "The Final Solution may have been unstoppable by American Jewry," they wrote, "but it should have been unbearable for them. And it wasn't."[50] A more enduring example was historian David Wyman, whose 1984 book *The Abandonment of the Jews* argued that the Roosevelt administration consciously deserted European Jewry. Highly moralistic, the book focused on what the U.S. could have and should have done according to Wyman. Following its publication, *Abandonment* became a staple of bookshelves in American homes and libraries.

Relearning history and American exceptionalism were not the only historical trends and context. Israel had been a country since 1948, but in 1967, Israeli forces occupied Gaza and the West Bank. Growing Holocaust consciousness attempted to justify that occupation, in both Israel and the U.S. Peter Novick argues that "American Jews' anxiety about Israel's security, and their viewing Israel's situation within a Holocaust framework" was the "single greatest catalyst of the new centering of the Holocaust in American Jewish consciousness."[51] The period of the 1970s to 1980s served as a bridge from the 1960s—a key moment in historical memory of the Holocaust in which consciousness was on the rise, but not in a victim-centering way—to the 1990s, another pivotal stretch. In 1993, the opening of the United States Holocaust Memorial Museum (USHMM) signified a federal, national platform for remembering the Holocaust in the U.S.

But first, a few additional events helped pave the way to make that happen. In 1977, the U.S. Supreme Court ruled in *National Socialist Party of America v. Village of Skokie* that the First Amendment protected Nazis' right to march in Skokie, Illinois, a predominantly Jewish community.[52] The decision provoked increasing efforts at Holocaust awareness and education, including a new legislative effort. In 1980, the U.S. Congress unanimously passed a law to establish a U.S. Holocaust Memorial Council, which would institute annual Days of Remembrance and oversee plans for USHMM.[53] The U.S. Holocaust Memorial Council, the Days of Remembrance including a ceremony at the Capitol, and the federal museum all signified American collective memory verging into national, official memory.

The President, Oprah, and Disney Want You to Watch Schindler's List, 1990s

USHMM's address in Washington, D.C., is 100 Raoul Wallenberg Place, named for a Swedish businessman who saved tens of thousands of lives by issuing protective papers in 1944 before his disappearance in 1945. The building sits between the Bureau of Engraving and Printing and a U.S. Forest Service building. Standing outside you can see the Jefferson Memorial and the Washington Monument.

At its dedication in April 1993, President Bill Clinton remarked that USHMM would stand alongside the Lincoln and Jefferson memorials.[54] Fifty years earlier, in April 1943, the Jefferson Memorial opened as part of a Roosevelt administration effort to connect the New Deal–era government interventions with Jeffersonian republicanism in the American consciousness. Later that year, in October 1943, the Union of Orthodox Rabbis of the United States and Canada marched on the National Mall to draw attention to the plight of Jewish people in Nazi territory.

At the heart of Washington, D.C., the National Mall is a stage both literally and metaphorically. It's likely the most influential physical setting for laying out American collective memory and a sense of history. Structures like the Washington Monument, Lincoln Memorial, Jefferson Memorial, FDR Memorial, and MLK Memorial symbolize important moments and values. Since the National Mall is a dynamic, evolving space, historical events like the "I Have a Dream" speech on the steps of the Lincoln Memorial further embed the Mall into national narratives.[55]

While the Smithsonian museums serve more substantial exhibition and research purposes, their history and placement connote symbolism, too. For example, though not part of the Smithsonian system, USHMM predated both the National Museum of the American Indian and the National Museum of African American History and Culture. Historian Edward Linenthal explains that USHMM found a home on the National Mall because of "lessons worthy of inclusion in the official canon that shaped Americans' sense of themselves."[56] These lessons have included "dignity, social, justice, and civil rights," according to historian Tim Cole.[57]

Opening USHMM was not without controversy. Thought leaders worried that the Holocaust would overshadow a longer, vibrant Jewish history, and that Americans would use the museum for partisan politics, among other concerns.[58] Despite ongoing criticism, such as the fetishization of Jewish victimhood and the overemphasis of American roles in liberation, USHMM has become invaluable for both advancing education and making research accessible.

Thus, two pivotal events for Holocaust memory in the U.S. both took place in 1993: the opening of USHMM and the premiere of *Schindler's List*. While the former provided a platform for education and remembrance on a national stage, the latter shaped what narrative that venue would convey, beyond what director Steven Spielberg intended. Spielberg, who claimed that he was trying to portray only one story, produced a narrative that people viewed as definitive.

The film presents a real-life story of Oskar Schindler, who saved over a thousand Jewish people from almost certain death. Tim Cole explains how *Schindler's List* "tells of a 'Holocaust' where one 'good' man makes a difference, rather than a 'Holocaust' characterized by the banality of evil and the indifference of many." Spielberg directed a film "about power rather than powerlessness," Cole continues, "a celebration of the freedom of the individual to act, rather than a reflection on the fate of powerless individuals in the face of a regime which decided that Jews should die."[59] *Schindler's List* had all the marks of extreme success in the mid-1990s. It grossed over $300 million at the box office, and President Bill Clinton, Oprah Winfrey, and Walt Disney studio boss Jeffrey Katzenberg all recommended it strongly.[60]

Despite several decades of ever-evolving historical memory of the Holocaust, in 1999, Cole's book pointed out that no depiction abandoned the prevalence of "human dignity." In the 1950s, Anne Frank validated readers' belief that "people are really good at heart." As the Holocaust in American memory evolved from ambiguity, to raising consciousness while erasing Jewishness, to a fixture of collective memory, developments throughout the twentieth century continued to center people's goodness.[61]

So, where is Frances Perkins? Motivated by morals, she pushed against the grain of restrictive immigration policy. She does not play a role in any of the television, plays, movies, or books of the Holocaust zeitgeist of the twentieth century. One might think that Congress and the State Department thwarting her valiant efforts could have fit into Wyman's *Abandonment of the Jews*. But she's left out of this chronology. Why? The answer is because of what thwarted her: not only antisemitism, but also a broader xenophobia and bigotry so foundational to American governance that she could not always see it herself. The story of Frances Perkins's efforts to aid refugees from Nazi Germany is representative of historical factors, yet antithetical to twentieth-century trends in historical memory.

"More Could Have Been Done," Twenty-First Century

By the turn of the twentieth-first century, Holocaust memory had undoubtedly become embedded within American collective consciousness. However, more time playing a central role does not automatically mean that the memory is better or worse, or more or less accurate. More time just means that there's more time for more developments, including books—fiction and nonfiction—exhibits, films, memorials, oral histories, popular cultural references, and much more.

We face numerous challenges in our attempts to remember the Holocaust as accurately as possible. The number of survivors and other eyewitnesses to the Holocaust is dwindling. Honoring their memory necessitates people avoid voyeurism—which fuels the insatiable market for the more exploitive movies, fiction, and exhibits—while remaining sensitized to the profound human tragedy. Sadly, desensitization is almost unavoidable when the traumatic history is so prominent.

Since its opening, USHMM has served as a powerful agent of education and research into the Holocaust era. The museum is a staple of school field trips and tourism to Washington, D.C. Its permanent exhibit covers significant ground literally and metaphorically. In 2018, USHMM added a temporary special exhibit entitled *Americans and the Holocaust.* "The United States alone could not have prevented the Holocaust, but more could have been done to save some of the six million Jews who were killed," the opening to the exhibit reads. "This exhibition examines the motives, pressures, and fears that shaped Americans' responses to Nazism, war, and genocide."[62] It explores American responses, consciously incorporating Americans more broadly, not just the U.S. government. The exhibit portrays dual narratives of the rise of Nazi Germany and the persistence of xenophobic American immigration law, establishing political context on both sides of the Atlantic Ocean.

USHMM staff built online educational resources to complement the 2018 exhibit. Since then, Frances Perkins has her own page on the USHMM domain. "During her tenure as labor secretary, Perkins advocated on behalf of German-Jewish refugees seeking to immigrate to the United States—often in opposition to the prevailing public sentiments," it educates readers, dividing the story into sections of "charge bonds," "helping refugees," "personal attacks," and "end of control over INS."[63] The page is among the top results when googling "Frances Perkins," likely the reason behind more recent mentions of refugee policy in the infographics and social media posts that mark Perkins-related historical anniversaries each year.

By the 2010s, Frances Perkins was slowly becoming a supporting character in books and documentaries depicting American responses to the German-Jewish refugee crisis. She graces page thirty of Erik Larson's 2011 narrative nonfiction book, *In the Garden of Beasts*:

> Secretary of Labor Frances Perkins, the first
> woman in American history to hold a cabinet
> position, was energetic in trying to get the ad-
> ministration to do something to make it easier
> for Jews to gain entry to America. Her depart-
> ment oversaw immigration practices and policy
> but had no role in deciding who . . . received or
> was denied a visa. That fell to the State Depart-
> ment and its foreign consuls, and they took a
> decidedly different view of things. Indeed,
> some of the department's most senior officers
> harbored an outright dislike of Jews.[64]

While a great start, this excerpt captures neither Perkins's
story nor her role in the broader events.

In 2022, filmmakers Ken Burns, Sarah Botstein, and
Lynn Novick directed a three-part documentary entitled
The U.S. and the Holocaust, which aired nationally on PBS.
USHMM partnered with them on research and interpretation. Of the six-hour fifty-eight-minute total series run time,
slightly under one minute of the first episode mentions Perkins: "Frances Perkins, Roosevelt's Secretary of Labor,
sided with critics of the State Department. The first woman
ever to serve in a presidential cabinet, she had known and
worked with immigrants all her life, believed the United
States should be a haven for refugees, and promoted a plan
to make their entry easier. But the State Department refused to relax its rules."[65] She stood between two men in
the first image of her on-screen, wearing her signature tricorne hat. Her floral brooch and pearl necklace catch
viewers' eyes as she turns her head slightly to the side, look-

ing almost displeased with everyone around her. The camera then pans to Perkins and her fellow members of FDR's cabinet—all men—posing for an official photograph.

Including Perkins in the documentary, and in broader historical narrative, advances the story. For Perkins, the humanitarian intent and interest in helping were there. Antisemitism, isolationism, and xenophobia—widespread in the American populace and deeply embedded into the U.S. governmental institutions—thwarted many of her efforts. The story of her efforts therefore invites the historical reality of antisemitism and its contemporary legacies back into the narrative.

The 2022 documentary has earned a plethora of award nominations, rave reviews, and widespread popularity. It uses familiar symbols and robust historical research to present a narrative that avoids both voyeurism and desensitizing viewers. The documentary opens with Anne Frank, age three, strolling with her sister and parents in Germany in 1933. The following year, her father settled the family in the Netherlands, a promising move for German-Jewish refugees. The family of Anne Frank—a symbol of relatable victimhood to white American audiences and author of "people are good at heart"—applied for immigration to the U.S. "Most Americans did not want to let them in," the film clarified to conclude its vignette.[66] The camera panned next to an image of the Statue of Liberty, for dramatic effect, as the narrator read Emma Lazarus's poem, "The New Colossus": "I lift my lamp beside the golden door!"[67]

Maybe at least some American audiences are ready for new narratives in which the U.S. could have and should have done more for someone like Anne Frank, in which

Lazarus's "send these, the homeless, tempest-tost to me" is ironic in retrospect. The obstacle to refuge was more than a politically calculating president or a heartless and ignorant State Department. The obstacle was comprised of all the bigoted systems and structures that a wide-eyed Labor Secretary from New England with progressive credentials, including a belief in immigration, came to understand. Since World War II, American attitudes toward international affairs and toward Judaism and Jewishness have continued to shape historical memory of the Holocaust in the U.S. Alas, every step in historical memory reflects the place and time of remembering.

CHAPTER TWELVE

Remembering American Immigration Law

*E*TCHED—LITERALLY—INTO AMERICAN COLLECTIVE memory of immigration law is a verse that Jewish-American poet Emma Lazarus wrote in 1883, barely a year after the Chinese Exclusion Act: "With silent lips. 'Give me your tired, your poor / Your huddled masses yearning to breathe free / The wretched refuse of your teeming shore / Send these, the homeless, tempest-tost to me / I lift my lamp beside the golden door!" Her words remain mounted inside the pedestal of the lower level of the Statue of Liberty.

Yet the American immigration story has always been full of contradictions. President Calvin Coolidge designated the Statue of Liberty a national monument the same year, 1924, that he signed the National Origins Act ("Quota Act") which established racist, xenophobic immigration quotas that would dictate U.S. immigration law.

Americans are slowly beginning to peel back the layers to contemplate the truths that lay underneath. The three two-hour episodes of the 2022 documentary *The U.S. and the Holocaust* are entitled "The Golden Door," "Yearning to Breathe Free," and "The Homeless, Tempest-Tossed," after the poem. Together they depict the American responses to the plight of European Jewry throughout the Nazi regime.

Frances Perkins pushed against the xenophobic quota laws through innovative implementation with varying degrees of success. Because of her efforts, hundreds of Jewish children who departed Germany through a collaboration between the Labor Department and the German-Jewish Children's Aid (GJCA) passed the Statue of Liberty—and Lazarus's poem—on their way into New York.

A quarter century later, President Lyndon B. Johnson performed a signing ceremony for the Immigration Act of 1965, at the base of the Statue of Liberty. The statue's European features gazed down at him as he equalized U.S. immigration law, at least for European immigrants. The law abolished the quota system, instead privileging people with valued skills and people with family in the U.S. After the Immigration Act of 1965—because of it and thanks to it—the myth of the U.S. as a nation of immigrants became more challenging to debunk. It advanced the ideas of American democracy, diversity, freedom, and multiculturalism in American collective consciousness. The Statue of Liberty remains a frequent school field trip, a tourist destination, and a symbol of what many Americans believe the U.S. to be and have been.

Our reality is much murkier. The reasons why the U.S. was *not* a nation of immigrants are the same reasons why Perkins was unable to do more for the Jewish refugees: xenophobia, nationalism, and broader bigotry. According to historian Roxanne Dunbar-Ortiz, the U.S. "has always been a settler state with a core of descendants from the original settlers."[1] The myth of a "nation of immigrants" works to "erase the scourge of settler colonialism and the lives of Indigenous people."[2] It also obscures the immigrants denied, including the Holocaust victims who'd wanted to immigrate to the U.S. Further, the increasing prevalence of the myth of a "nation of immigrants" from 1965— through the twenty-first century—contributed to obscuring the story of Perkins's efforts.

The year 1965 marked both the death of Frances Perkins and the abolishment of the racist, rigid quota system. Although U.S. immigration law became more progressive by abolishing the quotas, historians such as Mae Ngai remind us that the progressivism of the Act that Johnson signed at the Statue of Liberty was limited. "Nationalism resists humanitarianism and remains blind to the causal connections between the United States' global projections and the conditions abroad that impel emigration," Ngai writes, commenting on how the 1965 Act strengthened nationalism and the nation-state as an agent of restrictionism.[3]

The idea of the U.S. as a nation of immigrants from the end of the quota system through the twenty-first century illuminates both why we didn't know that Perkins tried to

help, and why, in many cases, restrictionism and xenophobia thwarted Perkins's efforts.

The Demise of the Quota System

In 1933, when the Under Secretary of State called the Secretary of Labor on the phone intending to explain U.S.
immigration law to her, she shot back that her department
would have a say in the matter and that it would carry on
an American tradition of welcoming immigrants and refugees. She was imagining the tradition, but she believed it
to be true. There was significant evidence for her belief,
not in law or practice, but in poetry and popular culture.
In 1855, American poet Walt Whitman wrote in *Leaves of
Grass*, "Here is not merely a nation, but a teeming nation
of immigrants."[4] In 1908, British-Jewish playwright Israel
Zangwill popularized the phrase "melting pot" through a
play about a Russian-Jewish family in the U.S.[5]

The reality was more sobering. In the earliest years of the
U.S., displacing Indigenous people and enslaving Africans
drove the nation's wealth. Following the Civil War, the Fourteenth Amendment attempted to establish ethnic and racial
equality for citizens. Consequently, lawmakers turned their
attention toward imposing ethnic and racial inequality on
noncitizens. The Chinese Exclusion Act of 1882 emerged
from this context.

Following sixty years of Chinese exclusion, Congress repealed it in 1943, at the height of U.S. involvement in World
War II. By then, white Americans' attitudes toward Chinese
people were changing because of their common enemy, the

Japanese Empire. Even more, the decision represented a "wartime measure to counter Japanese propaganda that held up Chinese exclusion as evidence of Americans' anti-Asiatic race policies."[6] Following World War II, the U.S. increasingly made decisions to project a more benevolent, moralistic image on the world stage, as a superpower and as a foe of the Soviet Union. The U.S. "was sensitive to charges of racial discrimination," Mae Ngai writes, "knowing that the charges damaged the international image... and may have felt particularly vulnerable to criticism of the Chinese quota, which was based on race."[7] Dunbar-Ortiz added that the U.S. "scrambled to conceal any trace of... colonialist roots."[8] Curating a national image on the world stage accelerated the process of mythmaking.

It was in this postwar context that the McCarran-Walter Immigration Act of 1952 bridged the quotas with the post-quota era. The 1952 Act repealed Japanese and Korean exclusion while also preferencing people with special economic skills from within each quota. Half of each country's quota went to immigrants with special skills in short supply. Although it did not repeal the quota system based on nation origins, the 1952 Act set precedent for the privileging of economic skills. Overall, the 1952 Act was more of a reinforcement than an overhaul, and as a result, it provoked resistance against the quota system. An important arena of resistance against the 1952 Act was among lawmakers and politicians. President Harry Truman vetoed it, though Congress overrode.

The late 1950s was a time of reframing U.S. history with an emphasis on a "nation of immigrants." Lawmakers still wanted to restrict immigrants, but they didn't want the restrictions to appear to be about ethnicity or race. This trend was politically advantageous for a young Irish-Catholic senator who wanted to be president. In 1958, the short book *A Nation of Immigrants* by John F. Kennedy (JFK) was emblematic of the moment between the 1952 Act and the 1965 Act, when Americans were starting to re-conceptualize the U.S. as more receptive to immigrants, if only certain ones.

Part of JFK's motivation for presenting the U.S. as a nation of immigrants was that he sought acceptance as an Irish-Catholic person running for the presidency. In her opposite title, *Not a Nation of Immigrants*, Roxanne Dunbar-Ortiz writes that as the "first Catholic president in a Protestant-dominated culture," JFK "introduced a clear context and narrative in which he could transform this negative into a positive."[9] JFK's book aligned with the beliefs and hopes of a critical mass of voters at the time of publication in 1958.

JFK's *A Nation of Immigrants* unintentionally epitomizes why the phrase "nation of immigrants" is a myth and the problems with perpetuating it. JFK omits the Chinese Exclusion Act, fitting because it wouldn't match his narrative. While including two total paragraphs on immigration from the continent of Asia and the region of Latin America, the future president never mentioned Mexicans, Mexico, or the words "Hispanic" or "Latino."[10] As Dunbar-Ortiz explains in her counterargument, the U.S. seized what's now the Southwestern U.S. from Mexico by force.[11] Americans settled the territory through subsequent massacres of Indigenous people—such as the Camp Grant Massacre and the Sand Creek Massacre—and throughout the quota era the U.S. limited Mexican immigration to the Bracero Program, which allowed Mexican laborers to perform labor to benefit the American economy. Astonishingly yet unsurprisingly, JFK included enslaved Africans in his definition of immigrants. It's not that JFK lacked documentation of images of enslavement. He included in his book, as Dunbar-Ortiz describes, the "infamous drawing of a slave ship, with humans chained down on their backs, scarcely an inch between each."[12] Erasing the pain and reality of enslaved experiences, JFK's caveat in his own words was "Immigration was not always pleasant."[13]

JFK removed the influence of laws from his idealized history of immigration. The table of contents distinguished between prerevolutionary and postrevolutionary immigrants—before and after American independence from England—as if one could legally immigrate to a nation that did not exist yet. "Another way of indicating the importance of immigration to America is to point out that every American who ever lived, with the exception of one group, was either an immigrant himself or a descendant from immigrants," JFK pontificated. He then added that "anthropologists believe that the Indians themselves were immigrants from another continent who displaced the original Americans—the aborigines."[14] JFK constructed an alternative—albeit well-liked—history to justify settler colonialism, soften enslavement, and romanticize American immigration law.

Perkins would not recognize her own experiences of working with U.S. immigration law in JFK's book. "The search for freedom of worship has brought people to America from the days of the Pilgrims to modern times," he wrote, "for example anti-Semitic [sic] and anti-Christian persecution in Hitler's Germany and the Communist empire have driven people from their homes to seek refuge in America."[15] Here the author and presidential hopeful simultaneously grouped Jewish victims with Christians and grouped Nazism with Communism, fusing the postwar trends of decentering Jewish people while increasing whiteness, as well as linking Nazism with Communism to forgive West Germany and to villainize the Soviet Union. Even more, he used German-Jewish refugees as an example of continuing the Pilgrims' tradition.

Still, JFK hinted at Christian nationalism and xenophobia. "Minority religious sects, from the Quakers and Shakers through the Catholics and Jews to the Mormons and Jehovah's Witnesses, have at various times suffered both discrimination and hostility in the United States," he wrote. By grouping Jewish immigrants together with a hodgepodge of predominantly white Christians, JFK ensured that the realities of U.S. immigration law in the 1930s and 1940s were nowhere to be found in his book. Rigid, restrictionist U.S. immigration quotas contributed to dooming the masses of European Jewry.

The U.S. ended its quota system in summer 1965. Perkins died a few months too early to witness the change. The Immigration Act of 1965 was by any measurement a watershed moment in the history of American immigration law and formative for historical memory of it.

JFK also did not live to see the end of the quota system. A few months before the 1965 Act's passage, however, Harper reprinted *A Nation of Immigrants* with a new introduction by the beloved, deceased president's younger brother, U.S. Senator Robert F. Kennedy. Senator Kennedy's words were emblematic of the stance of progressives in Congress upon the passage of the Act. "We have always believed it possible for men and women who start at the bottom to rise as far as their talent and energy allow," RFK wrote, hoping to bolster a different myth, meritocracy, and to protect the U.S. government's privilege of deciding who brings enough merit to immigrate. Sentences later, RFK described the quota system as "a source of embarrassment to us around the world," a "source of anguish to many of our own citizens with relatives abroad," and a "source of loss to the economic and creative strength of our nation as a whole."[16] Here RFK articulated a key motivation behind the Immigration Act of 1965—American reputation on the world stage during the Cold War—and its two primary effects: privileging immigrants with family in the U.S. and immigrants with economically beneficial skills, while continuing to restrict mostly everyone else.

Indeed, the Immigration Act of 1965 helped the U.S. to appear less bigoted to other countries by restructuring U.S. immigration law to privilege family ties and professional opportunities. The Act "established preferences for family and occupationally based immigration," adding spouses and unmarried minor children as possible non-quota immigrants.[17] It increased an annual immigration ceiling to 290,000, which would later increase to 300,000. As a result, immigration increased from a wider range of places since then: 6,244,379 documented immigrants in the 1980s and 9,775,398 documented immigrants in the 1990s. Over a million refugees settled in the U.S. from Cambodia, Laos, and Vietnam.[18]

There were limits to the progressivism of the Immigration Act of 1965. For example, it set the first numerical cap on immigration from the Western Hemisphere, limiting immigration from Latin America, especially Mexico, barely a year after the Bracero Program ended. The effect was "restricting [immigration] from Mexico, the Caribbean, and Latin America," despite the benefits of "greater opportunities for migration from Asia and Africa."[19] The American Legion, which had supported the National Origins Act of 1924 and vehemently opposed both the Wagner-Rogers Bill for child refugees and the King-Havenner Bill for refugee settlement in Alaska in 1939, called the Immigration Act of 1965 "common sense" because it was truly quite moderate.[20]

The Immigration Act of 1965 followed on the coattails of civil rights movements in the 1960s. Indeed, lawmakers had overlapping motives for addressing both civil rights and immigration reform, such as considering international reputation during the Cold War. Some even had humanitarian motives. Throughout U.S. history, however, civil rights and immigration have had a complicated relationship. The Reconstruction Amendments, for example, contributed to backlash in the form of the racist immigration legislation of 1882. Ngai clarified regarding the Immigration Act of 1965: "That immigration reform and civil rights were cut from the same cloth of democratic reform . . . seems undeniable . . . Yet the strong similarities have perhaps obscured important differences . . . whereas the civil rights movement targeted the legacies of racial slavery, immigration reform in the 1940s to 1960s addressed . . . discriminations faced by ethnic Europeans."[21] Although abolishing the quota system was progressive and radical, the Act nevertheless "hardened the distinction between citizen and alien," and people adversely affected were not white.[22]

The Immigration Act of 1965 "repairs a very deep and painful flaw in the fabric of American justice," Lyndon Johnson stated at his signing ceremony beneath the Statue of Liberty, green and glowing. "It corrects a cruel and enduring wrong," he added righteously. But this was not the end of restrictionism. The Act introduced new preferences. "From this day forth," the president declared, "those wishing to immigrate to America shall be admitted on the basis of their skills and their close relationship to those already here."[23] Both categories of preference undoubtedly would have admitted more Jewish people from Europe. But as atrocities unfolded around the globe throughout the late twentieth century, making European immigration more equitable was less helpful to people in many parts of the world, predominantly people of color, many who tried to escape conflicts that American imperialism incited.[24]

Burned by the "Great American Melting Pot"

In 1976, the U.S. celebrated two hundred years of independence from England. As part of the bicentennial celebrations, *Schoolhouse Rock!*—a purveyor of educational music videos—packaged American historical narratives into musical form for a new generation to consume. Members of Generation X might remember videos such as "The Great American Melting Pot" in 1977. While in some ways an animated, melodious iteration of JFK's *A*

Nation of Immigrants, the video is emblematic of the myth of a nation of immigrants in a post-quota era.

In the opening notes, viewers see the narrator's white arms flipping through photographs of her grandmother from Russia and her grandfather from Italy. "And there [in the U.S.] they melted in," she sings. The narrator shifts into a chorus of "Lovely Lady Liberty," as an animated, green statue flashes a smile through white, European features.

The premise of the song's plot is that the Statue of Liberty is literally cooking a melting pot. The video lists ingredients: "Armenians, Africans, English, Dutch..." Keeping with JFK's failure to acknowledge that millions of Africans were, in fact, not immigrants—but coerced and enslaved laborers kidnapped from their homes without a choice—the song jumps from the list of ingredients into a bubbly "America was founded by the English." An animated Englishman with a flag appears on-screen, and then German, Dutch, and French men join him, steamrolling over any possible mention of Indigenous history, a leading casualty of the melting pot myth.

The phrase "principle still sticks" aims to convince viewers that American immigration law was always as inclusive as it was to European and Asian immigrants after the Immigration Act of 1965, while East Asian immigrants were still banned just decades earlier. "The principle still sticks / our heritage is mixed / so any kid could be the president," the video continues with an image of seven children. Without missing a beat, the narrator sings "You simply melt right in" as the animated children from the previous image leap into a pool of water contained within a pot. Although the narrator sings "It doesn't matter where you're from / Or your religion, you jump right in," a critical mass of the characters appear to be white.

National origin and religion did matter for Jewish refugee children in 1939, when the Wagner-Rogers Bill did not even make it out of committee onto the floor of Congress. Supporters of the bill tried to assure hesitant colleagues that only some of the children would be Jewish. Congress would not allow additional child refugees separately from the German quota, and the bill sponsors could not in good conscience legislate for the children to replace adult refugees' spots. The German quota was limiting, and American antisemitism prevented Congress from adjusting it, even for children who appeared like the ones in the video—no matter how catchy a tune tries to reframe the narrative.

Then the video cuts back to Indigenous erasure again: "America was the New World / And Europe was the Old" with a map of the Northern Hemisphere. Finally, it closes out with a refrain of "the great American melting pot," the kind that will be stuck in your head for at least a day and embedded within American collective consciousness even longer.[25]

In 1977, when animated children leapt into a melting pot, and a voice sang "Lovely Lady Liberty," U.S. immigration law still had no official refugee policy. Congress first introduced a legal definition of "refugee" in 1980. Ngai writes that it would "not be until 1980 that Congress passed legislation that defined refugees in the same terms as an international law defined them—that is, as persons unable or unwilling to return to their native country because of persecution or a well-founded fear of persecution.[26] Both the Immigration Act of 1965 and the U.S. legal definition of a refugee in 1980 provided evidence for an otherwise misguided claim that Americans historically welcomed immigrants.

This myth of America as a nation of immigrants became integral to the ascent of multiculturalism during the 1990s. In theory, multiculturalism describes the political philosophy of different cultures, ethnicities, races, and religions coexisting peacefully in a society. In practice, multiculturalism is not always as equal and equitable among the groups as it might be among the animated children in *Schoolhouse Rock!* Or put otherwise, viewers of *Schoolhouse Rock!* grew into adults, they raised children who visited the Statue of Liberty on field trips, and the myths of "Lovely Lady Liberty" and the "great American melting pot" snowballed.

Museums and cultural institutions presented multiculturalism to their patrons, who bought into ideas of history through gift shops. In the 1990s, the telling of history looked like figurines lined up in a museum gift shop—Harriet Tubman, George Washington, Davy Crockett, Sacagawea, and don't forget the miscellaneous heroes like Harry Houdini, Amelia Earhart, and at times even Charles Lindbergh—a nonsensical hodgepodge of enslaved persons and enslavers, colonizers and colonized, some thrill seekers, and a xenophobe. Ideals of equality and justice in the face of unequal and unjust historical circumstances erased the realities of slavery, settler colonialism, and xenophobia. The 1990s made progress on inclusivity and representation at the expense of accuracy and adjusting structures. The melting pot was a staple dish of multiculturalism.

Regardless of intentions, the 1990s brand of multiculturalism was not a complete antidote to white supremacy, antisemitism, or xenophobia. It often reinforced white supremacy by adding people of color without changing the traditional narrative. Meanwhile, antisemitism is a separate social force from racism. Of course, antisemitism and racism can intersect. But antisemitism is a distinct force in history that, generally, Americans have not spent much time considering or learning the unique challenges faced by a relatively small Jewish population. Equalizing opportunities for immigration to the U.S. throughout Europe has obscured the fact that Jewish immigration to the U.S. was once quite difficult. In the 1920s and 1930s, the rise of Nazi Germany happened at the same time and for some of the same reasons as American isolationism and tightening American immigration restrictions.

Xenophobia never disappeared from American society. They close to disappeared, however, from American historical narratives that appeared in the 1990s and early 2000s, in formal education, popular culture, and political rhetoric. "We in America are immigrants, or the children of immigrants," Mitt Romney pontificated while running in the 2012 presidential election. "We are a nation of immigrants, and that means we are constantly being replenished with fighters who believe in the American dream, and it gives us a tremendous advantage over other nations," his opponent President Barack Obama trumpeted. "The Statue of Liberty [reminds] us of who we are and where we came from. We are a nation of immigrants," agreed the next Democratic presidential nominee, Hillary Clinton.[27]

Clinton's opponent did not. Donald Trump built his campaign and presidency around xenophobia, from the wall to the Muslim ban to the responses to the pandemic.

Historian Erika Lee writes: "Despite its many inaccuracies, Trump's message resonated with voters, propelled him to the White House, and shaped his domestic policy agenda."[28] Supporters were reacting against an increase of diversity among American citizens since the Immigration Act of 1965. The U.S. had been undergoing what journalist William Booth described in *The Washington Post* in 1998 as a "movement of people that has profound implications for a society that by tradition pays homage to its immigrant roots at the same time it confronts complex and deeply ingrained ethnic and racial divisions." These immigrants were not of European descent, and the article predicted that the demographic shifts would "severely test the premise of the fabled melting pot, the idea, so central to national identity, that this country can transform people of every color and background into 'one America.'"[29] Trump's message and support for him represented both a backlash against the diversification of American society through immigration from populations that were once excluded, as well as resistance against the "fabled melting pot" itself.

A Trump brand of nationalism rejected the centrality of the "nation of immigrants" myth in American collective memory. Once elected president, Trump turned this rhetoric into a redirection of the formal narrative. Prior to February 2018, the U.S. Citizenship and Immigration Services mission statement said it "secures America's promise as a nation of immigrants by providing accurate and useful information to our customers, granting immigration and citizenship benefits, promoting an awareness and understanding of citizenship, and ensuring the integrity of our immigration system."[30] In February 2018, the Trump administration edited the mission to drop the phrase "a nation of immigrants." Trump's beliefs about immigrants as people were false. His goals for the treatment of immigrants were inhumane. His interpretation of the history of U.S. immigration law, however, was likely more sobering, historically consistent, and aligned with the spirit of U.S. immigration law throughout U.S. history than his predecessor's. Dunbar-Ortiz explains that the "Democratic Party politicians and liberals in general insisted that Trump and his supporters were un-American in denying the 'nation of immigrants' ideology that has been a consensus for more than a half century and remains a basic principle of the Democratic Party."[31] In 2020, the Biden campaign responded with "The Biden Plan for Securing Our Values as a Nation of Immigrants."

"History wars" have been unfolding over competing interpretations of the American past and how they shape the present.[32] For different reasons, each side seems eager to challenge traditional narratives, hungry for facts to substantiate the truths they might intuit. Both sides might succumb to cherry-picking evidence to support claims. The more xenophobic side, however, wants with increasing explicitness a nation for white European immigrants. A nation of white European immigrants would have been a more fitting title for JFK's book, too. But JFK twisted the myth all the way into progressive zeal that helped launch him into the presidency. White supremacists today might embrace a more accurate narrative of exclusion, quotas, and restrictions, if they could see it repeat.

A wide range of progressive activists and audiences are ready to fight the history wars, armed with fresh interpretations of the past. They want multiculturalism to work. They want to welcome immigrants. Frances Perkins did, too. But anyone who takes the beautiful, increasing diversity of the U.S. population in the post-quota era and tries to fit that square peg into the circular hole of a longer U.S. immigration history—as defined by JFK's book or *Schoolhouse Rock!*—will end up with a narrative that, while happier, just doesn't track. The details of the story of Perkins's efforts to aid refugees from Nazi Germany wouldn't make sense if U.S. laws were actively welcoming them, or if the Statue of Liberty with a smile across her face were stirring a melting pot gleefully.

With the "nation of immigrants" as a dominant narrative, Perkins's efforts against the grain would be obscure, as for a long time they have been.

CHAPTER THIRTEEN

Remembering
Frances Perkins

*F*RANCES PERKINS INTENTIONALLY GAVE THE historical record precious little about her.

She did not keep a diary. She was most candid either in person or on the phone. She was more interested in the work that she did and in her and her family's personal safety than in being remembered.

She wrote herself out of history in her memoir about FDR, and predominantly male scholars didn't need to be asked twice to follow her lead. Despite standard commemorations like biographies, building dedications, oral histories, and even a postage stamp, Perkins receded from view and memory in the late twentieth century as little more than a quirky fun fact. *The Woman Behind the New Deal* by journalist Kirstin Downey and the founding of the Frances Perkins

Center in Maine transformed historical memory of Perkins in the early 2000s, giving her an entrancing narrative and bringing her memory home. Both were well prepared for the post-2016 national reflections on what it meant to be the first woman in an important position.

Still, memory is limited. "I know who she is. Isn't she the handkerchief lady? Yes, Triangle Shirtwaist Fire. See, I know my stuff," a tourist remarked to their partner in front of the charcoal portrait of Perkins as I sat nearby at the National Portrait Gallery in Washington, D.C., in fall 2023.

To the extent that she's known, Perkins is an ideal tour guide for the historic catastrophes that she weathered and the milestones that she influenced. Writing early in her career, she felt like she was "on the switchboard of contemporary history," and indeed she was. A primary goal of studying history is to wrestle with the social forces, not to absorb them passively. And when American xenophobia came head-to-head with the rise of Nazism, she was desperately trying to operate the switchboard, with odds against her and lives at stake. She held on tight, and she felt the weight, until ultimately more bigoted, conservative forces wrestled the switchboard from her.

"Oh, Do It, Mother. Don't Be So Stupid. Just Do It!": Publishing The Roosevelt I Knew

Perkins never sought out a literary agent, but she did have a friend named George Bye who worked as one. Bye decided that Perkins should author a memoir, and once Bye decided this, he was undeterred. Much like her initial reaction to the cabinet nomination twelve years earlier, Perkins initially refused. She traveled to London, where a representative of Bye's literary agency appeared at her door with a book deal from the famed Viking Press. Her daughter, Susanna, sided with the agent: "Oh, do it, Mother. Don't be so stupid. Just do it!"[1] Perkins signed the contract and received a $20,000 advance—higher than her government salary and the equivalent of a six-figure advance today.

She agreed to the project in large part because after her tenure, with her husband struggling with his mental illness and dependent, and twenty-nine-year-old Susanna recently divorced, she needed to earn money. As Secretary of Labor, her salary had been $15,000, nothing extra to save.[2]

Viking was excited for Perkins's book of recollections about the recently deceased president. But Perkins had to write it first. She hired typists and a research assistant and purchased a recording device. Yet she struggled to narrate recollections without an audience. So, she hired World War II veteran and writer Howard Taubman to essentially write the book based on her narration.[3]

Published in 1946, *The Roosevelt I Knew* was full of the accomplishments of Frances Perkins repeatedly credited to Franklin Delano Roosevelt (FDR). For example, she wrote that after Kristallnacht he'd extended the visitor visas of Jewish Germans in the country. She didn't mention that she'd been pushing for this measure for years. Anyone claiming that Perkins left someone or something out of *The Roosevelt I Knew* should remember that she barely included herself. She wrote on a specific topic—FDR—for a specific purpose: to support herself and her family financially after she submitted her resignation to the new president, Harry

Truman. After all, she'd expressed that she "came to Washington to work for God, FDR, and the millions of forgotten, plain common working men."[4] She cared about her work for the country, her faith, and the presidential administration, rather than receiving recognition.

In the early to mid-1950s, Perkins sat for oral history interviews with the newly formed Columbia Center for Oral History Research, established in 1948. Thirty-one-year-old Dean Albertson interviewed her. Journalist and historian Allan Nevins spearheaded the project, which interviewed lawmakers from modern American history. While digitized and made accessible by Columbia, the audio is intelligible but less than easy listening.[5]

In the interviews, Perkins discussed key New Deal legislation, as well as earlier episodes in her career, but not refugee policy. Most likely, neither the interviewer nor the interviewee would have thought to include refugee policy because American collective memory of Nazi atrocities was in its earliest stages, barely scratching the surface of consciousness. *Refugee* would not even be an American legal term until 1980. Early biographers omitted Perkins's efforts on behalf of refugees.

Perkins lived for another decade after the oral history interviews. *The Roosevelt I Knew* sold so well that Perkins's agent and publisher regretted not advising her on tax withholdings. She worked for the Civil Service Commission during the Truman administration, resigning when her husband, Paul Wilson, died in 1952. The following year, Perkins relocated halfway across the country for a teaching position at the University of Illinois. For Perkins, Illinois was a familiar state for an unfamiliar stage. She taught a series of twelve seminars on labor movements and policy, and she delivered a university lecture titled "The Roosevelt I Knew."

"Forasmuch as Ye Know That Your Labor Is Not in Vain": Death of Frances Perkins

Like a half-century earlier, the move to Illinois was not permanent. Perkins returned to New York, where she accepted a teaching position at Cornell University to be closer to her family and friends spread across the Northeast from Maine to Washington, D.C. Living in New York and newly remarried, Susanna Wilson Coggeshall gave birth to Perkins's only grandchild in 1954, Tomlin Coggeshall. Perkins's relationship with her daughter was difficult at times. In 1952, for example, she'd advised Susanna and her friend to wear black dresses and pearls to a reception in New York for Princess Juliana of Holland. Susanna instead wore "a watermelon skirt with green top, Capezio shoes tied up to the knees, her hair piled on her head with a huge red rose and another huge red rose on a black velvet ribbon around her neck."[6] Perkins's face betrayed shock and outrage for a moment, a second longer than normal on personal matters.

In her final years, a highlight of Perkins's time at Cornell was that in 1960, an academic society known as the Telluride Association invited her to live in their house as an honor without payment or other responsibilities. She appreciated feeling part of a community with the undergraduate and graduate students living there. Now eighty years old, she enjoyed their social gatherings where people discussed events and ideas, reminding her of Washington society.[7]

On May 14, 1965, while visiting Midtown Hospital in Manhattan for a routine appointment, Frances Perkins passed away from a stroke. Forever avoiding unnecessary attention, she'd always carefully curated her appearances when they were unavoidable. Her funeral was no exception. It took place at an Anglo-Catholic congregation, the Church of the Resurrection, in Manhattan. She'd chosen a biblical passage from First Corinthians: "Be ye steadfast, unmovable, always abounding in the work of the Lord, forasmuch as ye know that your labor is not in vain in the Lord."[8] Through the verse we catch a glimpse of how Perkins wanted to be remembered: steadfast, unmovable, and for work not in vain.

It was the same verse that she'd selected during senior year as class president at Mount Holyoke. In 1902, she'd meant to inspire classmates to take on righteous causes and important work. By the time of her funeral, in 1965, she'd done that work. Spoken during senior year of college and at her funeral, the phrase "be ye steadfast" bookended Perkins's career. The years in between were infused with the same sentiment.

"In recent years time had mellowed the opposition to her," *The New York Times* obituary commented, recalling the conservative opposition to her policies and the sexist backlash against her tenure as cabinet secretary. "Miss Perkins, who kept sewing needles and thread in her drawer next to Presidential memorandums, was often the target of much criticism and some abuse," the obituary continued, perhaps unintentionally demonstrating how subtle phrasing habitually undermined taking women seriously. Quoting a misogynist who'd once called her "a colorless woman who talked as if she swallowed a press release," the obituary clarified that Perkins spoke clearly because she didn't, in her own words, "believe men would long tolerate vague women in public office."[9] Staying cool and calculated had been the best option for a trailblazing woman whose historic first would provoke backlash no matter what.

Frances Perkins lies to rest beside her husband, Paul Wilson, down the street from the Perkins family homestead in Newcastle, Maine. Susanna selected a simple stone, classic and humble like her mother. To visit the gravesite, cars must persevere parking on a rocky slant. In the summer of 2023, an author accompanied by a Frances Perkins Center board member—both of Jewish heritage—participated in the Jewish tradition of laying stones atop a grave, to honor Perkins's efforts on behalf of Jewish communities.

A Biography, a Building, and a Postage Stamp

In the early 1970s, Perkins's personal papers, including the 1950s oral history interviews, became open to the public at Columbia University. Their accessibility led biographer George Martin to produce the first book-length volume on Perkins. Drawing from 102 tape-recorded interviews and more, Martin selected punchy and precise anecdotes to weave into a readable narrative.

In the preface of *Madam Secretary*, Martin reflects on the historical memory of Perkins at the time of the biography's publication. "Her achievements have been too little appreciated. She disliked personal publicity and often would do nothing to counter criticism even when it was patently unfair," he writes. "Then, just as the legislation for which she was chiefly responsible began to bear fruit, World War II intervened, and after it few people bothered to recall the source of legislation already a decade old."[10] He attributed scholars' treatment of her to her own decisions not to correct contemporaries who undermined her, and he identified wartime as having doubled down on the erasure.

Martin's 1976 *Madam Secretary* offered a gripping read as the centennial of Perkins's birth approached in 1980. Alas, *Madam Secretary* alone wasn't enough to launch Perkins into collective consciousness in the way that a subsequent biography would in the twenty-first century. For the bicentennial of American independence in 1976, perhaps Americans preferred focusing on much earlier American history. Notably, when Martin was writing the biography, Susanna Wilson Coggeshall was not yet willing to share.

Susanna and Tomlin did attend the formal dedication of the Frances Perkins Department of Labor Building on April 10, 1980, Perkins's hundredth birthday. In the 1960s, the executive branch had begun efforts to consolidate a series of Labor Department office buildings into one, located on Constitution Avenue. Overlooking the Capitol and parts of the National Mall, President Jimmy Carter delivered an address to mark the occasion: "Looking back at the history of our Nation," he remarked, "it's significant that from time to time there came upon the American scene an outstanding and courageous and farsighted and sensitive human being who literally transformed for the better the life of all Americans." Carter and Perkins would have shared ideals of American humanitarianism and Christian moralism. "Nobody deserves this ceremony and this honor more than Frances Perkins," he added.[11]

If Perkins's hundredth birthday were a year later, President Ronald Reagan might not have delivered a speech, or at least a very different speech. Perkins had been a key architect of New Deal initiatives that the Reagan movement desired to reverse. Historical commemorations like Carter's speech at the Frances Perkins Department of Labor Building always reflect the politics of the contemporary moment.

Much like commemorating anniversaries and naming buildings, the images on U.S. postage stamps offer glimpses into how the nation wants to see itself and its history at the precise moment when they're printed.[12] On the same day as the dedication of the Frances Perkins Department of Labor Building, the U.S. Postal Service (USPS) marked the centennial of Perkins's birth with a commemorative postage stamp. The stamp was designed by F. R. Petrie from New Jersey, the *Philatelic News* reported, and "rendered based upon several photographs of the former labor secretary."[13]

Petrie depicted Perkins in old age still wearing a tricorne hat and respectable pearls, turning her face to the side with an open-lipped smile.

Maybe USPS chose an image where Perkins looked slightly older to signal that the first female cabinet secretary appointment happened long ago enough that she'd grown old, while so few female cabinet secretaries followed her between 1945 and 1980.

NAME	DEPARTMENT	ADMINISTRA-TION	YEARS
Oveta Hobby	Health, Education, and Welfare	Eisenhower	1953–1955
Carla Hills	Housing and Urban Development	Ford	1975–1977
Juanita M. Kreps	Commerce	Carter	1977–1979
Patricia Harris	Housing and Urban Development; Health and Human Services	Carter	1977–1979; 1979–1981
Shirley Hufstedler	Education	Carter	1979–1981

Between Perkins's tenure as Labor Secretary and the dedication of the Labor Department in her name, only five out of countless appointed secretaries were women. Carter appointed three of them in the 1970s. None served in a position longer than two years.

Though pursuing initiatives that might cause more conservative Americans of her ancestry to clutch their pearls, Perkins wore pearls frequently throughout her career. In 1980, the commemorative stamp could have cropped her neckline above the pearls, yet it included the necklace, perhaps to signal respectability. Regarding Perkins's smile, perhaps Petrie sought to ascribe to her the emotion and personality that she'd gone to great lengths to keep private. He might have sensed that she needed to convey more feeling to play a greater role in collective memory. Alternatively, maybe just an unoriginal *women should smile more* guided the choice.

By 1980, anyone who wanted to engage with the first female cabinet secretary would have had a biography to read, a building to visit, and a stamp to collect. Yet interest in Perkins lingered beneath the surface, popping up only occasionally as a quirky fun fact. It would continue to recede for the next two decades.

"Nobody Puts Baby in a Corner": But What About Frances Perkins?

In 1987, *Dirty Dancing* portrayed the story of a Jewish teenager called "Baby" who fell in love with a dancing member of the staff at a resort in the Catskills, where her family was spending the summer. The choreography, the relationship arc, the societal commentary on abortion, and the soundtrack captivated audiences, becoming the number-one best-selling VHS in 1988. In the film, Baby explains that her real name is "Frances, after the first woman in the Cabinet." Starting college—"Baby's going to Mount Holyoke in the fall"—when the movie took place in the 1960s, the fictional character would have been born in the 1940s, shortly after the Roosevelt administration. Still, including the name "Frances" signified not much more than a catchy fun fact.

Historical memory of Frances Perkins was relatively quiet in the 1990s. She never appeared in either of the widely distributed, multiculturalist, children's biography series: *Childhood of Famous Americans* and *Who Was?* While assessing memory is always imprecise, determining why someone or something recedes from view can be the most challenging. One strategy is to consider what people needed at that time.

In the 1990s, Newt Gingrich's reign as Speaker of the House built on the conservative legacies of the Reagan presidency. Perkins for many reasons was never going to be a modern Republican hero. And as Democrats looked to redefine their party, President Bill Clinton announced during his State of the Union address in 1996: "The era of big government is over." Despite accusations of Communism, Perkins was a mainstream Democrat with mild socialist leanings throughout her tenure as Labor Secretary. As a key architect of the New Deal, she helped to expand the power of government into the economy and society. "The era of big government is over" was not her time to shine.[14]

Frances Perkins: The Woman Behind the New Deal

Journalist Kirstin Downey first heard about Frances Perkins on a bus tour of Washington, D.C., where the tour guide joked that Perkins spent "twelve years in labor."[15] On business, economics, and labor beats at *The Washington Post*, Downey kept hearing of this elusive historical figure. She embarked on a decade-long research journey to find out more. Downey applied Perkins's adage "leave no stone unturned," tirelessly interviewing sources, reading books and articles, and researching archives up and down the East Coast. She became a regular at the Library of Congress's night hours after her day job. Downey's method of storing research was endless photocopies. If Martin gave Perkins a long-overdue biography, Downey gave Perkins her heart, and eventually the hearts of her readers.

In *The Woman Behind the New Deal*, readers follow Perkins trying on hats with her mother, who told her that her cheekbones were too wide for anything besides a tricorne hat; how much Perkins felt at home at Mount Holyoke; how she flailed around after college figuring out what to do; how she taught school to earn a living while volunteering at settlement houses; how she found her calling in labor investigation and public service. In the prologue, Perkins brought to FDR a list of demands to which he must agree before she accepted the cabinet position, and those demands translated into some of the most progressive and influential legislation of the New Deal. The book contains two chapters on Perkins's efforts to aid refugees from Nazi Germany: one on charge bonds from 1933 to 1935, and one on the flurry of efforts after Kristallnacht. Those chapters built on a 2001 academic article by historian Bat-Ami Zucker entitled "Frances Perkins and the German-Jewish Refugees, 1933-1940."

Rather than shying away from the familial difficulties that Perkins faced throughout her adult life, Downey empathetically traces the onset of Paul Wilson's battles with bipolar disorder. Susanna Wilson Coggeshall granted Downey interviews that she never trusted previous biographers to handle.

Downey cited them and maintained a relationship with the family. Susanna died in 2003, but Tomlin became central to establishing the Frances Perkins Center.

Located in Newcastle, Maine, the Perkins family homestead sits only a few hours north of Boston by car, but from a New England vantage point, it's far out there. With her family, Perkins traveled from Worcester to Newcastle by train in her youth. Despite years in Chicago, New York, and Washington, D.C., Frances Perkins was always a New Englander at heart.

The Frances Perkins Center was founded in 2009 with a mission that "honors the legacy of Frances Perkins by sharing her commitment to the principle that government should provide all its people with the best possible life, and by preserving the place that shaped her character." The homestead itself includes the Brick House—the family's historic home—and fifty-seven acres of land on the Damariscotta River. When the Frances Perkins Center was founded, Tomlin and his spouse were still living in the family home. The Perkins family homestead joined the National Register of Historic Places in 2009, Secretary of the Interior Sally Jewell designated it a National Historic Landmark in 2014, and the Frances Perkins Center completed its capital campaign to purchase the home from Tomlin in 2020. House tours and educational programming, which began in 2011, were reinvigorated in 2023 after a preservation project to make the buildings safe and accessible, including exhibits, lectures, talks, tours, undergraduate internships, and additional outreach for K–12 education. A tightknit core of early participants on the original Frances Perkins Center team included Tomlin

Coggeshall; Christopher Breiseth, who'd lived with Perkins at Cornell; retired National Park Service planning chief and expert preservationist Sarah Peskin; and author Kirstin Downey, among others. Together they expand the narrative of *The Woman Behind the New Deal.*[16]

Any historical figure needs a narrative to integrate more fully into national memory. Downey gave Frances Perkins that narrative. Perkins had gone to great lengths to hide from public scrutiny and attention. The remnants of her career and life were scattered across archival and other sources. Downey stitched together as many threads as possible. And to endure, that memory must find additional vehicles.

When progressive political strategists Joe and Georgia Rospars were deciding what to name their daughter, Georgia remembered a portrait of Frances Perkins she had encountered at the National Portrait Gallery. They acquired a copy of *The Woman Behind the New Deal* and were deeply moved by Perkins's story and unacknowledged impact on America. After the birth of Frances Rospars in December 2017, they gave copies of the book to family, friends, and colleagues—among them Senator Elizabeth Warren.

So, when Joe Rospars became Elizabeth Warren's chief strategist for her 2020 presidential run, he could not help but notice the parallels. Both Perkins and Warren were brave, brilliant, detail-oriented female leaders striving to channel their empathy and talents into improving life for people in need, for people lacking necessities and security amid structural inequality. Perkins's words "be ye steadfast," "leave no stone unturned," and "social justice would be my vocation" could have been Warren's. Warren's words "only righteous fights" could have belonged to Perkins.

As a presidential candidate in September 2019, Warren delivered a speech to a crowd of more than twenty thousand people in Manhattan's Washington Square Park, overlooking the site of the Triangle Shirtwaist Factory fire of 1911. Supporters watched Warren's speech feet away from where Perkins had witnessed poor immigrants, mostly women, jump to their deaths. Warren embraced the symbolism, physically leaning on a podium made of wood salvaged from the Perkins homestead. Her words connected how the fire ignited something within Perkins to Warren's own commitment to improving living and working standards for Americans. At the time of the speech, Warren was starting to surge in the polls and was especially popular among younger Democrats. As a result, Perkins and her narrative— as told by Warren as guided by Rospars as researched by Downey—found favor with new audiences.[17]

Social media is a prevalent tool for politicians drawing on Perkins's historical memory to signal female trailblazing and progressivism. "Frances Perkins saw what was broken in our country and had a plan to fix it. One woman— backed by millions of people—was able to make big, structural change. And we can do it again in 2020," the Warren presidential campaign tweeted on October 28, 2019, with an accompanying educational video about Perkins as a "driving force" behind the New Deal.[18] The Warren campaign delved into Perkins's policies to communicate her own priorities: building a social safety net and enacting structural change.

On March 4, 2021, Vice President Kamala Harris tweeted: "In 1933, Frances Perkins made history as the first woman appointed to the US Cabinet. As Secretary of

Labor, she helped implement social security, unemployment insurance, and a federal minimum wage. Today, we
honor her legacy. #WomensHistoryMonth."[19] Two of the
vice president's motives were explicit: the historical anniversary of Perkins's appointment on March 4 and
Women's History Month. The more implicit reason was
to validate, legitimize, or at least identify Harris's historic
first as a female vice president with Perkins's historic first.
People employ historical anniversaries and a theme of the
month like women's history as tools in service to broader
goals, such as representation and building solidarity among
the first women to serve in high offices.

Barely four years earlier, Hillary Clinton became the first
female presidential nominee for a major political party in
U.S. history. When her social media referenced Perkins, it
focused on the cabinet secretary's status as the first woman,
rather than any detailed policies or political philosophy.
"Sec. of Labor Frances Perkins was our first woman cabinet
member and an architect of the Fair Labor Standards Act,"
Clinton tweeted on September 5, 2016, with two months remaining in her campaign.[20] Clinton's loss in 2016, and the
misogyny of the Trump movement, likely contributed to
motivating three separate children's book authors to bring
the first woman in the cabinet to younger audiences.
Jennifer J. Merz's *Steadfast: Frances Perkins, Champion of
Workers' Rights* explores Perkins's childhood, her career in
social work, and her policy achievements as Labor Secretary. The book emphasizes Perkins's work with immigrant
communities and the life-changing experience of witnessing
the Triangle Shirtwaist fire, on which *Steadfast* spends
twelve of its thirty-eight pages. "'This is not the America of

dreams!' fumed Frances," Merz writes, hinting at a patriotic progress narrative.[21] A page of supplementary notes at the end of the book includes the line, "Immigration: Saved thousands of refugees by limiting deportations to Nazi Germany," but not a full chapter in Perkins's story yet.[22] Merz's bibliography includes Downey, David Brooks's 2015 essay on Perkins and the Triangle fire, and the Frances Perkins Center, and it excludes Martin.

That same year, 2020, Kathleen Krull's *Only Woman in the Photo: Frances Perkins & Her New Deal for America* tells Perkins's story through the lens of finding her speaking voice. In Krull's book, Perkins started out shy, learned to speak publicly in high school and college, and consistently spoke out on causes important to her ranging from fire safety to the New Deal. *The Only Woman in the Photo* is packed with captivating illustrations by Alexandra Bye, bearing a resemblance to Warner Bros.' *Anastasia* with her hat, coat, and animated eyes. In one image, Perkins wards off a man with the tip of her umbrella, and in another, she stomps on a paparazzo's camera. "She actually stomped on the camera of one photographer who took her picture despite her pleas not to," Krull writes, "so when Frances died after suffering a stroke in 1965, at age eighty-five, not many people remembered who she was and what she had accomplished."[23] Krull's Perkins was eager to use her voice but less willing to be seen, contrasting Perkins's historic contributions with her receding from historical records. Krull's bibliography is nearly identical to that of Merz.

Finally, also in 2020, Deborah Hopkinson's *Thanks to Frances Perkins: Fighter for Workers' Rights* is more compact. It starts and ends with social security, sandwiching a brief biography of Perkins between them. Hopkinson's bibliography cites two primary sources, *The Roosevelt I Knew* and the Columbia oral histories, and one secondary, *The Woman Behind the New Deal*. Downey's book provided a narrative arc for children's authors and illustrators to translate Perkins's life story for younger generations.[24]

As of March 2022, West 46th Street between 9th and 10th Avenues is now called "Frances Perkins Place." As a young adult, Perkins had worked in that neighborhood, Hell's Kitchen, serving and studying the "languishing, overcrowded" settlements and tenements in early-twentieth-century Manhattan.[25] The McManus Midtown Democratic Club first proposed the street name change in 2017, in the aftermath of the 2016 presidential election and on the coattails of the Women's March. The street renaming aligned with the Democratic Party's task of self-reinvention after its stunning loss on a national scale. A member of the Democratic Club explained that "at a time when the Democratic Party is struggling for an identity, to look at a woman like Frances Perkins who was really a progressive and believed in a social safety net shows that we don't always have to look forward—we can look backwards and find out what was good about the Democratic Party."[26] Local elected officials, including the mayor, were present, along with Tomlin Coggeshall and representatives of the Frances Perkins Center. Frances Perkins Place is blocks away from the Richard Rodgers Theatre, where *Hamilton* does similar work in shaping American historical memory and identity.

Frances Perkins: The Woman Behind American Efforts to Aid Refugees from Nazi Germany, 1933–1940

O N PERKINS'S BIRTHDAY IN 2022, the Department of Labor's Facebook post included: "Among her many accomplishments, she helped draft the New Deal and helped thousands of European refugees flee Nazi persecution on special visas."[1] Aiding victims of Nazism is widely accepted as something that should have been done. What hasn't changed, however, is xenophobia. Recent xenophobia is reminiscent of what anyone who sought to help was up against in the 1930s.

This is a story of how a high-ranking governmental official identified a problem, proposed solutions, built alliances among key players, and yet still faced defeat amid an overwhelming tide of bigotry. Both her desire to help noncitizens and the structural and societal obstacles in the way of supporting them are quintessentially U.S. history. American responses to the rise of Nazism ranged from American Nazism and U.S. race laws inspiring Nazis how to codify antisemitism to the genuinely humanitarian endeavors of people like Perkins.

Despite perceptions in the 1980s and 1990s, she is more than a quirky fun fact. She is a product of historical forces: a descendent of English settlers in Maine and Massachusetts Bay Colony whose Puritan values remarkably passed down through several generations to characterize her, yet she shaped herself away from their conservatism. She channeled individual responsibility toward structural change. In a time when other white Anglo-Saxon Protestants maintained vehement nativism, Perkins was a progressive against whom they crusaded. In that fight, she watched American bigotry rear its ugly head. She saw it, and it changed her. She, too, viewed the fight as a moral crusade. "Do you remember the priest that walked beside Joan of Arc when she went to the stake?"[2] Perkins asked her colleagues as they stood by her side at her impeachment hearing.

Often being the only woman in the room was almost always a factor worth considering. Even more, she built relationships with female allies. Notably, Cecilia Razovsky was the pinnacle of the German-Jewish Children's Aid program that the Labor Department backed.

Consuming the books and media that are now available about Perkins, she stands out for her righteousness. Yet she was not a superwoman saving people left and right. She was a professional whose innovative policies and solutions shaped real people's daily lives. Her ideas pushed against the limits and tested the boundaries of the society where they took place.

When they wrote "Dear Miss Perkins," family and friends of refugees overseas did not know what would happen or if she would be able to solve their problems. They had good reason to believe that she would try.

Acknowledgments

Spring semester didn't feel like spring yet in Western Massachusetts, when the Mount Holyoke College Career Development Center sent an email with the subject line, "paid U.S. history summer internship in Washington, DC." I sprang from my dorm to inquire and apply. I interviewed with Leslie Fields at the Mount Holyoke Archives and Special Collections, and I became the Inaugural Mount Holyoke intern for the Frances Perkins Center. The opportunity was funded by the Frances Perkins Center in Maine—thank you Betty Allen and Sarah Peskin—coordinated by the Mount Holyoke Archives and Special Collections, and located at the home of Kirstin Downey, author of *The Woman Behind the New Deal*, in Old Town Alexandria, Virginia.

While organizing Kirstin's research as her intern, I came across Bat-Ami Zucker's 2001 article "Frances Perkins and the German-Jewish Refugees, 1933-1940" in *American Jewish History*. Walking by at that moment, Kirstin told me that someone should do more research on that subject. At the same time, I was looking for a senior thesis topic. Kirstin accompanied me to the National Archives at College Park, where she introduced me to the archival research process and to the letters that Perkins received from the family and friends of refugees.

Many thanks to Professor Jeremy King for agreeing to work with the overeager undergraduate who showed up in his doorway with a stack of photocopied archival documents. Professor Daniel Czitrom contributed expertise in U.S. history, and Professor Emeritus Joseph Ellis encouraged me, reminding me that I had "grit" during challenging moments. Professor Katia Vavova taught in my philosophy classes that clarity matters in writing, and that when writing is unclear, that does not signify brilliance, even if written by famous men. She also modeled being a woman scholar. My "4am footnotes" group with fellow thesis-writers Kristin Johnson, Emily Wells, and Kathryn Gullen holds a special place in my heart, and shout-out to the underclasswoman who—after we asked her to be quiet in the library—left on my carrel a "you can do it" note, which I keep with my undergraduate thesis.

Between graduating Mount Holyoke in 2015 and when I began earnest work on this book in 2022, a combination of History PhD training and American politics transformed my perspective. Like many white millennials, my perceptions changed, and my thinking sharpened, throughout the chaos and heartlessness of the Trump administration. Increasingly, the bigotry and xenophobia that Perkins pushed up against seemed quintessentially American. The Trump years had wide-ranging consequences and effects, and one was that more audiences seemed interested in how the past shaped the present. They looked toward historians to help. Although my dissertation was on a different topic—American nineteenth-century religion-state relations through the lens of Sunday mail delivery—I benefited from opportunities to write about Perkins's refugee policy for *The Washington Post* and *Contingent Magazine*. Many thanks to Brian Rosenwald and Erin Bartram, respectively.

I am a historian because my doctoral advisor, Gautham Rao, believed that I could be. He taught me to value my own insights and to harness them. He intuited through empathy and instinct how best to advise me before I had proper learning diagnoses, which happened after my PhD. As a teacher, I've sat through professional development sessions on pedagogy, but what Gautham brings to teaching cannot be taught. If one of my students ever benefits from my teaching as much as I have from Gautham, I'd react in stunned silence. When I told Gautham barely a year after defending my dissertation that I was applying to fellowships to research a different topic, he was immediately supportive.

Also at American University, thanks to Richard Breitman for pointing me in useful directions both in spring 2015 and summer 2023.

I genuinely intended to pursue an academic monograph on Sunday mail delivery when I was defending my dissertation. A few weeks later, I was browsing in the Clarendon Barnes & Noble when *The Warburgs* by Ron Chernow caught my eye. I remembered Jeremy King explaining to me that Perkins's Solicitor of Labor Charles E. Wyzanski's wife, Gisela Warburg, wouldn't have needed a charge bond because her family was affluent. I flipped to the index to see Wyzanski and realized as the pages turned how much I cared. I remained energized enough about my undergraduate thesis topic to write a book.

Sarah Peskin from the Frances Perkins Center reached out to her Smith College classmate and friend Carol Mann, who'd founded the Carol Mann literary agency. Carol connected me with my agent, Dani Segelbaum. Despite this logical chain of connections, I don't know how I got so lucky to sign with Dani as my literary agent. She is masterful and shared my vision for the book throughout the process. Many thanks to Elisabeth Griffith and Rebecca Erbelding for contributing blurbs to my book proposal.

I'm grateful for funding from the Cokie Roberts Fellowship for Women's History from the National Archives Foundation coordinated by Valerie McVey; a Rubenstein Center Research Fellowship from the White House Historical Association coordinated by Matt Costello, Sarah Fling, and Lina Mann; and research funds from the American University Department of History coordinated by Gabriella Folsom.

On an early research trip to New York City, I slept on an air mattress in Emily Niekrasz's studio apartment and benefited from the assistance of Vianca Victor to access the Frances Perkins papers at the Columbia University Rare Book and Manuscript Library. On the same trip, I enjoyed an evening with Perkins aficionados Joe, Georgia, and Frances "Frankie" Rospars, as well as their dog, Salty. I remain grateful for their continued support.

In Western Massachusetts, my research benefited from the gracious staff in the Mount Holyoke Archives and Special Collections and from the opportunity to present a chapter in the UMass Amherst Department of History. Many thanks to Sam Redman and the public history program for inviting me. Thank you, Alison Russell, for good writing company and for trying to decipher Frances Perkins's handwriting together. Stepping foot in the Pioneer Valley—riding the PVTA bus, sipping London Fog at the Thirsty Mind, and surrounded by kind people and mountains—I felt a flood of gratitude to my parents, Betsy and Jeff Brenner, for having sent me to college at Mount Holyoke and for always encouraging my education.

Thank you, Fawn Carter, archivist at the Alaska and Polar Regions Collections & Archives, for scanning and sending a crucial document to me, helping me to glimpse Alaskan history from across the country.

On a trip to Maine, thank you, Sarah Peskin, Giovanna Gray Lockhart, and Emma Wegner for a wonderful tour of the Perkins homestead. Many thanks to Bill Kelley and again to Sarah for research support and Maine lobster.

At the U.S. National Archives, I'm thankful for assistance from archivists Cate Brennan, William Creech, and Julie Hawks. Shout-out to Archivist of the U.S. Colleen Shogan for intervening when a rogue reference employee responded to Perkins's she/her pronouns with his thoughts and feelings about pronouns, as well as Sarah Handley-Cousins for the opportunity to reflect on that experience in an essay for *Nursing Clio*.

Thank you, Patrick Fahy, for your enthusiastic and knowledgeable research support at the Franklin D. Roosevelt Presidential Library in Hyde Park, New York.

I drafted chapters one and ten on trips to visit my sister, Lexi Brenner, during her internships in Cincinnati. I rewrote chapter seven in Santa Monica while visiting my brother, Matthew Brenner, during his internship in L.A. I also worked on my book at my grandparents-in-law Karen and Melvin Mednik's kitchen counter in Delray Beach, as well as my in-laws Kim and Shawn Graham's couch in the Hudson Valley. My brother-in-law Andrew Graham's support included postage stamps and a T-shirt, both with Frances Perkins's face on them.

Lauren Lassabe Shepherd, Tim Lacy, Katy Hull, and Holly Genovese's note-taking bot, my Society for U.S. Intellectual History writing group, proved invaluable for edits and insights throughout the process. Libby Tyson and Laura Auketayeva also edited a few chapters. Neil Hernandez generously fact-checked the immigration-specific chapters, and Sarah Peskin did the same for the Perkins-specific ones. I don't know where to begin to thank Ron Coleman for endless research support from the U.S. Holocaust Memorial Museum and for editing and fact-checking at least seven different chapters, as well as helping with photos. All errors are undoubtedly mine.

Rather than writing this book despite teaching full time at the Madeira School, I wrote this book because of teaching full time at the Madeira School. My students have taught me what's engaging, what's important, and what's not. Some of my twelfth graders from the class of 2024 read a draft of chapter eleven, and others listened to a test run of the introduction before I wrote it. Proximity to my colleagues has made me a better educator, person, thinker, and writer. Thank you to my History Department colleagues Nacola Smith, Larry Pratt, Shields Sundberg, Andy Lehto, Emily Dowd, and Lucy Pollard. Shout-out to Karen Joostema for inquiring about my writing often. Thanks to my breakfast table, Paul Bednarowski, Chelsea Land, Matt Goldman, Jeff Dayton, and whoever else has joined us; we're an inclusive bunch, and I don't know how I got so lucky to start five days a week with you.

In fall 2023, I was racing toward my December 1st manuscript deadline while teaching full time at Madeira and part time at American University. My therapist, Amanda, made balancing these competing demands possible. My outstanding American University Teaching Assistant, Henry Dickmeyer, helped significantly. Rebecca Erbelding provided three guest lecturers to my classes during that stretch, brightening my days, lightening my load, and generously sharing historical anecdotes in the process. For example, I first learned about the original verse of "God Bless America," which I mention in the introduction, during one of Becky's visits. I drafted the After-word on Thanksgiving 2023, in the good company of Andrea Brenner, Rick Brenner, Talia Brenner, and Nathan Schultz.

I'm grateful to Kensington for providing an ideal home for *Dear Miss Perkins* at the Citadel imprint. Endless thanks to my editor James Abbate, publicist Ann Pryor, publisher Jackie Dinas, cover designer Kristine Noble, and copy editor Sheila Higgins. *Dear Miss Perkins* began as an undergraduate thesis, it was refined through doctoral training, and it's told to you by a high school teacher.

It's dedicated to my husband, Brandon Graham. In 2015, Brandon dragged my suitcase full of library books around New York City while I was writing my thesis. He brought me Skittles from the Mount Holyoke library café and sat at the edge of my carrel to help me focus. Fast-forward nearly a decade, and Brandon was the first reader for each chapter, providing invaluable editing and commentary. "Nice try," he joked in the margin, removing a detail about the proxim-ity of the L.L.Bean flagship store to the Frances Perkins Center in chapter thirteen. By the end, I was literally writing for Brandon.

Notes

Introduction

1. Kate Smith, "God Bless America" (composed by Irving Berlin), first radio performance, Armistice Day (10 November 1938), Accessed via YouTube, https://www.youtube.com/watch?v=b1rKQ ReqJZg&list=LL&index=3.
2. Letter from Walter Campbell to Katherine Lenroot (28 May 1939) Children's Bureau, RG 102, Box 672, U.S. National Archives, College Park, MD.
3. Moffat Diary (20 April 1933) Moffat Papers, Harvard University, Quoted in Alan M. Kraut, Richard Breitman, and Thomas W. Imhoof, "The State Department, the Labor Department, and German Jewish Immigration, 1930-1940," *Journal of American Ethnic History* Vol. 3 No. 2 (Spring 1984) 9; Barbara McDonald Stewart, *United States Government Policy on Refugees from Nazism, 1933–1940* (Garland Publishing, 1982) 55; Frances Perkins, Letter to an unclear recipient (1938) RG 174, U.S. National Archives, College Park, MD.

Chapter One: Becoming Frances Perkins

1. For Perkins's birthplace, Birth #5896 (1880) Massachusetts Births, Vol. 315, p. 132, New England Historic Genealogical Society; William S. Kelley, "Birthplace of Frances Perkins," Unpublished Report (May 2011); William S. Kelley, "Chronology of the Abner

Perkins Farm, 1630-2021," Unpublished Report. For Perkins's ancestors at the onset of the Seven Years' War in Maine, Rev. David Quimby Cushman, *The History of Ancient Sheepscot and Newcastle, Including Early Pemaquid, Damariscotta and Other Contiguous Places, from the Earliest Discovery to the Present Time; Together with the Genealogy of More than Four Hundred Families* (Bath, ME: E. Upton & Son, 1882) 410-413.

2. Marion Fitch Connell, Conversation with the author (July 2016) Washington, D.C.

3. Frances Perkins, Quoted in John Louis Recchiuti, *Civic Engagement: Social Science and Progressive-Era Reform in New York City* (The University of Pennsylvania Press, 2006) 137.

4. Penny Colman, *A Woman Unafraid: The Achievements of Frances Perkins* (New York: MacMillan, 1993) 7.

5. Frances Perkins, *The Roosevelt I Knew*, Originally Published 1946 (New York: Penguin Classics, 2011) 12.

6. David Brooks, *The Road to Character* (New York: Random House, 2015) 34.

7. Michelle L. Kew, "Frances Perkins: Private Faith, Public Policy," Frances Perkins Center website (Accessed 31 May 2022), 4, https://francesperkinscenter.org/wp-content/uploads/2022/08/Frances-Perkins-Private-Faith-Public-Policy-by-Michelle-Kew.pdf.

8. Perkins, *The Roosevelt I Knew*, 10.

9. George Martin, *Madam Secretary: Frances Perkins* (Boston: Houghton Mifflin Company, 1976) 61.

10. Brooks, *The Road to Character*, 16.

11. Brooks, *The Road to Character*, 17.

12. Tony Michels, "Uprising of 20,000 (1909)," *Jewish Women's Archive* (Accessed 11 June 2022), https://jwa.org/encyclopedia/article/uprising-of-20000-1909.

13. Kirstin Downey, *The Woman Behind the New Deal: The Life and Legacy of Frances Perkins—Social Security, Unemployment Insurance, and the Minimum Wage* (New York: Random House, 2009) 54-60.

14. Downey, 27.

15. Letter from Frances Perkins to Mrs. Marshall Wilson (1913) Family Correspondence, Frances Perkins Papers, Columbia University Library, Quoted in Downey, 58.

16. Downey, 62.

17. Frances Perkins, "Lots of fun!" Fourth letter of the Class of 1902, Mount Holyoke College, Special Collections, South Hadley, MA, Quoted in Downey, 61.

18. For Susanna and Paul Wilson's struggles with bipolar disorder, see Downey, 72-73, 247. For Charles Wyzanski's struggles with bipolar disorder, see Ron Chernow, *The Warburgs: The Twentieth Century Odyssey of a Remarkable Jewish Family* (New York: Random House, 1993) 519.

19. Susanna Wilson Coggeshall, interviewed by Kirstin Downey (early 2000s), Quoted in Downey, 73.

20. Quoted in Martin, 136.

21. Quoted in Downey, 83.

22. Downey, 82-83.

23. Downey, 84.

24. Perkins, *The Roosevelt I Knew*, 11.

25. Quoted in Perkins, *The Roosevelt I Knew*, 12.

26. Perkins, *The Roosevelt I Knew*, 20-29.

27. Perkins, *The Roosevelt I Knew*, 21.

28. Quoted in Martin, 16.

29. Ibid.

30. Quoted in Martin, 17.

Chapter Two: Becoming
American Immigration Law

1. Nicholas T. Pruitt, *Open Hearts, Closed Doors: Immigration Reform and the Waning of Mainline Protestantism* (New York University Press, 2021) 13.

2. U.S. Reports: *Chy Lung v. Freeman et al.*, 92 U.S. 275 (1875), Library of Congress. For the president as immigration policymaker-in-chief, see Adam B. Cox and Cristina Rodriguez, *The President and Immigration Law* (Oxford University Press, 2020).

3. Roxanne Dunbar-Ortiz, *Not A Nation of Immigrants: Settler Colonialism, White Supremacy, and a History of Erasure and Exclusion* (Boston: Beacon Press, 2021) xxi-xxii.

4. Dunbar-Ortiz, 190.

5. Mae M. Ngai, *Impossible Subjects: Illegal Aliens and the Making of Modern America* (Princeton University Press, 2005) 58.

6. Dunbar-Ortiz, xxi-xxii.

7. Dunbar-Ortiz, 4.
8. Erika Lee, "Immigration," *Myth America: Historians Take on the Biggest Legends and Lies About Our Past,* edited by Kevin M. Kruse and Julian E. Zelizer (New York: Basic Books, 2022) 58-59.
9. Quoted in Lorraine Boissonealt, "How the 19th-Century Know Nothing Party Reshaped American Politics," *Smithsonian Magazine* (26 January 2017).
10. Shari Rabin, *Jews on the Frontier: Religion and Mobility in Nineteenth-Century America* (New York University Press, 2017).
11. "14th Amendment to the U.S. Constitution: Civil Rights (1868)," U.S. National Archives.
12. Dunbar-Ortiz, xix, 191.
13. The Chinese Exclusion Act of 1882 (6 May 1882) Library of Congress; Erika Lee, "'The Chinese Must Go!': The Anti-Chinese Movement," *The Making of Asian America: A History* (New York: Simon & Schuster, 2015) 89-108.
14. Erika Lee, "Chinese Immigrants in Search of Gold Mountain," *The Making of Asian America: A History* (New York: Simon & Schuster, 2015) 59-88.
15. Lee, *The Making of Asian America,* 72.
16. Dunbar-Ortiz, 189.
17. Dunbar-Ortiz, 186.
18. Lee, 94.
19. Ngai, xxiv; For U.S. immigration policy from the American Revolution through Reconstruction, see Kevin Kenny, *The Problem of Immigration in a Slaveholding Republic: Policing Mobility in the 19th-Century United States* (Oxford University Press, 2023).
20. Ngai, xx.
21. Emma Lazarus, "The New Colossus" (1873) *Selected Poems and Other Writings* (Broadview Press, 2002).
22. Dunbar-Ortiz, 162.
23. Immigration Act of 1917, 39 Stat. 874 (1917); For immigration officials coupling the public charge provision with other immigration provisions to deport newcomers, see Deirdre Moloney, *National Insecurities, Immigrations, and U.S. Deportation Policy Since 1882* (The University of North Carolina Press, 2012).
24. Ibid.

25. Immigration Act of 1924, Proclamation by the President of the United States, no. 1872 (22 March 1929) 46 Stat. 2984, Quoted in Ngai, 29.

26. Ngai, 31.

27. Calvin Coolidge, quoted in Dunbar-Ortiz, 191.

28. Ngai, 49.

29. Ngai, 57.

30. Ngai, 37; For more on deportation, see Adam Goodman, *Deportation Machine: America's Long History of Expelling Immigrants* (Princeton University Press, 2020).

31. Ngai, 26.

32. Ngai, 35.

33. Ngai, 68; For the INS on the US-Mexico border, see S. Deborah Kang, *Making Immigration Law on the US-Mexico Border, 1917-1954* (Oxford University Press, 2017).

34. Ngai, 3.

35. Neil V. Hernandez, "Labor Secretary Frances Perkins Reorganizes Her Department's Enforcement Functions, 1933-1940: 'Going Against the Grain,'" *Journal of Policy History*, Vol. 35, No. 1 (2023) 42.

36. Hernandez, 42.

37. Hernandez, 38.

38. Hernandez, 39; Daniel W. MacCormack, *The Spirit of the Service* (Washington, D.C.: Government Printing Office, 1934) 4.

39. Hernandez, 44-45.

40. Ngai, 84.

41. Frances Perkins, "Address Before the Commonwealth Club of California: 'Deportations and Aliens'" (19 February 1940), Box 52, Frances Perkins Papers, Columbia University Rare Book & Manuscript Library. Quoted in Hernandez, 39.

42. Daniel W. MacCormack, *The Spirit of the Service* (Washington, DC: Government Printing Office, 1934). Quoted in Ngai, 83.

Chapter Three: Becoming Nazi Germany

1. Johnny Harris, "How Europe Stole Africa (so quickly)," YouTube (Accessed 21 January 2023) https://www.youtube.com/watch?v=LjieOlWXwTw&t=150s.

2. Hannah Arendt, *The Origins of Totalitarianism* (New York: Schocken, 1951).

3. Benedict Anderson, *Imagined Communities: Reflections on the Origin and Spread of Nationalism* (New York: Verso Books, 1983).

4. Samuel R. Williamson, Jr., "The Origins of World War I," *The Journal of Interdisciplinary History* (Spring 1988) Vol. 18, No. 4, pp. 795-818; "Military Technology in World War I," Library of Congress Website (Accessed 15 January 2023) https://www.loc.gov/collections/world-war -i-rotogravures/articles-and-essays/military-technology-in-world-war-i/.

5. Peter Hayes, *Why?: Explaining the Holocaust* (New York: Norton, 2017) 29.

6. Hayes, 29.

7. For recent scholarship on antisemitism, see Deborah E. Lipstadt, *Antisemitism Here and Now* (New York: Schocken Books, 2019); Samantha Vinokor-Meinrath, *#antisemitism: Coming of Age during the Resurgence of Hate* (Santa Barbara, CA: ABC-CLIO, 2022); Ari Kohen and Gerland J. Steinacher, eds., *Antisemitism on the Rise: The 1930s and Today* (The University of Nebraska Press, 2021).

8. Jeremy Noakes and Geoffrey Pridham, eds., *Nazism 1919-1945: A Documentary Reader*, Vol. 1: The Rise to Power 1919-1934 (Liverpool, UK: Liverpool University Press, 1998) 15-16.

9. Hannah Arendt: The Last Interview and Other Conversations (Brooklyn, NY: Melville House, 2013) 14, Quoted in Anne C. Heller, *Hannah Arendt: A Life in Dark Times* (New York: Houghton Mifflin Harcourt, 2015) 48.

10. Benjamin Carter Hett, *The Death of Democracy: Hitler's Rise to Power and the Downfall of the Weimar Republic* (New York: Henry Holt and Company, 2018) 54.

11. Hayes, 61.

12. Hett, 86.

13. Nancy F. Cott, *Fighting Words: The Bold American Journalists Who Brought the World Home Between the Wars* (New York: Basic Books, 2020) 182.

14. Dorothy Thompson, *I Saw Hitler!* (New York: Farrar & Rinehart, 1932).

15. Hayes, 71.

16. Erik Larson, *In the Garden of the Beasts: Love, Terror, and an American Family in Hitler's Berlin* (New York: Random House, 2011) 54.

17. Quoted in Hett, 2.

18. Cott, 189.

19. Larson, 16.

20. Larson, 66-67.

21. Quoted in Larson, 50.

22. Larson, 11-13.

23. James Q. Whitman, *Hitler's American Model: The United States and the Making of Nazi Race Law* (Princeton University Press, 2017) 16.

24. Henny Brenner, *The Song Is Over: Survival of a Jewish Girl in Dresden* (The University of Alabama Press, 2000) xiv.

Chapter Four: Charge Bonds Controversy

1. Franklin D. Roosevelt, First Inaugural Address (1933), Avalon Project, https://avalon.law.yale.edu/20th_century/froos1.asp.

2. "Nazi Mobs Run Wild in the Heart of Vienna: Shouting Crowds Assault Jews," *The New York Times* (29 March 1933); "German Business Protests Boycott," *The New York Times* (31 March 1933).

3. "Nazi Boycott Against Jews Observed in Holiday Style," *The Dallas Morning News* (2 April 1933) Reprint by the United States Holocaust Memorial Museum.

4. George Martin, *Madam Secretary: Frances Perkins* (Boston: Houghton Mifflin Company, 1976), 31-32.

5. For Nazis drawing influence from the U.S., see James Q. Whitman, *Hitler's American Model: The United States and the Making of Nazi Race Law* (Princeton University Press, 2017).

6. David Brooks, "How the First Woman in the U.S. Cabinet Found Her Vocation," *The Atlantic* (14 April 2015).

7. Richard Breitman and Allan Lichtman, *FDR and the Jews* (Harvard University Press, 2013) 69.

8. Richard Breitman and Alan Kraut, *American Refugee Policy and European Jewry, 1933-1945* (Indiana University Press, 1988) 20.

9. Breitman and Lichtman, 69.

10. Immigration Act of 1917, 39 Stat. 874 (1917).

11. Charles Wyzanski, Memorandum to Perkins (10 February 1934) 6, Wyzanski Collection, Massachusetts Historical Society.

12. Letter from Paul C. Fletcher to Hodgdon (8 January 1934) RG 59, NA-WNRC, Quoted in Richard Breitman, Alan Kraut, and Thomas Imhoof, "The State Department and German Jewish Immigration, 1930-1940," *Journal of American Ethnic History* (Spring 1984) Vol. 3, No. 2, 13.

13. Breitman, Kraut, and Imhoof, 6.

14. Downey, 187; Breitman and Kraut, 13.
15. Arthur D. Morse, *While Six Million Died: A Chronicle of American Apathy* (New York: Random House, 1967) 29-33.
16, Breitman and Lichtman, 69.
17. Quoted in Erik Larson, *In the Garden of the Beasts: Love, Terror, and an American Family in Hitler's Berlin* (New York: Random House, 2011), 30.
18. Martin, 19; 23-25.
19. Jay Pierrepont Moffat Diary (20 April 1933) Moffat Papers, Houghton Library, Harvard University, Quoted in Breitman and Kraut, 14.
20. Breitman and Lichtman, 68.
21. Frances Perkins, "Eight Years as Madame Secretary," *Fortune* (September 1941), Quoted in Martin, 21.
22. Martin, 21.
23. Immigration Act of 1917, 39 Stat. 874 (1917).
24. Charles E. Wyzanski, Jr., Memorandum to Perkins on the Admission of Refugees from Germany (10 February 1934) 5, Wyzanski Collection, Massachusetts Historical Society.
25. Louis Adamic, "Aliens and Alien-Baters," *Harper's Monthly Magazine* (November 1936) Accessed in Subject Files of Frances Perkins, RG 174, Box 72, U.S. National Archives, College Park, MD.
26. Julian W. Mack, Confidential Report: Memorandum of Washington Trip (30 October 1933) Wyzanski Collection, Massachusetts Historical Society.
27. Charles E. Wyzanski, Jr., Letter to his mother (22 May 1933) Wyzanski Collection, Massachusetts Historical Society.
28. Quoted in Bat-Ami Zucker, "Frances Perkins and the German-Jewish Refugees, 1933-1940," *American Jewish History* (March 2001) 42.
29. Charles E. Wyzanski, Jr., Letter to his mother (12 January 1934).
30. Charles E. Wyzanski, Jr., Letter to Richard Breitman (12 August 1982) Wyzanski Collection, Massachusetts Historical Society.
31. Charles E. Wyzanski, Jr., "Opinion of the Solicitor of the Labor Department on the Secretary's Right to Accept Bonds Against Likelihood to Become a Public Charge Before Consuls Act on Applications for Visas" (3 November 1933) Vol. 597, 53-65, American Civil Liberties Union Archives, Mudd Library, Princeton University.
32. Homer Stiles Cummings, Letter to Frances Perkins (26 December 1933) U.S. National Archives, College Park, MD.
33. Cummings, 2.

34. Cummings, 4.
35. Charles E. Wyzanski, Jr., Letter to his mother (12 January 1934).
36. Breitman and Kraut, 26.
37. Breitman, Kraut, and Imhoof, 12.
38. Charles E. Wyzanski, Jr., "Immigration and the New Deal" (4 February 1934) 2, Wyzanski Collection, Massachusetts Historical Society.
39. Charles E. Wyzanski, Jr., Letter to his mother (12 January 1934).

Chapter Five: Child Refugees

1. Arthur D. Morse, *While Six Million Died: A Chronicle of American Apathy* (New York: Abrams Press, 1968) 162.
2. Bat-Ami Zucker, *Cecilia Razovsky and the American-Jewish Women's Rescue Operations in the Second World War* (Portland, OR: Vallentine Mitchell, 2008) 31.
3. Zucker, *Cecilia Razovsky*, 31.
4. Zucker, *Cecilia Razovsky*, 31-32.
5. Julia C. Lathrop, First Annual Report of the Children's Bureau (1912-1913), Quoted in U.S. Department of Labor, "The Children's Bureau and Its Relationships with Other Agencies" (October 1939) RG 174, Boxes 17-18, Subject Files of Frances Perkins, U.S. National Archives, College Park, MD; Zucker, *Cecilia Razovsky*, 2.
6. Morse, 161-162.
7. Mary McCune, "Cecilia Razovsky," *The Shalvi/Hyman Encyclopedia of Jewish Women*, Jewish Women's Archive (Accessed 4 May 2023) https://jwa.org/encyclopedia/article/razovsky-cecilia.
8. Zucker, *Cecilia Razovsky*, 13; 1-2.
9. Max Kohler (April 1934) Letter to Frances Perkins, "Affidavits, correspondence and statements of support from various organizations contributing money to the German-Jewish Children's Aid, 1934 May 11-1939 July 22," German-Jewish Children's Aid Records, Folder 21, Reel MKM 8.1 (RG 249) YIVO; Inflation calculator (Accessed 17 June 2023) https://www.usinflationcalculator.com.
10. Letter from Miss Colby to Miss Hanna (18 August 1939) Children's Bureau, RG 102, Box 672, U.S. National Archives, College Park, MD.
11. Immigration Act of 1917, 39 Stat. 874 (1917).
12. Zucker, *Cecilia Razovsky*, 34.

13. Letter from Miss Colby to Miss Hanna (18 August 1939) Children's Bureau, RG 102, Box 672, U.S. National Archives, College Park, MD.

14. Morse, 163; Bat-Ami Zucker, "Frances Perkins and the German-Jewish Refugees, 1933-1940," *American Jewish History* Vol. 89, No. 1 (March 2001) 49.

15. Zucker, *Cecilia Razovsky*, 36.

16. Letter from Miss Colby to Miss Hanna (18 August 1939) Children's Bureau, RG 102, Box 672, U.S. National Archives, College Park, MD.

17. Zucker, *Cecilia Razovsky*, 37.

18. U.S. Department of Labor, "The Children's Bureau and Its Relationships with Other Agencies" (October 1939) RG 174, Boxes 17-18, Subject Files of Frances Perkins, U.S. National Archives, College Park, MD.

19. Ibid.

20. Ibid.

21. For U.S. government coordination on the ground in Berlin, specifically Raymond Geist, see Richard Breitman, *The Berlin Mission: The American Who Resisted Nazi Germany from Within* (New York: Public Affairs, 2019).

22. James L. Houghteling and Katharine F. Lenroot, Letter to Frances Perkins (22 July 1939) "Affidavits, correspondence and statements of support from various organizations contributing money to the German-Jewish Children's Aid, 1934 May 11-1939 July 22," German-Jewish Children's Aid Records, YIVO.

23. Cecilia Razovsky, "Affidavits, correspondence and statements of support from various organizations contributing money to the German-Jewish Children's Aid, 1934 May 11-1939 July 22," German-Jewish Children's Aid Records, YIVO.

24. Pamela S. Nadell, *America's Jewish Women: A History from Colonial Times to Today* (New York: Norton, 2019) 207.

25. Fannie Brinn (March 1934) "Affidavits, correspondence and statements of support from various organizations contributing money to the German-Jewish Children's Aid, 1934 May 11-1939 July 22," German-Jewish Children's Aid Records, Folder 21, Reel MKM 8.1 (RG 249) YIVO.

26. "Nine German-Jewish Boys Taken into American Homes," *Jewish Post* (Patterson, NJ, 15 November 1934).

27. Joseph Eaton, Oral History interview (2010) United States Holocaust Memorial Museum, RG 50.030.0581 (Accessed 4 May 2023) https://collections.ushmm.org/search/catalog/irn41725.
28. Joseph Eaton, Oral History interview (2010) United States Holocaust Memorial Museum, RG 50.030.0581.
29. Joseph Eaton, Oral History interview (2010) United States Holocaust Memorial Museum, RG 50.030.0581.
30. "Correspondence and cables, 1934-1935," German-Jewish Children's Aid Records, Folder 490, Reel MKM 8.28 (RG 249) YIVO.
31. Zucker, *Cecilia Razovsky*, 39.
32. Joseph Eaton, Oral History interview (2010) United States Holocaust Memorial Museum, RG 50.030.0581.
33. Joseph Eaton, Oral History interview; "Joseph Eaton was professor of social work, committed Zionist," *Pittsburgh Jewish Chronicle* (16 October 2012).
34. Letter to Mr. F. Maybaum, General Passenger Agent, United States Lines, New York City (On board SS *Manhattan*, November 27, 1934); Thank you notes received by Lotte Marcuse and Cecilia Razovsky of the German-Jewish Children's Aid, 1934 November 6-1938 July 11, German-Jewish Children's Aid Records, Folder 102, Reel MKM 8.6 (RG 249) YIVO.
35. Thank you notes received by Lotte Marcuse and Cecilia Razovsky of the German-Jewish Children's Aid, 1934 November 6-1938 July 11, German-Jewish Children's Aid Records, Folder 102, Reel MKM 8.6 (RG 249) YIVO; "Correspondence and cables, 1934-1935," German-Jewish Children's Aid Records, Folder 490, Reel MKM 8.28 (RG 249) YIVO; Martin Meyer, Letter to Cecilia Razovsky (July 1939); Thank you notes received by Lotte Marcuse and Cecilia Razovsky of the German-Jewish Children's Aid, 1934 November 6-1938 July 11, German-Jewish Children's Aid Records, Folder 102, Reel MKM 8.6 (RG 249) YIVO.
36. Letter from Miss Colby to Miss Hanna (18 August 1939) Children's Bureau, RG 102, Box 672, U.S. National Archives, College Park, MD.
37. "Daniel MacCormack Dead in Capital; Head of Immigration and Naturalization Service Since March of 1933," *The New York Times* (1 January 1937).
38. "Correspondence and cables, 1934-1935," German-Jewish Children's Aid Records, Folder 490, Reel MKM 8.28 (RG 249) YIVO.

39. Richard Breitman and Alan Kraut, *American Refugee Policy and European Jewry, 1933-1945* (Bloomington, IN: Indiana University Press, 1987), 66; Barbara McDonald Stewart, *United States Government Policy on Refugees from Nazism, 1933-1940* (Garland Pub., 1982), 411-412; quoted in Neil V. Hernandez, "Labor Secretary Frances Perkins Reorganizes Her Department's Enforcement Functions, 1933-1940: 'Going Against the Grain,'" *Journal of Policy History*, Vol. 35, No. 1 (2023), 51.

40. Jay Pierrepont Moffat, Diary Entry (25 May 1939), Quoted in Rafael Medoff, "The Wagner-Rogers Bill to Save Children," *America and the Holocaust: A Documentary History* (The University of Nebraska Press, 2022) 103.

41. Anthony Read and David Fisher, *Kristallnacht: The Nazi Night of Terror* (New York: Random House, 1989) 68-69.

42. Morse, 253.

43. Clarence E. Pickett, Diary Entry (10 January 1939) Clarence E. Pickett Diary, American Friends Service Committee (AFSC) Archives (Philadelphia, PA).

44. Morse, 258; Statement from John Brophy, National Director of the Congress of Industrial Organizations (CIO), Wagner-Rogers Bill (S. J. Resolution 64) *Congressional Record* 84: 13 (24 May 1939) 91-92; "Wagner-Rogers Bill," *Holocaust Encyclopedia*, United States Holocaust Memorial Museum.

45. Morse, 259-261.

46. John Thomas Taylor (1939), Quoted in Morse, 259-260; Mrs. Agnes (1939), Quoted in Morse, 260.

47. "Refugee Children" News Clipping (1939) Children's Bureau, RG 102, Box 672, U.S. National Archives, College Park, MD; "Admission of German Refugee Children," *Joint Hearings*, 76th Congress 1st session, quoted in David Wyman, *Paper Walls: America and the Refugee Crisis, 1938-1941* (University of Massachusetts Press, 1968), 80.

48. Letter from H. J. Owen to Katherine Lenroot (7 June 1939) Children's Bureau, RG 102, Box 672, U.S. National Archives, College Park, MD; Letter from Walter Campbell to Katherine Lenroot (28 May 1939) Children's Bureau, RG 102, Box 672, U.S. National Archives, College Park, MD.

49. Robert R. Reynolds, "Our Country—Our Citizens First—Extension of Remarks," Wagner-Rogers Bill (SJ Resolution 64) *Congressional Record* 84: 13 (24 May 1939) 2424-2425.

50. David Wyman, *Paper Walls: America and the Refugee Crisis, 1938-1941* (Amherst, MA: The University of Massachusetts Press, 1968) 94-96.

51. Press Release, "'Suffer Little Children': Special Broadcast to Dramatize Plight of Child Refugees on Nationwide Hook-up" (25 June 1939) Children's Bureau, RG 102, Box 672, U.S. National Archives, College Park, MD.

52. Morse, 268; Robert Wagner (1939), Quoted in Morse, 259.

53. James Houghteling and Katherine Lenroot, Memorandum to Frances Perkins (22 July 1939) Children's Bureau, RG 102, U.S. National Archives, College Park, MD.

54. Eleanor Roosevelt, Quoted in Morse, 255.

55. John B. Trevor, President of the American Coalition, Statement on the Wagner-Rogers Bill (S. J. Resolution 64) *Congressional Record* 84: 13 (24 May 1939) 213-215.

56. Joseph Eaton, Oral History interview; Nadell, 206.

Chapter Six: Resolution to
Impeach Frances Perkins

1. "Harry Bridges," ILWU Local 142 Website (Accessed 23 March 2023) https://ilwulocal142.org/blog/harry-bridges/; Kim Kelly, *Fight Like Hell: The Untold History of American Labor* (New York: Simon & Schuster, 2022) 178-179.

2. Harry Bridges, Interview (1984), Quoted in "Harry Bridges," ILWU Local 142 Website (Accessed 23 March 2023) https://ilwu local142.org/blog/harry-bridges/.

3. Robert Justin Goldstein, *Political Repression in Modern America from 1870 to 1976* (The University of Illinois Press, 2001); Robert Justin Goldstein, ed., *Little 'Red Scares': Anti-Communism and Political Repression in the United States, 1921-1946* (Ashgate Publishing, 2014).

4. Neil V. Hernandez, "Labor Secretary Frances Perkins Reorganizes Her Department's Immigration Enforcement Functions, 1933-1940: 'Going Against the Grain,'" *Journal of Policy History*, Vol. 35, No. 1 (2023) 41.

5. U.S. Constitution, Quoted in J. Parnell Thomas, Resolution to Impeach Frances Perkins, 76th Congress, 1st Session (January 1939) Frances Perkins Papers, Box 51, Columbia University Rare Books & Manuscript Library.

6. J. Parnell Thomas, Resolution to Impeach Frances Perkins, 76th Congress, 1st Session (January 1939) Frances Perkins Papers, Box 51, Columbia University Rare Books & Manuscript Library.

7. Kirstin Downey, *The Woman Behind the New Deal: The Life and Legacy of Frances Perkins—Social Security, Unemployment Insurance, and the Minimum Wage* (New York: Random House, 2009) 276.

8. "DIES, Martin Jr., 1900-1972," History, Art & Archives, U.S. House of Representatives (Accessed 2 April 2023) https://history.house.gov/People/Listing/D/DIES,-Martin,-Jr—(D000338)/.

9. Elisabeth Griffith, *Formidable: American Women and the Fight for Equality, 1920-2020* (New York: Pegasus, 2022) 72.

10. Mary T. Norton, "The Case of Harry Bridges Speech," *Congressional Record* (January 1939) Proceedings and Debates of the 76th Congress, First Session, Frances Perkins Papers, Box 51, Columbia University Rare Books & Manuscript Library.

11. Mary T. Norton, *Congressional Record* (January 1939) Proceedings and Debates of the 76th Congress, First Session, Frances Perkins Papers, Box 51, Columbia University Rare Books & Manuscript Library.

12. Frances Perkins, Written Statement to Congress (21 January 1939) *Congressional Record* (January 1939) Proceedings and Debates of the 76th Congress, First Session, Frances Perkins Papers, Box 51, Columbia University Rare Books & Manuscript Library.

13. *Kessler, District Director of Immigration and Naturalization, v. Strecker,* 307 U.S. 22, 59 S. Ct. 694, 83 L. Ed. 1082 (1939).

14. Perkins, Written Statement to Congress (21 January 1939).

15. Ibid.

16. U.S. Congress, National Labor Relations Act (July 1935) U.S. National Archives Milestone Documents (Accessed 8 June 2023) https://www.archives.gov/milestone-documents/national-labor-relations-act.

17. Perkins, Written Statement to Congress (21 January 1939).

18. George Martin, *Madam Secretary, Frances Perkins: A Biography of America's First Woman Cabinet Member* (Boston, MA: Houghton Mifflin Company, 1976) 16; Downey, 62.

19. Letter to Frances Perkins (1938-1939) Box 79, Frances Perkins Papers, Columbia University Rare Book & Manuscript Library.

20. Ibid.

21. Letter to Frances Perkins (2 February 1940) Box 79, Frances Perkins Papers, Columbia University Rare Book & Manuscript Library.

22. Letter from Frances Perkins to Mrs. W. MacMillan (1 April 1936) Box 5, Lowell Mellet Papers, Franklin D. Roosevelt Presidential Library, Hyde Park, NY.

23. Letter to Frances Perkins (27 April 1938) Box 79, Frances Perkins Papers, Columbia University Rare Book & Manuscript Library.

24. Letter to Frances Perkins (5 December 1938) Box 79, Frances Perkins Papers, Columbia University Rare Book & Manuscript Library.

25. Downey, 280-281.

26. Quoted in Downey, 281.

27. Frances Perkins, Statement before the House Judiciary Committee in reply to House Resolution 67, Impeachment of Frances Perkins, Transcript, fourth draft, with her autograph corrections, Washington (8 February 1939) Box 51, Frances Perkins Papers, Columbia University Rare Book & Manuscript Library.

28. Perkins, Statement before the House Judiciary Committee in reply to House Resolution 67.

29. Ibid.

30. Ibid.

31. Ibid.

32. Ibid.

33. Ibid.

34. Ibid.

35. Ibid.

36. Ibid.

37. "Dismissal of Impeachment Proceedings Against Frances Perkins, Secretary of Labor," Speech of Hon. John A. Martin of Colorado (3 April 1939) U.S. House of Representatives, *Congressional Record* (U.S. Government Printing Office Washington: 1939) Box 51, Frances Perkins Papers, Columbia University Rare Book & Manuscript Library.

38. Frances Perkins, Unsent note to Congressman Martin Dies (August 1939) Box 51, Frances Perkins Papers, Columbia University Rare Book & Manuscript Library.

39. Ibid.

Chapter Seven: Dear Miss Perkins

1. Subject Files of Frances Perkins, RG 174, Boxes 66-73, U.S. National Archives, College Park, MD.

2. David Wyman, *Paper Walls: America and the Refugee Crisis, 1938-1941* (Amherst, MA: The University of Massachusetts Press, 1968) 71-72.

3. Richard Breitman and Alan Kraut, *American Refugee Policy and European Jewry, 1933-1945* (Bloomington, IN: Indiana University Press, 1987) 66.

4. Franklin D. Roosevelt, Press Conference (18 November 1938); *Franklin D. Roosevelt and Foreign Affairs* (September 1938– November 1938) Vol. 7, Ed. Donald B. Schewe (New York: Garland Publishing, 1979), Quoted in Bat-Ami Zucker, *In Search of Refuge: Jews and US Consuls in Nazi Germany, 1933-1941* (Portland, OR: Vallentine Mitchell, 2001) 127-128.

5. Ibid.

6. Neil V. Hernandez, "Labor Secretary Frances Perkins Reorganizes Her Department's Immigration Enforcement Functions, 1933-1940: 'Going Against the Grain,'" *Journal of Policy History*, Vol. 35, No. 1 (2023) 48.

7. Kirstin Downey, *The Woman Behind the New Deal: The Life and Legacy of Frances Perkins—Social Security, Unemployment Insurance, and the Minimum Wage* (New York: Random House, 2009) 13.

8. Letter from Eugene Weissmann to Frances Perkins (14 October 1938) RG 174, Box 70, Subject Files of Frances Perkins, U.S. National Archives, College Park, MD.

9. Ibid.

10. Immigration Act of 1924, Proclamation by the President of the United States, No. 1872 (22 March 1929) 46 Stat. 2984, Quoted in Ngai, 29.

11. Letter from Eugene Weissmann to Frances Perkins (14 October 1938) RG 174, Box 70, Subject Files of Frances Perkins, U.S. National Archives, College Park, MD.

12. Letter from Frances Perkins to Eugene Weissmann (20 October 1938) RG 174, Box 70, Subject Files of Frances Perkins, U.S. National Archives, College Park, MD.

13. Ibid.

14. Ibid.

15. Ancestry.com, ITS Archives, document no. 48502421#1; *Persons Naturalized or Granted Citizenship in New Zealand, 1843-1981*, Microfiche 1-34, 34 rolls, BAB Microfilming (Auckland, New Zealand) Accessed through Ancestry.com, *New Zealand, Naturalizations, 1943- 1981*, Online (Provo, UT: Ancestry.com Operations, 2010).

16. Rabbi Stephen Wise, American Jewish Congress, Letter to Frances Perkins (1 November 1938) RG 174, Boxes 69-70, Subject Files of Frances Perkins, U.S. National Archives, College Park, MD.

17. Frances Perkins, Letter to Rabbi Stephen Wise (4 November 1938) RG 174, Boxes 66-73, Subject Files of Frances Perkins, U.S. National Archives, College Park, MD.

18. Henriette B. Randegg, Letter to Frances Perkins (1939) RG 174, Box 69, Subject Files of Frances Perkins, U.S. National Archives, College Park, MD.

19. Ibid.

20. Martha Ackelsberg, "Angelica Balabanoff," *Jewish Women's Archive* (Accessed 7 May 2022) https://jwa.org/encyclopedia/article/balabanoff-angelica.

21. Letter from James L. Houghteling to Frances Perkins (7 August 1939) RG 174, Box 69, Subject Files of Frances Perkins, U.S. National Archives, College Park, MD.

22. Letter from Perkins to Congressman Adolph J. Sabath (19 August 1939) RG 174, Box 69, Subject Files of Frances Perkins, U.S. National Archives, College Park, MD.

23. Letter from James L. Houghteling to Frances Perkins (7 August 1939) RG 174, Box 69, Subject Files of Frances Perkins, U.S. National Archives, College Park, MD.

24. Florence Harriman, Letter to Frances Perkins (May 1939) RG 174, Boxes 66-73, U.S. National Archives, College Park, MD.

25. Frances Perkins, Letter to Florence Harriman (12 May 1939) RG 174, Boxes 66-73, U.S. National Archives, College Park, MD.

26. Florence Harriman, Letter to Frances Perkins (6 June 1939) RG 174, Boxes 66-73, U.S. National Archives, College Park, MD.

27. Frances Perkins, Letter to Florence Harriman (21 June 1939) RG 174, Boxes 66-73, U.S. National Archives, College Park, MD.

28. Frances Perkins, Letter to an unclear recipient, RG 174, Boxes 66-73, U.S. National Archives, College Park, MD.

29. Ibid.

30. Dorothy Thompson, Telegram to Frances Perkins (19 June 1939) Box 67, U.S. National Archives, College Park, MD.

31. Ibid.

32. Frances Perkins, Letter to Dorothy Thompson (20 June 1939) Box 67, U.S. National Archives, College Park, MD.

33. Ibid.

34. Felix Weinheber, Letter to Dorothy Thompson (11 April 1940) Box 67, U.S. National Archives, College Park, MD.

35. "Declaration of Intention Number 107818" (7 May 1946) Immigration and Naturalization Service, Los Angeles, CA, Accessed via Ancestry; "Petition for Naturalization Number 128815" (14 June 1946) Immigration and Naturalization Service, Los Angeles, CA, Accessed via Ancestry; "Petition for Naturalization Number 129907" (8 November 1946) Immigration and Naturalization Service, Los Angeles, CA, Accessed via Ancestry; "Felix Wayne (1896-1975)," IMDB (Accessed 21 June 2023) https://www.imdb.com/name/nm1033576/.

36. Immigration Act of 1917, 39 Stat. 874 (1917); Charlotte Carr, Letter to Frances Perkins (22 January 1940) RG 174, Box 67, U.S. National Archives, College Park, MD.

37. Frances Perkins, Letter to Charlotte Carr (27 January 1940) RG 174, Box 67, U.S. National Archives, College Park, MD.

38. Harvey O'Connor, Letter to Frances Perkins (9 February 1940) RG 174, Box 67, U.S. National Archives, College Park, MD.

39. Charlotte Carr, Letter to Frances Perkins (29 February 1940) RG 174, Box 67, U.S. National Archives, College Park, MD.

40. Charlotte Carr, Letter to Frances Perkins (4 March 1940) RG 174, Box 67, U.S. National Archives, College Park, MD.

41. Elisabeth Bigelow, Letter to Frances Perkins (23 April 1940) RG 174, Box 66, U.S. National Archives, College Park, MD.

42. Ibid.

43. Ibid.

44. Edward J. Shaughnessy, Memorandum to Miss Jay (8 May 1940) RG 174, Box 66, U.S. National Archives, College Park, MD.

45. Ibid.

46. "Bertolt Brecht," *Holocaust Encyclopedia*, United States Holocaust Memorial Museum.

47. Hamilton Fish Armstrong, Letter to Frances Perkins (17 April 1940) RG 174, Box 67, U.S. National Archives, College Park, MD; For Hamilton Fish's imperialism during the Grant administration, see Thomas Bender, *A Nation Among Nations: America's Place in World History* (New York: Farrar, Straus and Giroux, 2006) 203.

48. Thomas Mann, Oscar Maria Graf, and Curt Riess, Telegram to Frances Perkins (19 April 1940) RG 174, Box 67, U.S. National Archives, College Park, MD.

49. Hamilton Fish Armstrong, Letter to Frances Perkins (24 April 1940) RG 174, Box 67, U.S. National Archives, College Park, MD.

50. James L. Houghteling, Memorandum to Frances Perkins (16 May 1940) RG 174, Box 66, U.S. National Archives, College Park, MD.

51. James L. Houghteling, Letter to Senator James H. Hughes (28 February 1940) RG 174, Box 66, U.S. National Archives, College Park, MD.

52. Subject Files of Frances Perkins, RG 174, Boxes 66-73, U.S. National Archives, College Park, MD; "Which Is Acceptable: 'Undocumented' vs. 'Illegal' Immigrant?" (7 January 2010) *NPR*.

53. Subject Files of Frances Perkins, RG 174, Boxes 66-73, U.S. National Archives, College Park, MD.

Chapter Eight: Alaska

1. Richard Breitman and Allan Lichtman, *FDR and the Jews* (Harvard University Press, 2013) 159.

2. Daniel Sharfstein, "The Namesake of Howard University Spent Years Kicking Native Americans Off of Their Land," *Smithsonian Magazine* (23 May 2017).

3. Daniel Immerwahr, *How to Hide an Empire: A History of the Greater United States* (New York: Picador, 2019) 8-9.

4. Ted Morgan, *The Wilderness at Dawn: The Settling of the North American Continent* (New York: Simon & Schuster, 1993) 23.

5. Morgan, 23.

6. Angie Debo, *A History of the Indians of the United States* (Norman, OK: The University of Oklahoma Press, 1970) 12-18.

7. Ned Blackhawk, *The Rediscovery of America: Native Peoples and the Unmaking of U.S. History* (Yale University Press, 2023) 262.

8. Immerwahr, 168.

9. Debo, 384-385.

10. Immerwahr, 183.

11. Immerwahr, 168-171.

12. Debo, 386.

13. David Wyman, *Paper Walls: America and the Refugee Crisis, 1938-1941* (Amherst, MA: The University of Massachusetts Press, 1968) 98.

14. "Aged Bishop Tells of Alaskan Tragedy," *The New York Times* (24 March 1933); Rev. Rt. Antonin, Letter to Frances Perkins (25 January 1935) U.S. Office of Territories Records Re: Settlement of Eu-

ropean Refugees in Alaska (1907-1951) RG 126, Archives, Alaska and Polar Regions Department, Rasmuson Library, The University of Alaska, Fairbanks, AK.

15. Rev. Rt. Antonin, Letter to Frances Perkins (25 January 1935), U.S. Office of Territories Records Re: Settlement of European Refugees in Alaska (1907-1951), RG 126, Archives, Alaska and Polar Regions Department, Rasmuson Library, University of Alaska, Fairbanks, AK.

16. Ibid.

17. Letter from Frances Perkins to Harold Ickes (7 February 1935), U.S. Office of Territories Records Re: Settlement of European Refugees in Alaska (1907-1951), RG 126, Archives, Alaska and Polar Regions Department, Rasmuson Library, University of Alaska, Fairbanks, AK; Letter from Frances Perkins to Harold Ickes (3 December 1938), RG 174, U.S. National Archives, College Park, MD.

18. "The United States of America, Alaska—Memorandums, Correspondence, and Minutes" (1938-1939) Organizational Correspondence, Subseries 9: President's Advisory Committee on Political Refugees (PAC) of the Joseph Perkins Chamberlain Papers, RG 278, Folder 80, YIVO.

19. Wyman, 99.

20. Derek Leebaert, *Unlikely Heroes: Franklin Roosevelt, His Four Lieutenants, and the World They Made* (New York: St. Martin's Press, 2023) 2; Harold Ickes, *The Autobiography of a Curmudgeon* (Westport, CT: Greenwood Press, 1985).

21. Leebaert, 59, 85.

22. Letter from Frances Perkins to Harold Ickes (3 December 1938) RG 174, U.S. National Archives, College Park, MD.

23. Confidential Memorandum of Meeting in the Office of Dr. Isador Lubin (14 January 1939) Joseph Chamberlain Papers, RG 278, Folder 80, Reel 4, YIVO.

24. Ibid.

25. Ibid.

26. Immerwahr, 168.

27. For Jewish refugees in Siberia, see Eliyana R. Adler, *Survival on the Margins: Polish Jewish Refugees in the Wartime Soviet Union* (Harvard University Press, 2020); Glenn C. Altschuler, "Deciding Life or Death: Polish Jews and the Wartime Soviet Union Dilemma," *The Jerusalem Post* (11 March 2021); "'Sad and Absurd': The U.S.S.R.'s Disastrous Effort to Create a Jewish Homeland," *NPR* (7 September 2016).

28. Breitman and Lichtman, 159.

29. Wyman, 102.

30. Ernest Gruening, Letter to Seth T. Gano, Treasurer of the Commission for Service in Czechoslovakia (21 October 1939) Martha and Waitstill Sharp Collection (1905-2005) Series I Correspondence, Reports, Notes, Box 8, Folder 65, United States Holocaust Memorial Museum.

31. Letter from Seth T. Gano to Rev. Waitstill S. Sharp, Martha and Waitstill Sharp Collection (1905-2005) Series I Correspondence, Reports, Notes, Box 2, Folder 9, United States Holocaust Memorial Museum.

32. Wyman, 101.

33. Letter from Seth T. Gano to Rev. Waitstill S. Sharp, Martha and Waitstill Sharp Collection (1905-2005) Series I Correspondence, Reports, Notes, Box 2, Folder 9, United States Holocaust Memorial Museum; Wyman, 105; *Alaska Weekly*, Quoted in Wyman, 106.

34. United Fishermen's Union, Sound Fishermen's Union, and Alaska Fishermen's Union, "Resolution on the Political Exiles of Germany" (1939) RG 174, U.S. National Archives, College Park, MD.

35. Alaska Fishermen's Union, Alaska Fishermen's Union Records (1919-1917) Museum of History & Industry, Seattle, Washington, https://archiveswest.orbiscascade.org/ark:/80444/xv36605/.

36. United Fishermen's Union, Sound Fishermen's Union, and Alaska Fishermen's Union, "Resolution on the Political Exiles of Germany" (1939) RG 174, U.S. National Archives, College Park, MD.

37. Bruno Rosenthal, Quoted in Gerald S. Berman, "From Neustadt to Alaska, 1939: A Failed Attempt of Community Resettlement," *Historical Studies in Ethnicity, Migration and Diaspora* Vol. 6 (1987) 75. For Jewish refugees in Neustadt, see Mitchell, 148-150.

38. Dalia Tsuk Mitchell, "First Americans, Misfits, and Refugees," *Architect of Justice: Felix S. Cohen and the Founding of American Legal Pluralism* (Cornell University Press, 2007) 148.

39. Wyman, 103-104.

40. Harold Ickes, Quoted in Wyman, 107.

41. Anthony J. Dimond, Quoted in Hannah L. Mitson, "The King-Havenner Bill of 1940: Dashed Hopes for a Jewish Immigration Haven in Alaska," *Alaska History* Vol. 14 (1999); Hannah L. Mitson, "The King-Havenner Bill of 1940: Dashed Hopes for a Jewish Immigration Haven in Alaska," *Alaska History* Vol. 14 (1999).

42. Mitchell, 151.

43. Wyman, 111.

44. Michael Chabon, *The Yiddish Policemen's Union* (New York: Harper Perennial, 2007) 28-29.

Chapter 9: The Transfer of the INS from the Labor Department to the Justice Department

1. Robert Houghwout Jackson, *Reminiscences of Robert Houghwout Jackson* (1952) 1006-1008, Quoted in Kirstin Downey, *The Woman Behind the New Deal: The Life and Legacy of Frances Perkins—Social Security, Unemployment Insurance, and the Minimum Wage* (New York: Random House, 2009) 295.

2. Neil V. Hernandez, "Labor Secretary Frances Perkins Reorganizes Her Department's Enforcement Functions, 1933-1940: 'Going Against the Grain,'" *Journal of Policy History*, Vol. 35, No. 1 (2023) 52.

3. Reorganization Plan No. III of 1940, Eff. 30 June 1940, 5 F.R. 2107, 54 Stat. 1231 by Act 4 June 1940 Ch. 231, 4, 54 Stat. 231 (Accessed 22 July 2023) https://uscode.house.gov/view.xhtml?req=granuleid: USC-1999-title5a-node78-leaf82&num=0&edition=1999.

4. Frances Perkins, "The Relation of the Immigration and Naturalization Service to the Department of Labor" (24 July 1939) Speeches & Articles, Frances Perkins Papers, Box 51, Columbia University Rare Books & Manuscript Library.

5. Ibid.

6. Ibid.

7. Brookings Institution, Quoted in Perkins, "The Relation of the Immigration and Naturalization Service to the Department of Labor."

8. Perkins, "The Relation of the Immigration and Naturalization Service to the Department of Labor."

9. Richard Breitman and Alan Kraut, *American Refugee Policy and European Jewry, 1933-1945* (Indiana University Press, 1988) 117.

10. Richard Breitman and Allan Lichtman, *FDR and the Jews* (Harvard University Press, 2013) 162.

11. Deborah Lipstadt, *Beyond Belief: The American Press and the Coming of the Holocaust, 1933-1945* (New York: The Free Press, 1986) 162.

12. Sumner Welles, Letter to Franklin D. Roosevelt (18 May 1940) Box 7, Department of Labor, Official File, Franklin D. Roosevelt Presidential Library, Hyde Park, NY, Quoted in Hernandez, 52.

13. Breitman and Kraut, 114.

14. Julia Lopez Fuentes, "Petain and the French: Authority, Propaganda, and Collaboration in Vichy France, 1940-1942" (Undergraduate Thesis, Mount Holyoke College, 2014) MHC Institutional Digital Archive.

15. Lipstadt, *Beyond Belief*, 125.

16. Quoted in Kirstin Downey, *The Woman Behind the New Deal: The Life and Legacy of Frances Perkins—Social Security, Unemployment Insurance, and the Minimum Wage* (New York: Random House, 2009) 296.

17. Kirstin Downey, *The Woman Behind the New Deal: The Life and Legacy of Frances Perkins—Social Security, Unemployment Insurance, and the Minimum Wage* (New York: Random House, 2009) 295.

18. Reorganization Plan No. V of 1940, Eff. 15 June 1940, 5 F.R. 2223, 54 Stat. 1238, By Act 4 June 1940, Ch. 231 1, 54 Stat. 230 (Accessed 22 July 2023); For purpose or function as a common thread in reorganization planning, see Peri Arnold, *Making the Managerial Presidency: Comprehensive Reorganization Planning, 1905-1996* (The University Press of Kansas, 1998) 20-21.

19. Reorganization Plan No. V of 1940, Eff. 15 June 1940, 5 F.R. 2223, 54 Stat. 1238, By Act 4 June 1940, Ch. 231 1, 54 Stat. 230.

20. Susan Dunn, *1940: FDR, Willkie, Lindbergh, Hitler—the Election amid the Storm* (Yale University Press, 2013).

21. Reorganization Plan No. V of 1940, Eff. 15 June 1940, 5 F.R. 2223, 54 Stat. 1238, By Act 4 June 1940, Ch. 231 1, 54 Stat. 230.

22. Downey, 295.

23. Quoted in Breitman and Lichtman, 163.

24. Quoted in Downey, 295.

25. Ibid.

26. Sylvan Bruner, Letter to Franklin D. Roosevelt (5 June 1940) Subject Files of Frances Perkins, RG 174, Boxes 66-73, U.S. National Archives, College Park, MD.

27. U.S. Department of Labor, Press Release (13 June 1940) Speeches & Articles, Frances Perkins Papers, Box 52, Columbia University Rare Books & Manuscript Library.

28. Ibid.

29. Frances Perkins, "Notes for Annual Report on the Transfer of the Immigration and Naturalization Service to the Justice Department" (30 June 1940) Speeches & Articles, Frances Perkins Papers, Box 52, Columbia University Rare Books & Manuscript Library.

30. Ibid.
31. Ibid.
32. Ibid.
33. Summary Statement of Proposed Transfers Under Reorganization Plan V for the Immigration and Naturalization Service," Subject Files of Frances Perkins, RG 174, Box 66, U.S. National Archives, College Park, MD.
34. Downey, 295.
35. Henry Wallace, *Reminiscences of Henry Wallace* (6 June 1940) page 1142, Quoted in Downey, 296.
36. Frances Perkins, *The Roosevelt I Knew* (1946) 360-361; Downey, 296.
37. Frances Perkins, Letter to Peter Macsarka (6 December 1940) Subject Files of Frances Perkins, RG 174, Box 66, U.S. National Archives, College Park, MD.
38. Frances Perkins, Letter to W. G. Hamilton (5 December 1940) Subject Files of Frances Perkins, RG 174, Box 66, U.S. National Archives, College Park, MD.
39. Frances Perkins, Letter to Alex Springer (9 December 1940) Subject Files of Frances Perkins, RG 174, Box 66, U.S. National Archives, College Park, MD.
40. Frances Perkins, Letter to Mrs. Patrick Byrne (9 December 1940) Subject Files of Frances Perkins, RG 174, Box 66, U.S. National Archives, College Park, MD.
41. Frances Perkins, Letter to Hon. George W. Norris, U.S. Senate (7 December 1940) Subject Files of Frances Perkins, RG 174, Box 66, U.S. National Archives, College Park, MD.

Chapter Ten: The Trapp Family Singers

1. Agathe von Trapp, *Memories Before and After the Sound of Music: An Autobiography with Sketches by the Author* (New York: Harper, 2004) 1.
2. Trapp, 11-12.
3. Trapp, 47.
4. Trapp, 85.
5. Trapp, 120-123.
6. Trapp, 129.
7. Trapp, 130-132.
8. Trapp, 133-134.

9. Trapp, 138-139.
10. Trapp, 141.
11. Trapp, 156-157.
12. Trapp, 158-159.
13. Gertrude Ely, Letter to Frances Perkins (12 March 1940) Subject Files of Frances Perkins, RG 174, Box 67, U.S. National Archives, College Park, MD.
14. Frances Perkins, Letter to Gertrude Ely (18 March 1940) Subject Files of Frances Perkins, RG 174, Box 67, U.S. National Archives, College Park, MD.
15. Frances Jerkowitz, Letter to Gertrude Ely (9 April 1940) Subject Files of Frances Perkins, RG 174, Box 67, U.S. National Archives, College Park, MD.
16. Gertrude Ely, Letter to Frances Perkins (19 April 1940) Subject Files of Frances Perkins, RG 174, Box 67, U.S. National Archives, College Park, MD.
17. Frances Jerkowitz, Letter to Edward J. Shaughnessy (24 September 1940) Subject Files of Frances Perkins, RG 174, Box 67, U.S. National Archives, College Park, MD.
18. Frances Perkins, Letter to Gertrude Ely (24 September 1940) Subject Files of Frances Perkins, RG 174, Box 67, U.S. National Archives, College Park, MD.
19. Letter from Lemuel B. Schofield to Frances Perkins (27 September 1940) Subject Files of Frances Perkins, RG 174, Box 67, U.S. National Archives, College Park, MD.
20. Lemuel B. Schofield, Letter to Gertrude Ely (30 September 1940) Subject Files of Frances Perkins, RG 174, Box 67, U.S. National Archives, College Park, MD.
21. Gertrude Ely, Letter to Frances Perkins (22 September 1940) Subject Files of Frances Perkins, RG 174, Box 67, U.S. National Archives, College Park, MD.
22. Joan Gearin, "Movie vs. Reality: The Real Story of the von Trapp Family," *Prologue Magazine* Vol. 37, No. 4 (Winter 2005).
23. Maria von Trapp, Interview, *Opera Magazine* (2003), Quoted in Joan Gearin, "Movie vs. Reality: The Real Story of the von Trapp Family," *Prologue Magazine* Vol. 37, No. 4 (Winter 2005).
24. Samantha A. Vinokor-Meinrath, *#antisemitism: Coming of Age During the Resurgence of Hate* (Santa Barbara, CA: ABC-CLIO, 2022) ix.
25. Vinokor-Meinrath, x.

26. Samantha Vinokor-Meinrath, Interview by the Author (16 July 2023); Sarah Margulies, Interview by the Author (16 July 2023); Talia Brenner, Interviews by the Author (16 July 2023; 25 November 2023).
27. Stuart Anderson, "The Trapp Family and the Sound of Music: An Immigrant Success Story," *Forbes* (17 October 2022).
28. Letters to Katherine Lenroot, Children's Bureau, RG 102, Boxes 672-673, U.S. National Archives, College Park, MD.

Chapter Eleven: Remembering the Holocaust in the U.S.

1. Barry Trachtenberg, *The United States and the Nazi Holocaust: Race, Refuge, and Remembrance* (Bloomsbury Academic, 2018) 124.
2. Peter Novick, *The Holocaust in American Life* (New York: Mariner Books, 1999) 25.
3. Novick, 20.
4. Novick, 3; Maurice Halbwachs, *On Collective Memory* (Lewis A. Coser, ed., The University of Chicago Press, 1992).
5. Esther Safran Foer, *I Want You to Know We're Still Here* (New York: Tim Duggan Books, 2020) 5.
6. Jonathan Safran Foer, *Everything Is Illuminated* (New York: Harper Perennial, 2002), Quoted in Esther Safran Foer, *I Want You to Know We're Still Here* (New York: Tim Duggan Books, 2020) 5.
7. Dwight D. Eisenhower, Cable to George C. Marshall (4 April 1945), Quoted in Novick, 64.
8. Quoted in Peter Hayes, *Why?: Explaining the Holocaust* (New York: Norton, 2017) 301.
9. Sandra Fox, *The Jews of Summer: Summer Camp and Jewish Culture in Postwar America* (Stanford University Press, 2023) 107.
10. Fox, 105.
11. Fox, 116.
12. Fox, 110.
13. Trachtenberg, 150.
14. Robert Jackson, Quoted in Trachtenberg, 151.
15. Novick, 85.
16. Fox, 109; For the founding of Israel and the acceleration of the modern Israeli-Palestinian conflict, see Michael Brenner, *In Search of Israel: The History of an Idea* (Princeton University Press, 2018); Cate Malek and Mateo Hoke, eds., *Palestine Speaks: Narratives of Life Under Occupation* (Chicago, IL: Haymarket Books, 2019); Sami

Adwan, Dan Bar-on, and Eyal Naveh Prime, eds., *Side by Side: Parallel Histories of Israel Palestine* (New York: The New Press, 2012).

17. Frances Perkins, *The Roosevelt I Knew* (Originally Published 1946) (New York: Penguin Classics, 2011) 333.

18. Perkins, 333.

19. Samantha Rose Hill, *Hannah Arendt* (Reaktion Books, 2021).

20. Richard H. King, *Arendt and America* (The University of Chicago Press, 2016) 19, 191.

21. Novick, 87.

22. King, 49.

23. King, 46.

24. Ibid. For whiteness over time, see Matthew Frye Jacobson, *Whiteness of a Different Color: European Immigrants and the Alchemy of Race* (Harvard University Press, 1999). For corporate and Christian America in the 1950s, see Kevin M. Kruse, *One Nation Under God: How Corporate America Invented Christian America* (New York: Basic Books, 2015). See also: Kevin M. Schultz, *Tri-Faith America: How Catholics and Jews Held Postwar America to Its Protestant Promise* (Oxford University Press, 2011).

25. Dara Horn, *People Love Dead Jews* (New York: Norton, 2021) 3.

26. Trachtenberg, 128; For more on Anne Frank and historical memory, see Tim Cole, *Selling the Holocaust: From Auschwitz to Schindler: How History Is Bought, Packaged, and Sold* (New York: Routledge, 1999) 23-46.

27. Trachtenberg, 131.

28. Anne Frank, *Diary of a Young Girl*, Quoted in Horn, 9.

29. Horn, 9.

30. Trachtenberg, 129-130.

31. Trachtenberg, 130-131.

32. Trachtenberg, 136.

33. Horn, 10.

34. Trachtenberg, 154; For more on Adolf Eichmann and historical memory, see Cole, 40-72.

35. Hannah Arendt, Application to the Rockefeller Foundation (1961), Quoted in King, 193.

36. Hannah Arendt, *Eichmann in Jerusalem* (1963), Quoted in Novick, 135.

37. Novick, 137.

38. King, 190.

39. Novick, 133.

40. King, 189.
41. Trachtenberg, 150-155.
42. Trachtenberg, 149.
43. King, 191.
44. Trachtenberg, 143.
45. Sore-Rukhl Schaechter, "Gedenk Der Umglik" (1968) Camp Hemshekh Collection, Box 4, Folder 5, Quoted in Fox, 118.
46. Margie Newman, "Resistance: Camp Hemshekh and a Survivor's Daughter," *Jewish Currents* (March 2009), Quoted in Fox, 116.
47. Cole, 12.
48. Trachtenberg, 173.
49. Elie Weisel, *The New York Times* (1978), Quoted in Trachtenberg, 174.
50. Haskel Lookstein, Report, American Jewish Commission on the Holocaust (1985), Quoted in Trachtenberg, 164.
51. Novick, 168.
52. *National Socialist Party v. Skokie*, 432 U.S. 43 (1977); Edward T. Linenthal, *Preserving Memory: The Struggle to Create America's Holocaust Museum* (New York: Columbia University Press, 1995) 11.
53. "An Act to Establish the United States Holocaust Memorial Council," Public Law 96-388, 96th Congress (7 October 1980) H.R. 8081.
54. Trachtenberg, 159.
55. Kirk Savage, *Monument Wars: Washington, D.C., the National Mall, and the Transformation of the Memorial Landscape* (The University of California Press, 2009).
56. Edward T. Linenthal, *Preserving Memory: The Struggle to Create America's Holocaust Museum* (New York: Columbia University Press, 1995) 12.
57. Cole, 159.
58. Linenthal, 14-15.
59. Cole, 78.
60. Cole, 73.
61. Cole, 77.
62. *Americans and the Holocaust*, United States Holocaust Memorial Museum (Washington, D.C., 2018-2024).
63. "Frances Perkins," *Americans and the Holocaust*, United States Holocaust Memorial Museum (Accessed 30 September 2023) https://exhibitions.ushmm.org/americans-and-the-holocaust/personal-story/frances-perkins. One of the sources behind it was my under-

graduate thesis: Rebecca Brenner, "'Dear Miss Perkins': A Story of Frances Perkins's Efforts to Aid Refugees from Nazi Germany, 1933-1940," Thesis (South Hadley, MA: Mount Holyoke College, 2015).

64. Erik Larson, *In the Garden of Beasts: Love, Terror, and an American Family in Hitler's Berlin* (New York: Crown, 2011) 30.

65. Ken Burns, Sarah Botstein, and Lynn Novick, "'The Golden Door' (Beginnings-1938)," *The U.S. and the Holocaust*, PBS (2022) 1:12:59-1:13:25.

66. Burns, Botstein, and Novick, "'The Golden Door' (Beginnings-1938)," *The U.S. and the Holocaust*.

67. Emma Lazarus, "The New Colossus," Quoted in Burns, Botstein, and Novick, "'The Golden Door' (Beginnings-1938)," *The U.S. and the Holocaust*.

Chapter Twelve: Remembering American Immigration Law

1. Roxanne Dunbar-Ortiz, *Not A Nation of Immigrants: Settler Colonialism, White Supremacy, and a History of Erasure and Exclusion* (Boston, MA: Beacon Press, 2021) 270.

2. Dunbar-Ortiz, xii.

3. Mae Ngai, *Impossible Subjects: Illegal Aliens and the Making of Modern America* (Princeton University Press, 2005) 264.

4. Walt Whitman, *Leaves of Grass* (1855) The Walt Whitman Archive (Accessed 25 October 2023) https://whitmanarchive.org/published/LG/1860/poems/5.

5. Joe Kraus, "How the Melting Pot Stirred America: The Reception of Zangwill's Play and Theatre's Role in the American Assimilation Experience," *Varieties of Ethnic Criticism* Vol. 24, No. 3 (Autumn 1999) 3-19.

6. Ngai, 212.

7. Ibid.

8. Dunbar-Ortiz, xiii.

9. Ibid.

10. Dunbar-Ortiz, xv.

11. Dunbar-Ortiz, 83-120.

12. Dunbar-Ortiz, xv.

13. Quoted in Dunbar-Ortiz, xv.

14. John F. Kennedy, *A Nation of Immigrants* (1958) 2-3.

15. Kennedy, 6.

16. Robert F. Kennedy, "Introduction," *A Nation of Immigrants* by John F. Kennedy (New York: Harper & Row Publishers, 1964) x.

17. Ngai, 227.

18. Erika Lee, "Immigration," *Myth America: Historians Take on the Biggest Legends and Lies About Our Past* (New York: Basic Books, 2022) 64.

19. Ngai, 263; For the INS on the US-Mexico border, see S. Deborah Kang, *Making Immigration Law on the US-Mexico Border, 1917-1954* (Oxford University Press, 2017).

20. Ngai, 260.

21. Ngai, 228-229.

22. Ngai, 229.

23. Quoted in Ngai, 259.

24. For American imperialism inciting conflicts from which people sought to escape, see Lee, "Immigration," 56.

25. Lynn Ahrens and Lori Lieberman, "The Great American Melting Pot," *Schoolhouse Rock!* (1976).

26. Ngai, 236.

27. Quoted in Dunbar-Ortiz, xiii.

28. Lee, "Immigration," 66.

29. William Booth, "One Nation, Indivisible: Is It History?" *The Washington Post* (22 February 1998).

30. Quoted in Dunbar-Ortiz, xi.

31. Dunbar-Ortiz, xii.

32. David Blight, "The Fog of History Wars," *The New Yorker* (9 June 2021).

Chapter Thirteen: Remembering Frances Perkins

1. Quoted in George Martin, *Madam Secretary: Frances Perkins* (Boston, MA: Houghton Mifflin Company, 1976) 472-473.

2. Martin, 469.

3. Martin, 473.

4. Quoted in "The Woman Behind the New Deal," Frances Perkins Center Website (Accessed 18 November 2023) https://francesperkinscenter.org/learn/her-life/; Frances Perkins, *The Roosevelt I Knew*, Originally Published 1946 (New York: Penguin Classics, 2011).

5. Frances Perkins, Oral History, Interview by Dean Albertson (1951–1955) Columbia University Digital Library Collections, https://dlc.library.columbia.edu/catalog/cul:3xsj3txc7v.

6. Martin, 471.

7. Martin, 485.

8. Quoted in Martin, 489.

9. "Frances Perkins, The First Woman in Cabinet, Is Dead," *The New York Times* (15 May 1965) Accessed via Times Machine.

10. Martin, ix.

11. Jimmy Carter, "Department of Labor Remarks at the Dedication of the Frances Perkins Building" (10 April 1980) The American Presidency Project (UC Santa Barbara).

12. Sheila Brennan, *Stamping American Memory: Collectors, Citizens, and the Post* (The University of Michigan Press, 2018).

13. Philatelic Release No. 16, News, U.S. Postal Service (11 March 1980) Accessed in the Mount Holyoke Archives and Special Collections (South Hadley, MA).

14. William Jefferson Clinton, State of the Union address (23 January 1996); For a genealogy of representations of Frances Perkins up to 2008, see DeLysa Burnier, "Frances Perkins' Disappearance from American Public Administration: A Genealogy of Marginalization," *Administrative Theory & Practice* Vol. 30, No. 4 (December 2008) 398-423.

15. Kirstin Downey, *The Woman Behind the New Deal: The Life and Legacy of Frances Perkins—Social Security, Unemployment Insurance, and the Minimum Wage* (New York: Random House, 2009).

16. "About Us," Frances Perkins Center Website (Accessed 21 November 2023) https://francesperkinscenter.org/about-us/; "Frances Perkins Homestead," National Park Service Website (Accessed 21 November 2023) https://www.nps.gov/places/frances-perkins-homestead.htm; Geoff Montes, "A New Chapter for the Frances Perkins Homestead," National Trust for Historic Preservation (23 September 2014); "Frances Perkins Center Acquires Perkins' Homestead," *Living New Deal* (10 November 2020).

17. Steve Collins, "Elizabeth Warren's Campaign Puts Maine's Frances Perkins at Center Stage," *Sun Journal* (23 September 2019); Bill Scher, "Why Warren's Big Crowds Are a Big Deal," *Politico Magazine* (24 September 2019).

18. Elizabeth Warren, Twitter (28 October 2019) https://twitter.com/ ewarren/status/1188864131576881153.

19. Kamala Harris, Twitter (4 March 2021) https://twitter.com/VP/ status/1367577589037092865?s=20.

20. Hillary Clinton, Twitter (5 September 2016) https://twitter.com/ HillaryClinton/status/772893252898983936?s=20.

21. Jennifer J. Merz, *Steadfast: Frances Perkins Champion of Workers' Rights* (Allendale, NJ: Jennuine Books, 2020) 15.

22. Merz, 39.

23. Kathleen Krull, *The Only Woman in the Photo: Frances Perkins & Her New Deal for America* (New York: Simon & Schuster, 2020).

24. Deborah Hopkinson, *Thanks to Frances Perkins: Fighter for Workers' Rights* (Atlanta, GA: Peachtree Publishing Company, 2020).

25. Sarah Beling, "Frances Perkins—'The Mother of Social Security'— Finally Takes Her Place on W46th Street," W42ST.NYC (28 March 2022).

26. Mickey Spillane, Quoted in Beling, "Frances Perkins."

Afterword:
Frances Perkins: The Woman Behind American Efforts to Aid Refugees from Nazi Germany, 1933–1940

1. Department of Labor, Facebook (10 April 2022), https://fb .watch/osudcT17w3/.

2. Quoted in Downey, 281.

Index

Bacon Academy, 11
Balabanoff, Angelica, 141–42
"banality of evil," 225–30
Barred Zone Act. *See* Immigration
   Act of 1917
Beer Hall Putsch, 55–57
Bering Land Bridge, 162–63
Berlin, Irving, 2–3
Berlin Conference (1884), 49–50
Berlin Summer Olympics (1936), 64
Biddle, Francis, 193, 205
Biden, Joe, 257
Bigelow, Elisabeth, 150–52
bipolar disorder, 18–19, 271
Bismarck, Otto von, 50
Blackhawk, Ned, 163
B'nai B'rith, 86, 169
Booth, William, 256
Border Patrol, 37
Boschan, Paul, 148–50
Botstein, Sarah, 238–39
Brecht, Bertolt, 152–55
Breiseth, Christopher, 272–73
Breitman, Richard, 68, 78, 101, 171,
   185
Brenner, Henny, 63
Brenner, Talia, 209
Bridges, Harry, 103
   Longshore Strike of 1934, 111–
      13, 118
   Perkins and, 4, 111–12, 114–25,
      131, 132
   Perkins and impeachment hear-
      ings, 4, 123–29, 182
Brinn, Fannie, 95
Brooks, David, 11, 14, 276
Brownell, Don Carlos, 175–76, 178
Bruner, Sylvan, 190
Buckley, Charles A., 168
Bureau of Immigration, 24, 36–37,
   44, 75
Burns, Ken, 238–39
Bye, George, 260–61

Campbell, Walter, 106
Carr, Charlotte, 148–50

Carr, Wilbur J., 72–73, 85
Carr, William J., 46–47
Carter, Jimmy, 266–67, *268*
Chabon, Michael, 177–79
charge bonds controversy, 74–82,
   86, 88–89
child labor, 90, 91–92, 115
child refugees, 2, 3, 5, 83–110, 242,
   253
   quotas, 2, 99–100, 102, 103, 108,
      109–10, 134, 253
   role of GJCA, 4–5, 83–101, 109–
      10, 135, 166, 192, 242
   Wagner-Rogers Bill, 101–10, 250,
      253
   Wechsler children, 96–98
Children's Bureau (CB), 83–84,
   89–90, 93, 100, 105–6, 195
Chinese Exclusion Act of 1882, 30,
   35–37, 69, 101, 241, 244–45,
   246
Chinese immigrants, 30, 31, 35–37,
   105, 183, 244–45
Christianity, 8, 11, 120, 128, 167,
   210, 248
Chy Lung v. Freeman, 31
civil rights movement, 230, 250
Civil War (U.S.), 9, 34
Clinton, Bill, 233, 235, 270
Clinton, Hillary, 255–56, 275
Coggeshall, Susanna Wilson, 18–19,
   24–25, 261, 263, 266, 271–72
Coggeshall, Tomlin, 263–64, 266,
   272–73
Cohen, Felix, 169–70, 171, 177
Cold War, 218–19, 222, 231, 249, 250
Cole, Tim, 234, 235
Columbia University, 13, 27
Communism, 58, 111, 114–22, 125,
   126, 154
Congress of Industrial Organiza-
   tions (CIO), 104
Connell, Marion Fitch, 10
conspiracy theories, 120–22
Coolidge, Calvin, 9, 41, 44, 241–42
Cornell University, 98, 263–64